The Internationalization of Capital

Henrik Secher Marcussen and Jens Erik Torp

The Internationalization of Capital

The Prospects for the Third World

Henrik Secher Marcussen and Jens Erik Torp

Zed Books Ltd., 57 Caledonian Road, London N1 9BU

in association with

Scandinavian Institute of African Studies, P.O. Box 2126, Uppsala, Sweden.

The Internationalization of Capital was first
published by Zed Press, 57 Caledonian Road,
London N1 9BU in 1982

Copyedited by Anna Hodson
Proofread by Penelope Fryxell
Typeset by Donald Typesetting
Cover Design by Gyda Andersen
Printed by the Pitman Press, Bath

First Reprint, 1985

British Library Cataloguing in Publication Data

Marcussen, Henrik Secher
The internationalization of capital.
1. International economic relations
I. Title II. Torp, Jens Erik
337'.09172'4   HF1413
ISBN Hb 0 905762 90 8
    Pb 0 905762 77 0

US Distributor
Biblio Distribution Center, 81 Adams Drive,
Totowa, New Jersey, 07512

Contents

	Introduction	9
	Our Central Argument	9
	The Case We Have Examined: The E.E.C. and Africa	12
	Methodology of Our Study	13
	Scope of this Book	15
1.	**The Internationalization of Capital and the Reproduction Process of the Periphery**	17
	West European Capital After 1945	17
	Three Periods in the Concentration and Centralization of Capital	20
	New Patterns in the Internationalization of Capital	24
	The Reproduction Process in the Periphery	28
2.	**The Internationalization of French Capital**	32
	The Process of Internationalization of French Capital	33
	An Example: The Structure of the French Textile Industry	36
	French State Intervention	39
	The French Textile Industry and the Periphery	42
	Relations between France and the Ivory Coast	44
3.	**The E.E.C. and the International Division of Labour**	48
	Historical Background	49
	The Association Agreements Between the E.E.C. and the Developing Countries	53
	The Ivory Coast and the E.E.C.	60
	Conclusion	62
4.	**The Ivory Coast: Transcending Blocked Development?**	66
	The Role of the State in Ivorian Economic Development	69
	The Agricultural Development of the Ivory Coast	74
	Palm Oil Production as a Case Study	76
	Socio-Economic Consequences of Smallholders' Attachment to SODEPALM	89

Industrial Development in the Ivory Coast, 1960-76   97
The Ivorian Textile Industry   103
Concluding Remarks: Extended Reproduction of
     Capital   114

5.   **The Socio-Economic Consequences of Economic
Development in the Ivory Coast**   122
Social Differentiation in the Ivory Coast   123
The Ivorian Economy under Current Harsh World
     Market Conditions   129
The Class Nature of the State   132
Conclusions   135

6.   **A Changing Theoretical Paradigm? − From
Dependency Theory to the Internationalization of
Capital**   139
Dependency Theory Re-examined   140
Theories of the Internationalization of Capital   145
Theories of the Peripheral State   151
Towards a Changing Theoretical Paradigm   158

7.   **The Political Implications**   163

Statistical Annex   166
A. Foreign Direct Investment Flows by country,
     1961-79 (%)   166
B. Average Annual Growth Rates of Foreign Direct
     Investment from DAC Countries to LDC's, 1960-78
     (current $)   167
C. Total DAC Foreign Direct Investment by country of
     origin, 1967-76 ($ billion and %)   168
D. Net External Financial Receipts of LDCs by type of
     flow, 1970-79 ($ billion and %)   169
E. Total DAC Private Direct Investment in LDCs by
     country, 1978 ($ million)   170
F. LDC Share in Total Foreign Investment of Leading
     DAC capital-exporting Countries, 1966-77.   172

Bibliography   173
Index   179

List of Tables

1. The Exchange of Commodities between Centre and Periphery(%)   28
2. French Direct Investments in Selected Groups of Countries 1967-75   34
3. Turnover in Leading French Textile Companies (Millions of French francs)   36
4. French Imports of Certain Cotton Textiles, 1976 (Tons)   43
5. French Exports of Cotton Yarn, Fabric and Clothing, 1960-76 (Tons)   44
6. Direct Investments in the Ivorian Textile Industry by Main French Textile Groups, 1977   45
7. The Ivory Coast's Imports from and Exports to the E.E.C., 1973-77 (Billion C.F.A. francs and % of Total Trade)   60
8. The Ivory Coast State Investment Budget (Millions of C.F.A. francs)   71
9. Purchase of Inputs in the Industrial Sector (%)   98
10. The Textile Production Process   104
11. The Development of Cotton Production, 1960-61 to 1975-76   105
12. The Three Dominant Groups in the Ivorian Textile Industry   109
13. Distribution of Share Capital in Ivorian Textile Industry, 1 January 1976 (%)   111
14. Investments and Turnover in West African Textile Industries, 1975   114
15. Agricultural Cash Incomes, 1971-73 and 1975 (C.F.A. Francs *Per Capita*)   130

List of Figures

1. Long Term Changes in the Structure of Developing Countries' Total Net External Financial Receipts, 1960-78   27
2. The Palm Oil Production Process   86

Map
67

Introduction

Our Central Argument

The main argument of this study is that changing historical conditions for capital accumulation in the Western industrialized countries (the Centre) in the 1970s have led to new ways in which the developing countries (the Periphery) are integrated in the reproduction of the Centre's capital.

Our main conclusion is that the economic crisis in Western Europe, since the oil price rises following 1973, has led to new forms of internationalization of capital. From Europe, capital is now directed towards the peripheral countries in order to find *new* areas of investment and *new* markets. The consequence of this process is an increased differentiation among the countries in the Periphery. A few are for the first time in the process of establishing the basis for national capital accumulation within a framework of capitalist development. Other countries seem to be remaining in the situation characterized as 'blocked development' by the theorists of the Dependency School.

To stress the relationships between the accumulation process in the Centre and in the Periphery is certainly not a brilliant, new idea. In the theoretical controversy of the 1950s and 1960s, it was precisely the merit of writers like Andre Gunder Frank and Samir Amin that they did emphasize this relationship in contrast to the prevailing liberal development thinking.

The liberals did not see — or did not want to see — the causes and consequences of the operation of the international capitalist system. They preferred to divide the world into two separate and dualistic categories, 'developed' and 'developing' countries. The implication was that the developing countries unfortunately had not yet reached their growth or 'take-off' stage, mainly due to low investment rates, inherent traditionalism and lack of entrepreneurship.

Consequently, it was seen to be the task of the then newly set-up international aid organizations to spread to the developing countries the values and techniques of the modern world. A self-perpetuating growth process would then in due course become a reality, it was thought.

Gunder Frank, Samir Amin, and in their wake a whole school of development thinking, focused instead on the *global accumulation process* as the main determinant of underdevelopment. Their analysis of the way in which this global accumulation process actually functioned and the concepts necessary to analyse it were not very elaborate and sophisticated. Their basic assumption, however, was that the international capitalist system had created an international division of labour, with the Periphery supplying raw materials to the Centre and also acting as markets for manufactured goods from the Centre. Through this division of labour whatever economic surpluses existed were extracted by way of repatriation of profits to the Centre countries. Hence, the peripheral countries were assumed to be locked in a 'development trap', the cause of this underdevelopment system and its persistence being the global accumulation process and the established international division of labour.

Samir Amin, in particular, analysed at length the worldwide socio-economic consequences of the integration of the peripheral economies into the international capitalist system. As a result of many detailed and useful empirical studies. Amin and other representatives of the Dependency School concluded that the underdeveloped world was in a 'blocked development' situation, due to its orientation to the world market and the consequent exogenous nature of its economies.

To focus on the relations for global capital accumulation and the development prospects of the Periphery is clearly not at all revolutionary. What distinguishes our study from that of Marxist theorists like those mentioned above is that we have reached the conclusion that dynamic elements exist in the changing historical conditions for capital accumulation in the Western countries, particularly the economic crisis since 1973, and that these elements are responsible for the creation of *new reproductive structures in parts of the Periphery which may very well break with the 'blocked development' situation.*

The period after World War II has been mainly characterized by the dramatically accelerated internationalization of productive investment, the developing countries taking around a third of total foreign direct investment. The second half of the 1960s and the whole of the 1970s have, however, shown an increasingly differentiated pattern of internationalization of capital.

Regarding foreign direct investments made by companies from the Centre, the share of developing countries has been in relative increase in recent years compared to investments in the Western industrialized countries themselves, a tendency which has marked itself in the years following the beginning of the crisis. At the same time, there has been a remarkable growth in the internationalization of other forms of capital like portfolio investments, private and public export credits, bank loans, and commodity exports in the form of turn-key projects intended to build up production and reproduction processes in the Periphery.

The decline in the share of foreign direct investment in the total picture of the internationalization of capital is, however, probably exaggerated. New forms of co-financing the transnational corporations' activities in the Third World (like borrowing on the private capital market, export credits and the co-finance offered by the peripheral state) are areas which are not easily distinguishable in the statistics. The standard definition of private direct foreign investment is investment in enterprises located in one country but effectively controlled by residents of another. According to I.M.F. regulations, effective control is inferred from 50% or more ownership of voting stock by residents in an investor country, or 25% or more ownership by a single holder or organized group of such residents. The change in the predominant character of private foreign direct investment from one of equity participation to the use of loans and suppliers' credits (that is, from direct control over management to participation in management, technical agreements, production-sharing, supply contracts etc.) is, therefore, not reflected in the statistical categories at present in use.

In spite of this statistically underestimated role of private direct foreign investment in developing countries, there *has* been a shift in the pattern of the internationalization of capital. The most remarkable change is the shift from official (i.e. public) sector commitments, like overseas development assistance, to the now dominant role of the private sector in total net external financial receipts of developing countries. In particular, private bank lending has been drastically on the increase during the 1970s, comprising more than 30% of developing countries' total capital receipts as against virtually none in 1960.

Another change in the internationalization of capital pattern – and one equally difficult to ascertain from the available statistics – is the increasing importation by peripheral economies of large-scale producer goods complexes, often in the form of turn-key projects. This introduction into the Third World of large, highly developed and technologically sophisticated production complexes has taken place, as has the growth in private bank lending, particularly in the years of world economic crisis provoked by the increase in oil prices (and often financed by the huge oil revenues piling up in the Western banks). Already these new investments are reflected in the changing export pattern of some peripheral countries. At the aggregate level, the Periphery's export statistics are still dominated by raw materials, agricultural as well as mineral. But for these Third World countries with a development strategy based on creating 'sound investment climates' (*inter alia*, low wage levels, infrastructure built by the state, tax and custom duties exemptions) the export of finished or semi-finished manufactured goods to the Western world has been increasing drastically. The share of developing countries in total trade in manufactured goods was only 10% in 1978, but given certain conditions for growth, this share may grow to 14% during the 1980s. Moreover the share of manufactured goods in total exports from the developing countries could increase from the present 24% to 39% in 1990. At the same time the ongoing industrialization of the developing countries has also implied a rapid increase in exports from the industrialized countries — especially in means of production. In 1978 the developing countries bought one-third of the total exports of manufactured goods from North America, nearly half of Japan's, and 20% of Western Europe's.

The international division of labour has thus obviously changed in the years since 1973-74, from the traditional one with the peripheral countries acting as raw material suppliers and markets for Western manufactured goods, to a more complex pattern. Two basic questions thus arise: (1) Has the economic crisis in the Western industrialized world contributed to these new trends in the international division of labour? And (2) Is this emerging new international division of labour contributing to the creation of new patterns of *national* capital accumulation in the Periphery, possible breaking with the 'blocked development' situation in at least some countries?

When investigating these two questions, we will look into the changing historical conditions for capital accumulation in the countries of the Centre in order to determine whether these changes have forced new reproductive structures within the overall capitalist framework to emerge with the crisis. If new reproductive structures in the Periphery are observable, this obviously implies that the peripheral economies are not always simply appendices to the economies of the Centre and so placed in a deadlock situation — as many of the dependency theorists would have us believe. Instead it suggests that these peripheral economies can in addition contain some relatively autonomous factors, amongst which the role and function of the state has been given primary importance in our analysis.

Due to the normal absence — until now, at least — of a national bourgeoisie able to take on its natural role as the generator of capitalism, the peripheral state in a number of cases seems to have developed into an active, economically interventionist state. Not only does the state (with the assistance of the large international aid organizations) establish the material preconditions for capitalist production (infrastructure, investment codes and legal framework etc.), it also extracts economic surpluses from, primarily, the agricultural sector, presumably to be reinvested in agriculture and/or industry.

It is, therefore, our basic contention that the changing historical conditions for capital accumulation in the Centre (reflecting itself in changes in the process of the internationalization of capital), together with relatively autonomous forces in the Periphery like the state, are creating examples of new patterns of national accumulation of capital within a capitalist development process in the Periphery.

The Case We Have Examined: The E.E.C. and Africa

In our preliminary research into the role of the E.E.C. vis-à-vis the Associated African states (as evidenced in the Conventions of Association etc.), we intended to look into whether or not the peripheral nations were acting as suppliers of raw materials for the economies of the Centre, thus occupying a still largely traditional role within the international division of labour. Prevailing investigations in the field at that time produced the hypothesis that the Conventions could be interpreted as neo-colonialist measures intended to keep the Associated African states within the West European sphere of interest, so that the Associated countries thereby lowered the costs of production in the European countries. This way of looking at the problem was, of course, very much inspired by Samir Amin and other writers of the Dependency School.

In order to select one of the African Associated countries for further investigation, we briefly visited, among others, Senegal, the Ivory Coast and Ghana, and had discussions with persons of various views regarding these countries' association with the E.E.C. Our final selection of the Ivory Coast was determined firstly by an interest in looking further into what (at a superficial and impressionistic level) seemed to be an extraordinary and impressive case of economic growth *and* possibly transcending blocked development. Secondly, our choice was determined by the existence of studies carried out in the 1960s by members of the Dependency School emphasizing the Ivory Coast as the prototype of a blocked economy characterized by 'growth without development'. In other words, looking into the development experiences of the Ivory Coast in the period following the 1960s gave us an opportunity to test the Dependency School's analysis.

Also contributing to our interest in the Ivory Coast was the theoretical discussion within Europe at the time concerning the role, function and future direction of the E.E.C. The beginning of the 1970s witnessed a whole range of studies which analysed the prospects of the E.E.C. contributing to the strengthening of capitalism in Western Europe in a situation of increased competition on the world market among the leading economic nations — U.S.A., Japan — and the individual nations of Europe.

The theoretical paradigm used in these analytical studies seemed to have developed into a theory of the internationalization of capital, the outline of which was broadly agreed among writers taking different theoretical angles, though naturally there was divergence of opinion with regard to the theory's content and its political consequences. No studies within this framework, however, gave a satisfactory analysis of the role of the Periphery, so the question for us then was to what extent the theory gave room for the analysis not only of the creation and future development prospects of the E.E.C. and its member countries, but also of the Convention agreements with the Third World as well as the economic situation of our selected country, the Ivory Coast.

The Methodology of Our Study

In our study of the changing historical conditions for capital accumulation in the Centre and its impact on the accumulation pattern in the Periphery, we have been guided by the following three analytical aspects:

(1) the way in which capital reproduces its own structure in the Centre;
(2) the way in which the reproduction of peripheral capital is embodied in the reproduction of the Centre's capital;
(3) the way in which these two conditions set limits for and are influenced by the development of the Periphery itself.

By looking at these three levels of analysis, we intend to establish the theoretical and factual relationship between the Centre and the Periphery as one conceptual entity within the global accumulation of capital. It is in this way that 'the whole', the global capitalist production and reproduction process, determines the 'parts', the relations between capital and state in the Centre and the Periphery. At the theoretical level this implies that the processes of the internationalization of capital are the moving force behind the international structuring of the capitalist system, not ignoring, however, the possibility of influence and modification by relatively autonomous factors such as the peripheral state.

While the theory of the internationalization of capital expresses the dynamic factors behind single capitals or groups of capital seeking new profitable investment opportunities abroad, this tendency of capitalism to broaden its sphere of operation only becomes manifest to the extent that factors conducive to capital are present, that is to the extent that material preconditions for capitalist production in its wide sense guarantee economic viability. The state — and in this case particularly the peripheral state — is the instrument judged capable of realizing the tendencies inherent in the process of internationalization of capital to create new capitalist production and reproduction centres.

The relationship between capital and state is in this way seen more 'organically' and made more central to the analysis than has been the case in many previous studies on the internationalization of capital. Furthermore, while we stress the importance of the conditions which accumulation at the Centre sets for the accumulation process in the Periphery, at the same time we perceive a more independent role for peripheral economic development initiated by the peripheral state and/or the national bourgeoisie. This assessment of a more autonomous peripheral economic development is in contrast to most studies which only analyse the bourgeoisie as a comprador bourgeoisie, leaving no room for any other solution than that of being a simple appendix to international capital's transactions.

The key concept, theoretically and analytically, is therefore the internationalization of capital, with the relations between state and capital being seen as important forces in the processes studied.

Having said that, we want to stress that the choice of the internationalization of capital as the key concept also implies some limitations for the study. First of all, the concept is rooted in economic aspects, which has the danger of underestimating the importance of political relations and class contradictions. Examples of this are only too easy to find. Secondly, choosing the internationalization of capital as the theoretical framework might in itself lead to an underestimation of the contradictions between the bourgeoisie in the Centre and in the Periphery, and there could develop a tendency to see the capitalist mode of production as an ever-expanding process, with only minor contradictions involved.

In the same manner our conception of the peripheral state is mainly founded within an economic framework. The state has, of course, to be seen also in relation to the underlying class structures in the peripheral country in question. But our main conception of the state is as an instrument actively intervening in the economy, in the absence of a national bourgeoisie, in order to establish a national capital accumulation process.

The Scope of This Book

Chapter 1 starts out with a discussion of the relative strength of the respective capitals of the U.S.A. and Western Europe in the 1960s. It then examines how these relative strengths have changed, and how this has affected relations with the Periphery. After this introductory discussion, the remaining part of the chapter focuses on the E.E.C. countries, and discusses the way in which the accumulation pattern of the West European capitals and their tendency to internationalization have expressed themselves in the period 1958-78.

A distinction is made between three periods: 1958-62, 1963-73 and 1974 to the present. The central period for our analysis is 1963-73, which is characterized by a clear tendency for European national capitals to centralize within their own boundaries rather than to be absorbed under U.S. capital or under any domination of transnational companies. This has a special importance for the approach in the subsequent chapters, as it provides an argument for starting the analysis with the centralization of national capitals within each E.E.C. country in order to understand the main dynamics of the accumulation process in the period concerned.

In this first chapter we also discuss whether the new supra-governmental structures of the E.E.C. are likely to take over some of the functions which have traditionally been left to the individual nation states in Western Europe.

Besides the accumulation process in Western Europe from the 1950s until the 1970s, two other issues are dealt with in Chapter 1. First, an attempt is made to integrate the Periphery into the understanding of the accumulation process in the Centre — in particular, we investigate the effects on the reproduction process of the Periphery of its status in the world market. Secondly, the role of the peripheral state in the establishment of a more autonomous development is looked into.

In Chapter 2 we discuss the change after 1958 in the orientation of the French economy, specifically from a closed overseas market with its colonies towards an opening to the E.E.C. area. We also analyse what impact this change has had on the internationalization strategy of French companies, and the resulting consequences for economic relations between France and the developing countries. Finally, different forms of state intervention are discussed, concentrating on the example of the French textile industry.

In Chapter 3, the Association agreements between the E.E.C. and the developing countries are interpreted in the light of the E.E.C.'s accumulation pattern. The central issue is whether these agreements express a common E.E.C. interest in relation to the international division of labour, or whether they express considerations — economic as well as political — specific to particular E.E.C. countries. At the same time, we discuss whether the Association agreements contain elements which certain peripheral countries can take advantage of in their national economic development strategy.

Chapter 4 takes its point of departure in Samir Amin's analysis of development in the Ivory Coast in the 1960s. His conclusion was that the Ivory Coast is the prototype of a dependent and blocked economy. Its particular form of integration into the world market, i.e. the predominant export orientation of the economy, is seen as the most important problem. According to Amin, this fact causes linkages between different economic sectors to be blocked, so preventing the creation of a 'self-centred' economy. The logical strategy flowing from Samir Amin's analysis is, therefore, to recommend the Ivory Coast to break with the world market, so that a more substantial economic development can take place.

In this chapter we try to judge whether the kind of development that has taken place in the Ivory Coast since Samir Amin first analysed it has modified the validity of his conclusions. We look at both agricultural and industrial development and at the role of the Ivorian state.

Having so far tried theoretically and empirically to analyse the possibilities for a single peripheral economy to break away from the so-called blocked development situation, in Chapter 5 we discuss the social and political consequences of new capitalist reproductive structures. We consider what are the social and political preconditions for a development strategy based on the twofold purpose of both being fully integrated into the world market *and* succeeding in extracting economic surpluses in order to further national accumulation processes; and we examine the social and political implications of persevering with this strategy.

Finally, in Chapter 6 we briefly discuss the theoretical consequences of our study. The issue here is the obvious need for a new theoretical paradigm, with much more sophisticated concepts than have been presented in the literature of economic development so far, not least within the Dependency School.

1. The Internationalization of Capital and the Reproduction Process of the Periphery

West European Capital After 1945

The economic and political development of Western Europe since World War II has been very much influenced by the changed balance of power resulting from the Soviet Union's assumption of control over Eastern Europe and by the development of economic competition between Western Europe, the U.S.A. and Japan. These two factors were central in the creation of the E.E.C. In the beginning, political motives played a crucial role; the E.E.C. was seen as an attempt to limit the influence of the 'socialist' Eastern European countries. Later economic motives came to the fore; the creation of the E.E.C. was seen as an instrument to catch up with the productivity increases of the U.S.A. and Japan.[1]

By the end of World War II the major productive and infrastructural capacity of the European nations had been destroyed, resulting in a drastic decline in the accumulation rate and obvious shortcomings with regard to the supply of the most essential goods like foodstuffs and energy needed for keeping industry running. On the other hand, the U.S.A. not only had its productive potential intact, but had also succeeded in using the innovations in the armaments industry to raise the productivity and technological level of civil production, thereby creating a favourable and sustained accumulation rate.

After the War, therefore, Western Europe was weakened, economically, politically and militarily, while the U.S.A. had become the leading economic and political world power. At the same time socialist influence had increased in the East European countries due to the Soviet Union, and although the working class in the West European nations was disorganized and still very much affected by the repression of the previous fascist regimes, the War and the European resistance movements had opened up an increased belief in a more radical political change-over.

These favourable prospects for the U.S.A. could, however, only materialize to the extent that a reorganization of the capitalist world market took place. In other words, a rapid reconstruction of the West European nations was considered to be a prerequisite for the re-establishment of a global capitalist accumulation process. At the same time, this would contribute to the reduction of socialist influence from Eastern Europe (the so-called policy of containment).[2] The Marshall Plan was the means by which the U.S.A. would assist in the reconstruction of Western Europe, and at the same time secure an increasing demand for American products, without which the American economy would stagnate. And the dollar credits made available through the Marshall Plan did result in a sudden and immense increase in imports to Western Europe of American foodstuffs, raw materials, and means of investment.

Around 1951, the Federal Republic of Germany reached its 1938 level of industrial production. By 1955 the pre-war relative economic strength between the Federal Republic of Germany and France was re-established.[3]

German heavy industry based on coal and steel was considered to be absolutely essential for creating sustained growth in Western Europe. This was among the reasons for the first steps towards an economic and political integration process among the Western European countries. Dollar credits from the U.S.A. under the Marshall Plan were given on condition that a common organizational system should be created in order to facilitate a rational distribution of the means of production within a larger market. To this end the Organization for European Economic Co-operation (O.E.E.C.) was established, with the aim of reducing customs duties and other restrictions on trade flows.

The European Coal and Steel Union was the first effort to establish an institution in Europe with supra-national authority. As conceived by the French Foreign Minister, Robert Schumann, in 1950, the idea behind the Union was 'an act of solidarity' pooling the production and reserves of coal, iron, steel, etc. of the member countries in order to create a basis for economic development in Europe as a whole and to make any future war between France and Germany impossible.[4] For France, the policy of integration was an effort to prevent a new resurgence of West German expansionism by means of control of the German economy. That, at least, was the official reason given. The relative economic weakness of France compared to West Germany, however, led France to give up her ambition to be the leading economic power in a European context, and instead to look for a major political role to play. Still considering herself with her colonies as one of the world's leading powers, France naturally adopted the position as the country controlling the German economy. For West Germany, in contrast, the Union was the only way to overcome the narrowing of her territory after the partition of the country, and to regain a reliable political reputation.[5]

In spite of the overall bright economic prospects in the 1950s for the leading capitalist nations, and the West European nations in particular, there were still great disparities and inequalities among the European nations, reflected in the economic structure and state policies of the countries concerned.[6] The two leading and often mutually opposed nations within the Coal and Steel Union, France and West Germany, developed, not least due to their different historical backgrounds, different patterns of concentration and centralization of firms during the 1950s. Notably, the coal and steel industries, which were dynamic elements in the European economic recovery of the 1950s, were organized differently in the two countries. The coal and steel industry is characterized everywhere by a very large initial capital investment in order to start production, a rather high fixed capital, and a very long period of maturation of capital invested, all favouring a process of concentration and centralization of firms in order to stay in business. This process had to a large extent already taken place within the West German industry, while the position of the industry in France was only marginally viable.[7]

Although France had impressive growth rates during the 1950s, her manufacturing industry was in a structurally weaker position vis-à-vis West Germany, and its growth reflected the short-term advantages of her closed overseas market in her colonies. France was very much oriented towards a protectionist policy. The French colonies, mainly in Africa, supplied her with cheap raw materials and agricultural products for consumption and manufacturing, while she exported the major part of her industrial exports to the colonies at prices far above world market prices. At the time, between 75% and 94% of the total French exports of textiles went to the franc zone, 90% of shoe exports, 65% of pharmaceutical exports, 45% of electrical goods and 52% of automobiles.[8] Apart from this, France also had protectionist goals vis-à-vis the incipient E.E.C., as more than 50% of her agrarian exports went to Western European markets, while at the same time she was a net importer of machinery and equipment needed for the modernization of her industry.[9]

During the period of negotiation for the establishment of the E.E.C., France and West Germany often had opposed interests. West Germany, being internationally much more competitive, mainly due to the restructuring of her economy towards larger and fewer individual firms, was not exactly against a degree of protection of Western Europe from the world market, but underlined the importance of a global approach, i.e. considering the potential of the E.E.C. as an instrument capable of furthering the interests of the Federal Republic in the world market.

These conflicts were also reflected in the question about the supranationality of E.E.C. institutions. France still considered the national interest to be fundamental, while West Germany was in favour of a political and economic union with clearcut rights to intervene in national planning procedures as well as the power to resolve currency problems.

The result of the negotiations, the Treaty of Rome, was a compromise between: (1) partial and full integration; (2) regional protectionism and global economic liberalism; and (3) national autonomy and supra-national authorities.[10] In one of her more vital spheres of interest, however, France succeeded in convincing her future E.E.C. partners of the necessity to keep the French colonies in Africa within the influence of the new E.E.C.

The economic rationale behind the E.E.C. lay in the common wish among the European nations to cope with the productivity increase of the U.S.A. It was believed that by creating an enlarged market the strengthened competitive situation and thus higher productivity *within* this European market would create an economic bloc much more competitive world-wide.

Three Periods in the Concentration and Centralization of Capital

As described above, the period immediately after World War II up to the formal start of co-operation within the E.E.C. in 1958 was characterized by the furthering of the process of concentration and centralization of firms in Western Europe.

The rapid economic reconstruction of Western Europe was not least due to a huge reserve of labour, which kept the wage level down and made a rapid accumulation process possible. From 1951 to 1957, 1.8 million people migrated to West Germany from East Germany.[11] Together with their recent experience of the fascist regime, this kept the West German working class rather disorganized and easily controllable. But the War also left the French working class in a weak state. While French industrial production reached the 1938 level by around 1947, the purchasing power of the French weekly wage did not reach its 1938 level until 1954.[12]

Because France was economically screened off from the world market, and because it was still possible to drain off manpower from agriculture and later to employ foreign workers from the colonies, there was no incentive for French industry to replace manpower with machinery. This was probably one reason for the structural weakness of the French economy at the time of entering the E.E.C.

The process of concentration and centralization of capital is not only of importance when judging the economic strength of the different capital groups and the placing of the nations in a hierarchy of reproduction, but is also fundamental to the understanding of the subsequent process of internationalization of capital. In order to underline the conditions for this development, it is necessary to divide the process into periods, because the type of concentration and centralization differed from one period to another. We will describe the process in three periods: 1958-62, 1963-73 and from 1974 onwards.

(1) 1958-62: Economic Expansion, but no Strong Concentration or Centralization

In this period right after the start of the E.E.C., the accumulation process continued at a rather high speed, and the effects of the Community had not yet showed themselves. The relative strength of the units of production did not yet present any pressure towards a further centralization process.[13]

For France this period, in which the country still benefited from the advantages of its closed overseas market and the generally favourable economic circumstances, did not compel any process of capital accumulation based on technological development since the profits were high and secure. This was reflected in an investment rate far below that of many other European countries.[14]

As for the internationalization of capital, there were good investment and profit opportunities in the Western countries themselves, thereby leaving only a marginal role for direct investments in the Periphery. These were mainly limited to extraction of raw materials, together with a continued relatively high export of agricultural commodities.

Competition from the high productivity capital groups of the U.S.A. was not seriously felt in Western Europe during this period. First of all, the economic situation during the Korean War — and after — made it possible for West European firms to increase their exports of capital and commodities, since the U.S. economy was geared towards meeting the needs of the war and so required industrial and other inputs. At the same time markets formerly dominated by U.S. capital were now more open to West European capital groups. Secondly, the relations between the imperialist powers and the Periphery were still colonial, thereby protecting weak West European firms from the more competitive West European and U.S. capital groups.

The impact of the creation of the E.E.C. in 1958 was not really felt immediately, since a number of transitional arrangements in the early years delayed the introduction of the free movement of capital and labour.

(2) 1963-73: Rapid Accumulation and Accelerated Concentration and Centralization of National Capital Groups

In 1963 an accelerated process of concentration and centralization of capital started with the gradual reduction of tariffs and other restrictions on the movement of commodities, capital and labour within the E.E.C., and competition in the market-place became tougher. Individual capital groups transformed themselves into larger units of production in response to the competitive situation and the requirements of the expanded E.E.C. market. The state had to support this process.

One can distinguish three different types of centralization, all taking place in the E.E.C. countries in this period:

(1)   fusion of existing national capital groups;
(2)   fusion (or rather absorption) of individual national capital groups by American firms; and
(3)   fusion of national capital groups in different member countries into new units in which the nationally founded capital is no longer dominant, but ownership is split between two or three countries.

Ernest Mandel[15] is of the opinion that the centralization process dominating this period took place within West European capital groups themselves. This view is questioned by Nicos Poulantzas[16] who emphasizes the establishment of factories in Europe with American dominance as the prevailing type of fusion in the years 1962-68. It is Poulantzas's opinion that American capital was quantitatively dominant, and that this also implies a qualitative change in the economic structure of European industry with regard to ownership and control.

The European dependency on American capital is particularly obvious in the most advanced manufacturing sectors, which are the ones that attract foreign capital, as the example of the electronics industry in France indicates. As a countermeasure to this, it is, according to Poulantzas, not a viable strategy to support increased centralization of European capital, as this will only tend to bring about continued subordination to American capital.

In spite of having clearly formulated his conclusions, Poulantzas does not provide satisfactory empirical evidence to substantiate them. However, empirical evidence based on an analysis of 187 American multinational companies can be found in a study by Klaus Busch.[17] Busch's analysis shows that there seems to be a relatively equal distribution between expansion by means of buying up existing capitals (51%) and the founding of new capitals (48%). In contrast to this, in developing countries the buying up of existing capital plays a far less important role (38%) than foundation of new capitals (61%).

Apart from the forms of centralization mentioned above, the centralization of capital within the individual nation state is also important. Frank Deppe[18] stresses that, with the opening up of the European markets through the creation of the E.E.C., the national capital groups were forced to centralize in order to cope with outside foreign competition as well as with the competition of the most productive European capital groups. The consequent process of centralization allowed for a more rapid adaption of technological processes, which took place primarily in the industries already most advanced, and this allowed for a further expansion of production.

It is Deppe's conclusion, with which we agree, that in the West European countries the process of centralization has primarily been national rather than transnational.

The amount of U.S. investments was, however, felt very dramatically and seen as a threat by national capital groups in Western Europe. In the longer perspective this view was possibly an exaggeration, and the importance today of U.S. investments is partly that of an external pressure contributing to a fast concentration and centralization process among the national capital groups in Western Europe. Another factor contributing to this process, however, was the establishment of the E.E.C., which increased competition among the West European capital groups.

On the level of analysis of *capital in general*, therefore, one can attribute the major dynamics behind the internationalization process of capital in Western Europe in this period to U.S. investments and the coming into being of the E.E.C.

If — in addition — we look more carefully at the differences between *national capital groups*, we can observe two main patterns of internationalization. Countries like West Germany, the U.S.A. and Japan experienced an accelerated tendency towards productive capital export to Asia, Africa and Latin America. Countries like France and the United Kingdom undertook the reverse process, in the form of an orientation *away* from their former closed overseas markets within the Franc and Sterling zones and *towards* other West European countries and the U.S.A.[19]

In relation to the Periphery the process of internationalization of capital was characterized in this period by a continued effort to secure the necessary raw materials — at prices relatively stable and controlled — and by an increased export of productive capital to promote industrialization based on import substitution (often in co-operation with the peripheral state). There was also to a varying extent some industrialization oriented to exports.

(3) 1974 onwards: Crisis Leads to Rationalization and Large Capitals buying up Smaller Capitals

With regard to the period from 1974 onwards, the literature is scarce. The few available analyses[20] seem to show that investments were primarily aimed towards rationalization. This type of concentration process therefore seems to have been a dominant characteristic of the period, while at the same time exports of productive capital took place at an increased rate.

While at the beginning of the 1970s France had a relatively high growth rate (surpassing that of West Germany, Italy and the United Kingdom), she could not escape the crisis situation in 1973-74. Deficits on the balance of payments, inflation, and a decrease in the investment rate began to show.

The crisis was reflected in the foreign trade of the leading capitalist nations. 1975 was the first year since World War II which showed a decrease — around 6% — in the volume of exports. The crisis also resulted in a vast number of firms going bankrupt. According to estimates the number of bankruptcies in the capitalist nations of the Centre reached 121,000 in the years 1974 and 1975.[21] The large firms in the West European nations increasingly bought up small and middle-sized companies, increasing their total share of industrial turnover. In France, in particular, the process of concentration and centralization accelerated during 1976, primarily within the oil, aeronautical, nuclear, steel and electronics industries, all representing industries with a high level of technology and a high growth potential.[22]

Turning to the pattern of internationalization of capital in this period, the picture shows a conflict of interests among the national capital groups in the Centre, with on the one hand the weak capital groups demanding protection by their own nation states and the E.E.C., and on the other hand the already internationalized capital groups looking for support in their search for new investment areas and markets for commodities. This latter tendency represented an incentive for West European capital groups to invest or export to developing countries. Creating a 'favourable investment climate' in the Periphery might, therefore, in this period of worldwide recession attract investments geared towards the production of cheap manufactured products or semi-processed goods meant for export to the Centre.

Already during the 1960s there had been an increasing interest among U.S., Japanese and West German companies in making direct investments in the manufacturing sector of the Periphery; but this was not the case for the former colonial powers of France and the United Kingdom. These new productive investments were aimed at both the local market in the host country and markets in the U.S.A. and Western Europe. This tendency for West German, U.S. and Japanese capital groups to invest in the Periphery accelerated during the recession following 1974.[23] This period also showed a marked increase of British investments in the Periphery. And the already internationalized French capital groups also expressed a renewed interest in the Periphery, but on very different terms from the interest shown in the early

1960s, which had been based on an attempt to keep the advantages of a closed and secured market in the former colonies.

In the following pages we will go in more detail into the present trends in the internationalization of capital, ending up with an evaluation of their consequences for the reproduction process of the Periphery.

New Patterns in the Internationalization of Capital

The build-up of larger units of production capable of utilizing highly developed technologies, and thereby economizing on factors of production, is often seen as an absolutely necessary prerequisite for staying in business in a strongly competitive world situation. The overall tendency for different money capitals to merge with other capitals (centralization) or to extend the individual money capital through accumulation (concentration) has favoured the process of transnationalization. Once larger entities have been established, a continued exclusive anchoring of their economic activities within national boundaries is often an obstacle to further necessary expansion, as it precludes taking advantage worldwide of differences in the costs of factors of production, and hinders the exploration of new market and investment opportunities. It seems, therefore — and on this most theorists agree — that inherent in the conditions for continued profitable economic activity is the tendency for capital ever to broaden its sphere of operation, nationally as well as internationally. Of course, this is not a mechanical and linear process, but one which is liable to be furthered or hindered by a complex set of natural and socio-economic conditions.

The process of transnationalization, i.e. the internationalization of capital, is certainly not a new phenomenon, but one which has already been of considerable importance particularly in the post-war period, when exports of productive capital in the form of foreign direct investments have reached levels far above those of the pre-war period. In particular, the period from the early 1960s to the mid-1970s saw an increased rate of foreign direct investment, both in absolute terms and in proportion to foreign trade, G.D.P. and domestic investment.

For the period 1960-73 the average annual growth rate of total international direct investments was nearly 12%, i.e. approximately one and a half times the average growth rate of the O.E.C.D. countries' G.D.P. at current prices, and almost equal to the growth rate of international trade.[24] The growth rate of foreign direct investment flows from O.E.C.D. countries during 1974-78 was the same as in the preceding period, which when inflation is accounted for, however, represents a marked slow-down in real terms. But this slow-down was not more than the decrease in the rate of growth of real G.N.P. in the O.E.C.D. area since 1973, although it was much less than the increase in international trade which rose annually by about 19% in current prices during the period 1974-78.[25]

In absolute terms, the value of the worldwide stock of foreign direct investment increased from $ 158 to $ 287 billion between 1971 and 1976, representing an increase of 82%.[26] Foreign direct investments are still increasingly concentrated in the developed countries, which account at present for nearly three-quarters of the total compared with around two-thirds in the 1960s. The share of the developing countries in foreign direct investments has, however, been on the increase since 1973.

Although the share of the former colonial powers, France and the United Kingdom, in total direct foreign investments has been on the decline, these two powers together with the U.S.A. are still the main home countries of the transnational corporations despite the fact that the Federal Republic of Germany and Japan have in the 1970s drastically increased their rate of expansion.

After the standstill brought about by World War II, private direct foreign investments *in developing countries* made an upswing in the 1950s. By the end of the 1960s the average annual flow to these countries (including reinvested earnings) was around $ 3 billion. In constant 1975 dollars, the growth rate in the 1960s was about 4% per annum. The first half of the 1970s witnessed an accelerated rate of investment, reaching $ 10 billion in 1975. The annual growth rate in this period reached 10% at constant prices.[27]

When we look at the changes in the flows of international direct investment to developing countries in periods of economic prosperity and of crisis, the following picture emerges: the growth rate in real terms (that is using the O.E.C.D. consumer price index in current dollar terms as deflator) decelerated from the period 1960-68 to the period 1968-73, but regained its impetus in the period 1973-78, that is in the period characterized by increasing oil prices and subsequently the more widespread economic crisis in the Western countries. While the growth of direct investment flows to developing countries has been less rapid than to developed countries in the period 1960-73, it has been more rapid in the period 1973-78.[28]

According to O.E.C.D. reports, the share of developing countries in total foreign direct investment has increased in the post-1974 period, reversing the generally declining trend in earlier periods. The U.S.A. is still the dominant source of private investments in developing countries, accounting for just over 50% of total flows from 1960 to 1975. The United Kingdom and France retained a relatively high share (10% and 8% respectively), while the shares of Germany and Japan reached 9% and 8%. Private investment flows from these five countries accounted for more than 80% of total flows during the period 1960-76.[29]

Despite the increased rate of investment flows to developing countries, the rate of these flows in proportion to total flows remained small for most of the industrialized countries. For the U.S.A. the flow of foreign investment to developing countries was only 14% of the total (1966-76), for the United Kingdom 19% (1965-76), and for Germany and France roughly 30% in 1966-76, while it reached 60% for Japan in the period 1966-76.[30]

The bulk of foreign investments in developing countries has been to Latin America (with Brazil and Mexico as the main recipients) accounting for 37%

of the total. South East Asia and East Asia (with Indonesia as the major recipient) accounted for 27% of the total, while the African Continent only took 12%.[31]

In terms of sectors the investment flows have been increasingly directed towards manufacturing and associated services, notably banking (accounting for more than half of the total of foreign investments), while manufacturing alone accounted for about one-third of total investment. The petroleum sector (including natural gas) is, in spite of increased nationalization efforts on the part of the developing countries, still taking up a major share: 33% of the total.

However, the rate of foreign direct investments is only one part, albeit the major one, of the pattern of internationalization of capital. Full or partial control over foreign production is also developing along new lines, with investments based on non-equity arrangements, licensing and management contracts. Other new activities in recent years have been arrangements involving not only the transnational corporations, but also local enterprises, private or public, and other foreign investors. These new trends are at least in part an accommodation to policies pursued by the governments of developing countries, aimed at increasing their share and degree of control in realizing their national development goals.

At the same time there has been a shift away from equity participation to the use of loans and suppliers' credits, and a shift from direct control by the parent company to management participation, technical assistance, production-sharing, supply contracts etc., all of which contribute to blurring the picture of internationalization of capital as defined solely by the rate of direct foreign investments. It is clear that we must frame a much broader understanding of the internationalization of capital; this point is also brought out in Figure 1.

From Figure 1 it appears that the structure of financial receipts by developing countries has changed; whereas previously direct investments constituted the major private sector financial transfer, the picture now shows that private bank lending (which has grown from a few per cent of total receipts in 1960 to more than 30% in 1978), export credits and portfolio investments contribute increasingly to the financial transfers to developing countries.

This new trend — which has been labelled a 'new form' of investment in developing countries[32] — is a reflection of the new conditions for capital accumulation in the Western capitalist nations. The transnational corporations are not only investing abroad in the traditional sense, but are also using the recycling of the petrodollars (the huge financial reserves piling up in the international banks) and the support obtained from the state in the developed countries in the form of official export credits, to internationalize production in an effort to lessen the effects of the international economic crisis. The export of turn-key factories or other package programmes intended for the starting up of industrial production in the developing countries is an example of these 'new forms' of internationalization; these often huge sales contracts help keep the capital groups in business in the face of the contraction of their usual Western markets.

26

Figure 1 Long-term changes in the structure of developing countries' total
net external financial receipts, 1960-78

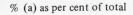

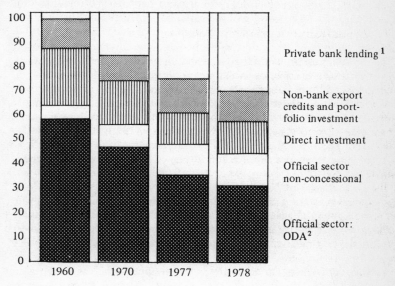

Private bank lending [1]

Non-bank export
credits and port-
folio investment

Direct investment

Official sector
non-concessional

Official sector:
ODA [2]

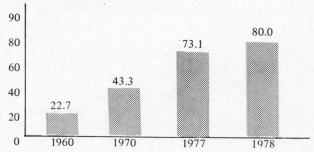

1. Including bond lending and export credits by private banks.
2. Including grants by private voluntary agencies.

Source: Development Co-operation: 1979 Review, (O.E.C.D., Paris, 1979), p. 67.

27

In addition, these new investment trends reflect the changes in the international division of labour, in which a certain number of developing countries have succeeded in achieving a rapid industrialization, most often by virtue of the intervention of the peripheral state.

We will now turn to some of the consequences for the developing countries of this changing international picture.

The Reproduction Process in the Periphery

Apart from the internationalization of capital in its more traditional sense — that is direct financial transfers from industrialized to developing countries — the internationalization of certain types of commodity capital has also become increasingly important in recent years. This is particularly true in the case of the export of machinery from industrialized to developing countries, which increased by 16% annually from 1966 to 1973, and by 27% annually from 1974 to 1976-77.[33] While the export of means of production to the developing countries thus has increased — and in particular has done so since the so-called oil crisis — the export of consumer goods, on the other hand, has stagnated.

The changing structure of commodity exchanges between industrialized and developing countries is shown in Table 1. As can be seen from the table, there has been in recent years an important increase in the export of industrial goods from developing countries to industrialized countries. Correspondingly,

Table 1. The Exchange of Commodities between Centre and Periphery (%)

| | As Percentage of Total Exports | | | | |
	1960	1965	1970	1975	1978
From Periphery to Centre					
Exports of industrial goods (SITC: 5+6+7+8)	13	16	22	15	21
From Centre to Periphery					
Exports of capital goods (SITC: 7)	35	38	41	46	47
Exports of other industrial goods (SITC: 5+6+8)	40	38	39	35	36

Source: UN Yearbook of International Trade Statistics, 1979.

there has been a remarkable increase in the export of means of production from the industrialized countries to the developing countries. Both these trends support the view that in a number of developing countries an export-oriented industrialization has taken root.

In a recent study of relations between the E.E.C. and the developing countries, these tendencies have been confirmed. Between 1972 and 1977 the export of capital goods from the E.E.C. to the developing countries rose nearly threefold, while the export of manufactured goods from the developing countries to the E.E.C. area rose equally fast.[34]

Not least in the period following the oil crisis, there seems to have been an increase in the internationalization of capital in its very broadest sense, including commodity capital. Obviously, the developing countries are increasingly involved in the global expansion of capitalist relations of production, resulting in new production and reproduction processes taking place in the Periphery. Certainly, a number of developing countries have succeeded in attracting foreign capital by means of particularly favourable investment conditions, such as export processing zones with a well-equipped infrastructure, a highly qualified, but low-paid (and unorganized) workforce, tax exemption regulations, or other liberal investment regulations. The so-called Newly Industrializing Countries (NIC) including Brazil and Mexico in Latin America and South Korea, Taiwan, Singapore and Hong Kong in South East Asia have developed into export-oriented industrializing nations. The key factors in this development process have been the internationalization of capital on the one hand, and the role of the peripheral state on the other.

The newly industrializing countries may represent atypical countries in the Third World — and it is true that only a handful of other developing countries have succeeded in becoming internationally competitive in industrial production. But it seems that in the Periphery *new examples* are appearing of countries showing tendencies towards the establishment of advanced capitalist production and reproduction processes. In an African context, this may be the case in countries like Nigeria, Kenya, and the Ivory Coast.

Whether the additional build-up of an export-oriented industrialization in any way reflects the establishment of broader capitalist development processes transcending the so-called blocked development situation is a question to which we will devote our attention in the following treatment of our example of the Ivory Coast.

There is no doubt, however, that the global picture reveals a pattern of increased differentiation. Capital's basic tendency to uneven development is manifesting itself in the developing world with a few relatively well-off nations at the top, with a certain predisposition to break out of the blocked development situation, while the majority of countries are still in a stagnant or perhaps even deteriorating situation but the tendency to uneven development is also reflected in the industrialized countries, where certain countries during the crisis are losing ground in a fiercely competitive international situation, while others are emerging from the crisis in a shape at least as good as they entered it. The basic contradiction between on the one hand equalization of production conditions, the rate of profit, technology used, etc., and on the other hand inequality or differentiation seems to be an inescapable element in the present-day tendency towards the uneven development of capitalism. This equalization/inequality contradiction in the very same process of uneven development is illustrated at the local and regional levels, the national as well as the international levels. With a further deepening of the economic crisis, the concepts of Centre and Periphery may very well have to be redefined. The traditional connotation of the concepts as linked to the notions of industrialized versus developing countries seems at least to be a superficial and unsatisfactory categorization of countries with quite different preconditions for undergoing or keeping pace with a capitalist development process. In the future the international reproductive hierarchy will perhaps be not only a hierarchy within the Western industrialized nations, but a much more intermingled hierarchy of nations, including some Western countries and a limited number of countries from the Third World.

Notes

1. See e.g. Dietmar Goralczyk, *Weltmarkt, Weltwährungssystem und westeuropäische Integration* (Giessen, Focus Verlag, 1975), pp. 148-9, Klaus Busch, *Die Krise der europäischen Gemeinschaft* (Frankfurt, EVA-Verlag, 1978, pp. 11ff., and Albert Statz, 'Zur Geschichte der westeuropäischen Integration bis zur Gründung der EWG' in Frank Deppe (ed), *Europäische Wirtschaftsgemeinschaft (EWG)*, (Reinbeck, Rowohlt, 1975), pp. 110-74.
2. See Frank Deppe, *Arbeiterbewegung und westeuropäische Integration* (Köln, Pahl-Rugenstein Verlag, 1976), pp. 19-28, and Ulrich Rödel, 'Die Verschärfung der internationalen Konkurrenz' in Volhard Brandes (ed), *Handbuch 1. Perspektiven des Kapitalismus* (Frankfurt, EVA-Verlag, 1974), pp. 193-4.
3. Statz, op. cit., p. 127.
4. Ibid., p. 123.
5. Deppe, 1976, op. cit., p. 25, and Statz, op. cit., p. 135.
6. Rödel, op. cit., p. 196.
7. Statz, op. cit., p. 131.
8. Georges H. Lawson, 'La Côte d'Ivoire: 1960-70. Croissance et diversification dans africanisation' in J. Esseks (ed), *l'Afrique de l'indépendance politique à l'indépendance économique* (Grenoble, 1975).
9. Goralczyk, op. cit., p. 149.
10. Deppe, 1976, op. cit., p. 31.
11. Statz, op. cit., p. 155.
12. Busch, op. cit., p. 135.
13. Ernest Mandel, 'International Capitalism and "Supranationality" ' in Hugo Radice (ed), *International Firms and Modern Imperialism* (London, Penguin, 1975).
14. Busch, op. cit., p. 140.
15. Mandel, op. cit.
16. Nicos Poulantzas, *Classes in Contemporary Capitalism* (London, New Left Books, 1975), pp. 50ff.

17. Klaus Busch, *Die multinationalen Konzerne. Zur Analyse der Welt-marktbewegung des Kapitals* (Frankfurt, Suhrkamp Verlag, 1974). The base material for Busch's analysis is the Harvard Multinational Enterprise Study.
18. Deppe, 1976, op. cit.
19. Grant, L. Reuber *et al., Private Foreign Investments in Development* (Oxford, Oxford University Press, 1973), pp. 262-94.
20. Folker Fröbel, Jürgen Heinrichs and Otto Kreye, *Die neue internationale Arbeitsteilung. Strukturelle Arbeitslosigkeit in den Industrieländern und die Industrialisierung der Entwicklungsländer* (Reinbeck, Rowohlt, 1977).
21. The estimates quoted in Autorenkollektiv, 'Die Okonomische Lage in den Imperialistischen Ländern 1975/Anfang 1976', *IPW-Berichte*, No. 9, 1976, pp. 26-41.
22. Ibid., p. 33.
23. See the annual *Reviews* of the Development Assistance Committee, the O.E.C.D.
24. O.E.C.D., *Recent International Direct Investment Trends* (Paris, O.E.C.D., 1980), p. 5.
25. Ibid., pp. 11-12.
26. U.N., *Transnational Corporations in World Development: a Re-Examination* (New York, U.N., 1978), p. 8.
27. The World Bank, *Private Direct Foreign Investment in Developing Countries*. World Bank Staff Working Paper No. 348, 1979, p. 4.
28. O.E.C.D., op. cit., p. 14.
29. The World Bank, op. cit., p. 4.
30. Ibid., p. 5.
31. Ibid., Table II.4, p. 6.
32. See Charles Oman, 'Changing International Investment Strategies: The "New Forms" of Investment in Developing Countries', O.E.C.D. Development Centre, Conference Document No. 2, 2nd Meeting of Experts on Foreign Investments and its Impact on Development, Paris, 1980.
33. U.N., *Yearbook of International Trade Statistics* (New York, U.N., 1977).
34. E.E.C., *Europe and the Third World − a Study on Interdependence*. E.E.C. dossier, Brussels, 1978.

2. The Internationalization of French Capital

We have observed in the previous chapter that the changing historical conditions for capital accumulation in Western Europe in the 1960s and 1970s led to new ways in which peripheral capital in its reproduction was embodied in the reproduction of the capital of the Centre. The internationalization of capital, broadly defined, has led to a situation in some of the peripheral countries where broader patterns of industrialization are emerging. This industrialization at least partly based on a local accumulation of capital is certainly putting a question-mark against the notion of blocked capital accumulation as defined by, for example, Samir Amin.

We have also referred to the increasing interest of U.S., Japanese and West German capital groups in undertaking direct investments in the manufacturing sector of the Periphery in the 1960s and the 1970s, although this has not been the case to the same extent with the former colonial powers of France and the United Kingdom.

In order to substantiate the main arguments presented in Chapter 1, we shall in this chapter examine the internationalization of French capital in relation to the Periphery. However, we shall only look into some aspects of this process. In particular, we shall examine certain groupings of peripheral countries, certain economic sectors, and the importance generally of commodity exports versus capital exports. We shall then turn to the question of the intervention of the French state in the Periphery. We will, in particular, deal with the Franc Zone which has been one of the major mechanisms binding the economic development of France to the Francophone countries in West Africa. However, the analysis of this special aspect of French state intervention must be related to other forms of state intervention as well. One important example is the state's role in furthering the process of concentration and centralization of French industry, which we shall discuss from the point of view of one industrial branch — the textile industry.

The Process of Internationalization of French Capital

The first period for investments abroad by French firms was 1945-58. The initial investments were primarily in those countries which had most contact with the French economy, i.e. other European countries and present or former French colonies. The first wave of investments was primarily in trade ventures, where the risk was limited and gradual (progressing from arrangements with a foreign sales agent to a fully fledged distribution subsidiary). This process did not involve risking a lot of capital or attempting to capture a large share of the market at the outset.

French enterprises which have established themselves abroad have been analysed in various ways by Charles Albert Michalet and Michel Delapierre.[1] The degree of control exercised by the parent company, the techniques of market penetration (ranging from acquisition of existing enterprises to development of new ones), and the extent of co-operation with other firms, whether French, host country or third party. Their general finding is that their sample firms, in whatever line of business, prefer to maintain majority control in the developed countries and seek — or have imposed upon them — minority positions in the less developed countries.

They also point to a distinction in the nationalities of joint-venture partners. In operations in developed countries there is a clear preference for local partners, but in less developed countries there is a significant tendency towards third-country partners.[2] In conclusion, the two authors point to the tendency in the structure of French investments towards an increasing proportion of joint ventures between French companies and others in the developing countries; this is the case to a much lower degree in developed countries.

Concerning markets, the developing countries do not offer attractions comparable to those of the developed countries. This reflects their lower purchasing power and consequent reduced attractiveness for commercial ventures.

It is interesting to note that, for an intermediate group of countries like Yugoslavia, Spain, Portugal and Brazil, the authors observe that the process of French companies locating their manufacturing capacity overseas instead of exporting to these markets continues, but more to avoid obstacles to exporting than to take advantage of any benefits associated with local operations. Tariff and other barriers, government protection of local producers, and nationalistic attitudes on the part of customers all received substantial attention from the respondents to the questionnaire.

On the basis of the findings in the study, it seems that the sample companies are much more afraid of being evicted from their established markets than they are attracted by any of the host countries' investment incentives.

Government assistance or local market potential were mentioned by less than 10% of the sample. Thus, production overseas is regarded more in terms of being able to carry on exporting by other means than as a basis for rationalizing manufacturing activities.[3]

An important investment incentive, however, is the availability of raw materials. French firms often use their foreign affiliates for the processing of raw materials or the manufacturing of components which, in turn, are further processed in France for sale at home and abroad. Countries hosting these activities must be able to cope with complex technology and minimize transport costs. However, the developing countries as a group have only few attractions for the French investor compared to countries like Spain, Portugal, Yugoslavia and Brazil.

In the period 1967-75, French direct investment in the Franc Zone amount to 15% of total French direct investments abroad. In the same period French investments in the E.E.C. ('the Six') amounted to 23%, while the total share of O.E.C.D. countries was 65%. Among the individual O.E.C.D. countries the highest share of investments went to the U.S.A. (11%).[4]

This figure of 15% for the Franc Zone in the period 1967-75 represents a continuous decline in importance; in the late 1960s it was 30-40% and it fell in the mid-1970s to only 2-5%. This decline is not only due to relative changes in the regional distribution of French direct investments but is also a result of the rapid absolute decline in French direct investments in the Franc Zone[5] as is apparent in Table 2.

Table 2 French Direct Investments in Selected Groups of Countries, 1967-75 (% and millions of francs)

%	1967	1969	1971	1973	1975	1967-75
E.E.C. (the Six)	16.7	–*	26.7	24.4	19.4	23.3
O.E.C.D.	43.4	37.9	57.5	71.7	75.8	65.1
Franc Zone	35.7	25.0	21.5	4.1	2.4	15.0
Total (%)	100	100	100	100	100	100
Total (francs)	1,747	943	1,923	3,245	4,136	21,651

* French disinvestments were in this year larger than investments.

Source: Ministère de l'Economie et des Finances, *Statistiques et études financieres*, vols. 20 (1968) to 28 (1976). Also Banque de France, 'Balance des Paiements de l'annee 1975 entre la France et l'exterieur', Paris, 1976.

This tendency is caused by a number of factors. But first and foremost it represents the result of a major shift in the political and economic orientation of France, implying a change in policy from a closed world market between France and the former colonies to a more open policy towards the

West European industrialized countries. The French Government in the VIth Plan (1971-75) deliberately encouraged direct investments in other E.E.C. countries and the U.S.A., and made other efforts to increase the competitiveness of the French industrial sector.

Turning to the policy of the Ivory Coast Government as a member of the Franc Zone, it has been able to attract French investment into import substitution activities. This is also the case for other countries in the Franc Zone, but it is a characteristic of the Ivory Coast that the investments there are much larger than in the other countries of the Franc Zone, and — more important — that the Ivory Coast is the only country that has been able to attract large industrial plants producing commodities for export.

Michalet and Delapierre conclude when discussing the profile of internationalization of French firms in relation to developing countries that a number of constraints exist in relation to direct investments, especially in terms of political risks and the limited market. The French businessmen's reaction to all this is to avoid long-term production commitments in these countries. They prefer to keep their activities there on a trading basis as much as possible. This is in clear contrast to the pattern of internationalization of U.S. capital groups, which 'are trying to develop a genuine international division of labour by assigning to each foreign subsidiary a pre-planned role in an overall operational scheme'.[6]

The most important findings of the study seem to be that the French firms primarily internationalize by *exporting* French products and generally limit themselves to this pattern of internationalization, and set up production subsidiaries only on a limited scale. However, an important reservation has to be made. The authors point to the prominence of two categories, lumber and textiles, in direct investments in Africa. The reason for this is to be found in the fact that the principal raw materials, tropical wood and cotton, are readily available there. They also emphasize that, for a number of years, there has been significant investment activity in Africa involving the development of textile plants to serve both local and the French markets.[7] This observation has a special importance in our study, since we look most carefully at textiles. In other words, this industry is atypical in relation to the internationalization pattern of other French industrial branches. For this and other reasons, the results of our case study on textiles, therefore, cannot be generalized to all French industry.

Turning to the French textile industry, the period from World War I until the end of the 1950s had been characterized by the establishment of a closed market between France and her colonies. For the textile industry this guaranteed secure markets for French textile products. However, it caused France to be turned into an area of high prices, since increases in productivity and structural development in the French textile industry were delayed.

In the 1950s and early 1960s two different events drastically eliminated the possibility of the continued operation of a closed market overseas. First, the French colonies representing the most important textile markets, i.e. Indochina and Algeria, won their independence, leading to a rapid decline in exports to these two countries. Secondly, the establishment of the E.E.C. led to the elimination of the protection of the French market from its European competitors. This marked the beginning of a change in policy of the French state towards the textile sector, gradually giving less importance to the protection of markets in the Periphery and more importance to the furthering of structural changes in the textile industry so as to lead eventually to the creation of an internationally competitive industrial sector.

An Example: The Structure of the French Textile Industry

Table 3 shows the size and growth of turnover for 1969-74 of the most important French textile companies. As can be seen, three main groups dominate the French textile industry: Dollfus-Mieg & Cie., Agache-Willot, and Boussac. In the following discussion these three companies will be used as the point of departure for outlining the main tendencies in the process of concentration and centralization of the French textile industry since World War II.

Table 3 Turnover in Leading French Textile Companies (Millions of French francs)

	1969	1974	1969-74, % change
Dollfus-Mieg & Cie. (D.M.C.)	846.6	2,152.1	+ 154.2
Agache-Willot	1,900.0	2,547.4	+ 34.1
Boussac (textile) *	550.0	630.0	+ 14.5
S.A.I.C. (Groupe Schaeffer)	94.4	315.1	+ 233.7
Cernay S.A.C. (Groupe Cernay)	70.6	160.0	+ 126.6
Texunion (Groupe D.M.C.)	328.8	594.5	+ 80.8
H. G. Perrin (Groupe H.G.P.)	108.5	163.6	+ 50.8
Consortium Général Textile (Groupe Agache-Willot)	565.6	831.6	+ 47.0
Motte Bossut	84.6	123.9	+ 46.5
Filt. Dollfus-Mieg (Groupe D.M.C.)	205.0	281.1	+ 37.1
Le Blan (Groupe Sofitex)	84.1	103.1	+ 22.6

* Estimate.

Source: Guirec Delanoë, *Etude sur l'évolution de la concentration dans l'industrie du textile en France* (Luxembourg, C.C.E., 1975), p. 37.

Two features of the French textile industry are particularly significant in the first period immediately after World War II. First was the existence of an extremely powerful, vertically integrated group, Boussac, which controlled approximately 10% of all aspects of French cotton textile production. Second was the excessive concentration of the majority of those textile-finishing activities not controlled by Boussac into two large firms, Gillet-Thaon and Schaeffer. Boussac kept its position as the leading group of French textile companies until the end of the 1950s, when imports of cheap cotton goods from Hong Kong and Japan made competition fierce, especially within the groups of commodities where Boussac had specialized.

Although it is not possible here to enter into a detailed analysis of the present organization of French textile interests, it is useful to note the major groups which have emerged to replace Boussac. Of these the leading one is the Groupe Agache-Willot. The other main group is Dollfus-Mieg & Cie. which in 1969 became financially associated with another result of central-ization, Rhône-Poulenc-Gillet (chemicals and synthetic fibres). They have a common affiliate, Texunion, which also ranks among the major French textile companies.

The centralization which took place in the period 1969-73 first and fore-most concerned Agache-Willot and Dollfus-Mieg & Cie. The fall of Boussac reached a dramatic culmination in August 1978, when Agache-Willot took over the Boussac group, thereby reducing the three leading French textile groups to two: Dollfus-Mieg & Cie, and Agache Willot.

Dollfus-Mieg & Cie.

This firm was established in Mulhouse in the 19th Century. Together with another firm les Ets. Thiriez et Cartier-Bresson, whose activities were concen-trated in the northern part of France, in the Vosges and the Paris area, it was the largest French producer of cotton yarn. From 1961 these two firms undertook close co-operation with each other. In the course of the last 15 years, they have acquired interests and affiliated plants and firms in cotton, textiles, wool, semi-textiles and printing of patterns etc.[8] The company Tex-union, which has important interests in the Ivorian textile industry, is controlled by the Groupe Dollfus-Mieg & Cie. through a 51% share-holding.[9]

Agache–Willot

This firm was established in 1967 by a fusion of Ets. Agache and La Société M.J. Willot & Cie. The two companies and their branches cover the full spectrum of textile products including spinning, weaving, colouring, printing on cotton cloth, wool, chemical fibres, jute, etc. In 1968 the firm was transformed into a holding company, and a subsidiary company Consor-tium Général Textile was formed, in order to regroup all its industrial and trading activities. Since then, the Groupe Agache-Willot has bought a number of textile firms and supermarkets[10] and has in the last five years continued this line of developing their activities in production as well as in distribution. Most recently, this can be seen in the take-over in 1978 of control of the Belgian retail chain Les Galeries Ansprach and of the textile factories of Boussac in the Vosges.[11]

It is characteristic that only a limited number of foreign firms have invested in the French textile industry. According to one source only six — one British, two Belgian, and three American.[12] Among the American firms is Riegel Textile, which has 32% of the shares in Schaeffer,[13] and together with Schaeffer has invested in the Ivory Coast in Blue Bell Côte d'Ivoire, producing blue jeans especially for the markets in Western Europe and the U.S.A.

The two largest French textile firms, Dollfus-Mieg & Cie. and Agache-Willot, have invested in all parts of the world, but especially in Western Europe and the U.S.A. Schaeffer has specialized in investments in Africa, while Boussac when still in existence had no investments outside France but simply supplied commodities for foreign markets by means of exports.

Of special importance for the analysis of the interrelation between the French and Ivorian textile industries are the firms Schaeffer and Texunion (affiliate of Dollfus-Mieg & Cie. (D.M.C.)). There is an interconnection of interests with the trading company C.F.A.O., which is deeply engaged in the Ivorian textile industry. Texunion (D.M.C.) has important financial interests in Ets. Confreville and in SOCITAS, both important textile firms operating in the Ivory Coast. Besides the firms mentioned, no other French textile companies have investments on a large scale in West Africa.

Historically, relations with West Africa have been the cause of conflict between the French textile companies in the 1960s. This conflict was not so much a struggle among the French firms, all of which had already benefited from privileged access to French colonial markets, as over the ways in which they could retain their former colonial privileges. Because it raised the vital issue of the competitiveness of the French textile industry, it aligned the less progressive firms (notably Boussac) which wished to keep production centralized in France, against those (Agache-Willot) which recognized the importance of decentralization not as much for reasons of production as of market control, and which were competitive enough to permit decentralization.

The issue led to Boussac's intervention at the French Ministry of Co-operation in 1968, in an attempt to block the establishment of industries overseas. Dollfus-Mieg & Cie., Agache-Willot and Schaeffer, however, were then in the process of jumping the protective tariff barriers erected by French-speaking African countries and locating import-substituting finishing operations within these overseas markets. As the larger French firms internationalized production to the former French colonies, these African markets were effectively closed to exports of cloth from the smaller French cotton textile firms during the 1970s. (For an empirical illustration, see Table 5.)

In what way has the process of concentration and centralization influenced employment and the work process in the French textile industry? J.Y. Darrake[14] has concluded that the development of the French textile industry in the period 1959-74 has led to four negative development trends for workers in the industry, namely:

(1)   a reduction in the number of workers employed;
(2)   a deskilling of the work force;
(3)   a modification in the structure of employment; and

(4)   a deterioration in the conditions of work.

First, Darrake points to the reduction in the workforce of 160,000 workers during the period 1959-74, i.e. 28% of the initial number of workers. The annual rate of decrease in the workforce has accelerated with time, being 1.5% in 1954-62, but increasing to 2% in 1962-68.

Secondly, he observes that, in the period 1954-62, the number of skilled workers in the French textile industry fell by 53%, while the number of unskilled workers increased by 13%. In terms of the ratio between unskilled and skilled workers, this led to a market predominance of unskilled workers. This process of deskilling is found in the French industrial sector generally, but most strongly in the textile industry.

Thirdly, a modification of the structure of employment can be observed, in the sense that an increasing percentage of the work force is male. This development is seen by Darrake as a consequence of the increase in hard physical labour in the production process, and the introduction of more shifts. This has also led to the replacement of many French workers by migrant workers, often young and male, from other countries.[15]

In conclusion, the recent concentration and centralization process in the French textile industry has led to increased productivity by a change in technique in the work process, an increased use of unskilled workers, and a deterioration in the conditions of work. As will become apparent, this process has also led to the possibility of transferring some of the work processes to the Periphery, where unskilled labour is abundant and relatively cheap compared to France.

French State Intervention

Three main phases of state intervention in relation to the French textile industry can be discerned.

The first phase, from the end of World War II until 1958, was — as mentioned above — characterized by the further protection of markets in the colonies and subsidies to textile production in France.

The second phase started in 1958, the year of the establishment of the Fifth French Republic, the establishment of the E.E.C., and the time when the dissolution of the French empire began to become obvious. These three events led in the coming years to a major re-orientation in the type of state intervention, giving more emphasis to structural transformation of the industry in order to create a competitive economic base. However, it was not an overnight change of policy, but a gradual introduction through the 1960s of new areas of state intervention, with the aim of creating a few large and internationally competitive firms within each industrial branch. At the same time, the formerly protected national market became more and more open as a result of the E.E.C. free trade zone in manufactured goods. In the first half of the 1970s, imports of textiles from the developing countries were also relatively open.

Thirdly, a major invasion of textile imports from developing countries led the French Government in 1976 to insist on a more restrictive E.E.C. policy in relation to those imports. This manifested itself in 1977 when the Multifibre Arrangement was renewed, and when the E.E.C. insisted on a much more restrictive practice than the one existing during the first period of the Multifibre Arrangement. At the same time the French state continues to support the merger of large textile companies, thereby undertaking an even more direct role in restructuration than before.

It is these three periods characterized by different types of state intervention, and their impact on the structure of the textile industry, that we must analyse.

In the post-war years, French industrialists were forced to adjust to the general liberalization of tariff barriers. Within the textile sector, certain branches (silk and wool) were able to adjust to the absence of trade restrictions. The same was not true, however, of the French cotton industry. Protectionist by tradition, this sector sought to update the former system of privilege. In this it anticipated far-reaching support from the state, and these expectations were fully justified.[16]

In the 1st Plan (1946-47)[17] the problem of the French textile industry was seen primarily as a structural problem, caused by the industry's being made up of many small firms, and as a problem about machinery, caused by the equipment being generally old and technically outdated. The importance of investments in new machinery was, therefore, underlined, in order to keep the domestic market and to be competitive in the markets of other West European countries.

In the IInd Plan, it was noted that the deficit on the balance of trade caused by the textile sector was rapidly increasing. In the period 1950-53, the textile sector alone was responsible for between 20 and 33% of the total deficit on the trade balance.[18] Therefore, the IInd Plan considered especially the best way to reduce the deficit.

As a result, state intervention in this first period continued to emphasize protected markets in the colonies, and began to enforce a supply of cotton from the colonies. This was a relatively new phenomenon, since most of the imports of cotton up till that time had come from the U.S.A. Cotton from the French colonies was not particularly cheap compared to U.S. imports. On the contrary, French textile producers paid some of the highest prices in Europe for cotton.[19] This was of special importance as raw material makes up 60-70% of costs in yarn and 30% in cotton fabric.[20]

French state intervention consequently took three different forms in this period. First, textile producers were given a price subsidy of 15-20% which equalized the difference between production costs in France and other countries. The subsidy was paid for by a tax on domestic sales of textiles.[21]

Secondly, a *Caisse de Stabilisation des Cours* was set up in the French West African area (the A.O.F. area) and in Togo. The aim of this was to subsidize the price of the cotton bought by France. This was done by enforcing duty on other export crops and by import duties and domestic taxes. This led to a reduction in the price of cotton from the French colonies by 15-20%, a reduction which in reality was paid for by the population in these areas to the advantage of the French trading companies and the French textile industry.[22]

Thirdly, the markets of the colonial areas were being monopolized by the French textile industry, both by tariffs and by monetary means. In spite of the recognition in the Ist Plan of the structural problems of the French textile industry, state intervention continued in the same way as before World War II. However, with hindsight, we can see that the state tended to weaken the industry by overprotecting it.

1958 seems to be the year from which the changes that took place in the next few years originated. However, when reading the IIIrd Plan, published in July 1958, one does not gain that impression. In their analysis of the preceding period, the authors of the plan note the increasing difficulties for exports of textiles in general, and specifically the ones caused by the independence of Indochina, but they consider the fall in textile exports to be a temporary setback. Although the IIIrd Plan mentions the problems of France in being an area of high prices and acknowledges the necessity of structural change, the major part of the report is concerned with how to maintain the existing textile industry by increasing exports to the colonies and increasing imports of raw cotton from the same areas.

This was clearly an intermediate period, when the consequences of the creation of the E.E.C. and the dissolution of the colonial empire led gradually to important changes in the form of state intervention.

In the Vth (1966-70) and VIth (1971-75) Plans, a deliberate attempt to attack some of the structural problems of the French manufacturing sector can be seen for the first time. In the Vth Plan it is clear that the state wanted to promote a process of concentration and centralization in order to create one or two internationally competitive groups.[23] A number of instruments were set up for this purpose. Of these the principal vehicle became the Economic and Social Fund (created in 1955), which was authorized to grant tax relief to firms engaged in takeovers and mergers and handled loans to the designated firms. One of the reasons for the importance of this fund was that the low level of self-financing in French industry made it practically impossible to finance a major industrial investment without state support. The state limited its support to those investments which conformed to the guidelines set out in the national plans and, therefore, the development of the textile sector as such depended upon the priorities of the state.

In order to implement the centralization processes foreseen in the Vth Plan, additional credits were made available in 1967 for restructuring through the Economic and Social Development Fund, and tax laws were modified to permit firms which merged to enjoy considerable advantages. In practice the larger part of these funds were used by the major textile firms. The creation of an additional fund for restructuring purposes in 1966 strengthened this tendency to support the mergers and investment activities of the large textile companies. During the first ten years of its existence, it financed one-third of all investments in the cotton-spinning and weaving branches of the textile industry. It thus facilitated the restructuring efforts of notably Agache-Willot, Dollfus-Mieg & Cie., and Schaeffer.[24]

Although it is difficult to assess clearly how far this state policy influenced the number of mergers taking place, it seems clear from different studies that it had less impact on the textile industry than on other industrial branches.[25] Examples of industrial branches in which state intervention was more active are energy, computers and steel, where the influence of the state was high, and the chemical industry and heavy industrial equipment, where it was only moderate.

State intervention has thus only to some extent taken the form of direct intervention in the industrial structure, but the authors of the VIth Plan envisaged that a gradual opening towards the world market would slowly bring about the necessary structural changes in the textile industry.[26]

In 1976 French exports of textiles increased by 6% compared to 1975, but imports increased an enormous 45%. The major part of the increase was caused by imports from developing countries participating in the Multifibre Agreement and thus limited in their exports to France in accordance with the so-called self-limiting agreement. However, during 1976 it was discovered that the import restrictions of the self-limiting agreements were being broken, through three different channels.[27] First, a number of countries in South East Asia, including Singapore and Hong Kong, used Mauritius as a re-export point, utilizing the free access of this country to the E.E.C. Secondly, re-export via the Netherlands and Germany also increased, taking advantage of the textile import quotas of these countries under the Multifibre Agreement. As soon as the commodities were inside the E.E.C. area, it was quite easy to export from one E.E.C. country to another and thereby avoid the fixed distribution of quotas among E.E.C. countries. Thirdly, a certain amount of re-exporting took place via Benin, Senegal, Cameroun and the Ivory Coast.[28]

All this led to the French Government's insistence that imports from the developing countries must be limited, and formed part of the background for the E.E.C.'s very tough position at the negotiations for the renewal of the Multifibre Agreement in 1977. In terms of French state intervention, this step meant that, once again, there was a return to a protectionist line in textiles.

The French Textile Industry and the Periphery

French imports of cotton yarn have increased rapidly, by as much as 494% in the period 1970-74. At the same time, imports from the E.E.C. only increased by 295%. French imports of cotton fabric have also increased rapidly, but with less speed than imports of cotton yarn. In 1970-74 the growth rate was 291%; and for this commodity the E.E.C.'s share has decreased, from 63% in 1970 to 54% in 1974.

Table 4 shows the distribution of French imports of yarn, fabric and

clothing among different groups of countries outside the E.E.C. As can be
seen from the table, the Mediterranean countries dominate with 38% of
French imports, followed by the Asian and Latin American countries (29%)
and the A.C.P. (Africa/Caribbean/Pacific) countries (12%). The increasing
importance of the developing countries in the imports of cotton textiles into
France is worth mentioning.

Table 4. French Imports of Certain Cotton Textiles, 1976 (Tons)

	Total Imports from outside E.E.C.	A.C.P.	Mediter-ranean	Asia/Latin America	Socialist Countries	General Scheme of Preferences – France
Yarn	18,760	819	11,330	4,442	685	1,484
Fabric	34,837	6,813	7,931	9,109	9,312	1,672
Clothing	16,489	454	6,988	5,544	3,419	84
Total	70,086	8,086	26,249	19,095	13,416	3,240
% of Total	100	11.5	37.5	29.3	19.1	4.6

Source: *F.C.A.M. Dossier d'information* (Abidjan, Ministère du Plan, 1978),
Table A.

On average France receives 12% of her textile imports from the A.C.P.
countries compared with 2% in the case of the E.E.C. Further, it appears that
it is fabric which is especially important in the French imports. For this commodity the market share for the A.C.P. countries is 20% in the case of France
and 3% for the E.E.C. as a whole. As was the case for the E.E.C., French
imports of cotton yarn (4%) and clothing (3%) from the A.C.P. countries
have relatively less importance than cotton fabric (20%).

There has been a smaller increase in exports from France of cotton yarn,
namely 106% in the period 1970-74. It is noteworthy that the figure for
exports for the E.E.C. area as a whole is greater than this (149%). For other
European countries the growth rate was 205%, while French exports to Africa
have actually declined in absolute terms. The share of the E.E.C. increased
from 55% in 1970 to 67% in 1974. Other European countries have had a
limited increase, from 9% in 1970 to 13% in 1974.

It is worth emphasizing that the export share of the African countries is
declining considerably. The export share of the countries in North Africa was
21% in 1970, but only 9% in 1974. For other countries in Africa it was 6% in
1970, and 3% in 1974.

The trends for cotton fabric are parallel to those outlined for cotton yarn.
French exports increased only slowly from 1970 to 1974 (130%), while
exports to the E.E.C. have increased more rapidly, by 187%. The increase in
exports to other European countries has been 201%, but again the record for
Africa is very bad. For the countries in North Africa there has been an increase
for the period 1970-74 of only 42%, and for other countries in Africa a direct
decline of 36%.

43

Turning to clothing, in terms of country groupings, we see again an increased concentration on the E.E.C. countries. The share of the E.E.C. in 1970 was already 61%, but increased by 1974 to 76%. Other European countries increased their share in the same period from 7 to 9%. On the other hand, we find again a direct decline in the share of exports to the African Continent. North Africa shows a decline from 2% in 1970 to 1% in 1974, while the share of other countries in Africa has fallen from 18 to 5%.

Relations between France and the Ivory Coast

As can be seen in Table 5, the Ivory Coast is not very important as a market for cotton yarn from France, and exports ceased altogether in 1976. For cotton fabric there has traditionally been quite a large French export, amounting in 1965 to nearly 8% of total French exports. But — as appears from the table — the export of this commodity from France to the Ivory Coast has, practically speaking, stopped in 1976.

Table 5. French Exports of Cotton Yarn, Fabric and Clothing, 1960-76 (Tons)

	1960	*1965*	*1970*	*1975*	*1976*
Yarn (C.C.T. 55.05)					
Total	9,993	13,993	16,876	14,248	16,102
Ivory Coast	97	99	87	27	0
Ivory Coast as %					
of total	0.97	0.70	0.51	0.18	—
Fabric (C.C.T. 55.09)					
Total	52,233	38,906	29,348	28,160	40,374
Ivory Coast	3,065	3,057	1,242	309	27
Ivory Coast as %					
of total	5.86	7.85	4.23	1.09	0.06
Clothing (C.C.T. 60 and 61)					
Total	19,750	18,699	29,647	56,513	50,096
Ivory Coast	347	408	413	409	237
Ivory Coast as %					
of total	1.76	2.18	1.39	0.72	0.47

Source: *Statistiques du commerce extérieur de la France* (various years).

Only in the case of clothing does France still export to the Ivory Coast, but this commodity too is of declining importance relative to total French exports. However, the importance of the Ivory Coast for the French textile industry becomes clear when French direct investments in the Ivorian textile industry are considered (see Table 6).

Table 6. Direct Investments in the Ivorian Textile Industry by Main French Textile Groups, 1977

Agache-Willot	*Dollfus-Mieg & Cie., Texunion*	*Schaeffer*	*Boussac/ CITEC*
Grantry-Abidjan 100% of 175 million F C.F.A.	Gonfreville 10% of 2,000 million F C.F.A. (via Gonfreville): SOCITAS SOFITEX	ICODI 8.3% of 1,700 million F C.F.A. (via ICODI): COTIVO Blue Bell Côte d'Ivoire	Nil

Source: 'Les 200 groupes francais d'Afrique noire', *Bulletin de l'Afrique noire*, Special No., 1978, pp. 4, 103, 210 and 296.

It should be noted that the investments in ICODI, COTIVO and Blue Bell Côte d'Ivoire by Schaeffer were in co-operation with the French trading firms C.F.A.O. and S.C.O.A. Similarly, the investments made by Texunion (Groupe Dollfus-Mieg & Cie.) in Gonfreville were undertaken in co-operation with the trading firm OPTORG.

In conclusion, it seems that French exports in textiles to the Ivory Coast decreased in the period 1960-76. However, at the same time the largest and most concentrated and centralized French textile companies have invested in the major textile companies of the Ivory Coast: Gonfreville and ICODI-COTIVO-Blue Bell Côte d'Ivoire. Besides these two groups, the only other large textile group in the Ivory Coast is UNIWAX-SOTEXI-UTEXI, which is dominated by Japanese capital. French participation in this group is limited to a French trading firm which is responsible for marketing the exports in France.

Changes in the strategy of internationalization of the French textile industry can be noted. In the early 1960s they exported yarn, fabric and clothing to the Ivory Coast, but since the end of the 1960s they have started to invest in the large Ivorian textile groups, involving also Ivorian state capital and U.S. capital. The motive behind these investments is on the one hand to keep a market formerly held through trade, and on the other to create a basis for exports to the world market. Naturally, as will be discussed more thoroughly in Chapter 4, the growing internal market in the Ivory Coast is a major factor in the decision of foreign capital to invest there; but equally important are the favourable investment conditions offered by the Ivorian state.

Summarizing the relations between the French textile industry and the

Periphery, the following main conclusions can be drawn. The French state has actively tried to change the most important external connections of the French textile industry, away from a closed and protected export market in the French colonies towards an outward-directed growth and direct competition with West European and American textile companies. The French textile industry has been made more competitive by French state efforts in supporting a process of capital concentration and centralization, with the aim of creating a few large companies which can cope with their major competitors on the world market. This process of concentration and centralization has led to changes in the work process and to the deskilling of the labour force. The change in technology employed has made it possible to transfer some of the work processes to the Periphery, where unskilled labour is abundant and relatively cheap.

Exports of productive capital from France to the Periphery are in the case of textiles only marginal, and decreasing with time. There are only a few French textile companies investing in Africa, but these are the ones which — in the period studied — have gone through a rapid concentration and centralization process. This is certainly the case with the two largest French textile groups Dollfus-Mieg & Cie. and Agache-Willot which, together with Schaeffer specializing in project deliveries in textiles, are also dominant in the Periphery.

The direct investments by French textile companies in the Ivory Coast seem to have the objective of creating a basis for exports for the world market, at the same time to keep a market formerly held through exports and trading activities. In cases where the French textile companies have made direct investments as a minority share-holder, the role of the French company is often to secure the marketing of products in the French market. As will be shown in Chapter 4, the choice between different developing countries as host countries for French direct investments in textiles depends more on the financial conditions offered and the presence of good quality cotton, than on the low level of wages. The Ivory Coast has succeeded in attracting foreign (mainly French) capital by means of favourable investment conditions and the production of high-quality Allen cotton to be used in modern factories. When French investments have been geared towards the local market in the host country, these investments have been made primarily by the French trading companies, or in co-operation with these trading firms.

Notes

1. Charles Albert Michalet and Michel Delapierre, *The Multinationalization of French Firms* (Chicago, Chicago University Press, 1975). This study was based on interviews with 50 companies among the 100 largest French companies, and by mailed questionnaires to 400 enterprises (of which only 18.3% replied). It was the aim of the study 'to seek out those factors which have motivated certain French firms to go multinational — that is, to establish production or sales subsidiaries abroad'.

2. Ibid., p. 37.
3. Ibid., p. 50.
4. Ministère de l'Economie et des Finances, *Statistiques et études financières, vol. 20 (1968) – vol. 28 (1976).* Ministère de l'Economie et des Finances; Banque de France, 'Balance des paiements de l'année 1975 entre la France et l'extérieur', Paris, 1976.
5. Ibid.
6. Michalet and Delapierre, op. cit., p. 94.
7. Ibid., p. 52.
8. Guirec Delanoë, *Etude sur l'évolution de la concentration dans l'industrie du textile en France* (Luxembourg, C.C.E., 1975), pp. 40-2.
9. Ibid., p. 79.
10. Ibid., pp. 45-6, where 25 different examples of buying up firms and interests in firms are listed for the period 1968-73.
11. *Le Monde*, 3 November 1978, p. 30 and *Le Monde hebdomadaire*, no. 1555, 17-23 August 1978.
12. Delanoë, op. cit., pp. 73-4.
13. In an interview undertaken in the Ministry of Planning in Abidjan, the Ivory Coast in May 1977, we were told that Riegel Textile first considered investing in France, but then decided in co-operation with Schaeffer to invest in the Ivory Coast in the textile firm Blue Bell Côte d'Ivoire.
14. J.Y. Darrake, 'Le lien entre rentabilité et modification de la structure des emplois', *Critiques de l'économie politique*, No. 23, 1976, p. 89.
15. Ibid., p. 94.
16. Bonnie Campbell, 'The Social, Political and Economic Consequences of French Private Investments in the Ivory Coast 1960-70. A Case Study of Cotton and Textile Production'. Ph.D. thesis, University of Sussex, 1973, p. 173.
17. République Francaise, Commissariat Général du Plan de Modernisation et d'Equipement, *Rapport général sur le Premier Plan de modernisation et d'équipement*, Novembre 1946-Janvier 1947, pp. 155ff.
18. Campbell, op. cit., p. 176.
19. Francois Capronnier, *La Crise de l'industrie cotonnière francaise* (Paris, Editions Génin, 1959), pp. 380-90.
20. Campbell, op. cit., p. 178.
21. J. Suret-Canale, *Afrique noire. De la colonisation aux indépendances 1945-1960* (Paris, Editions Sociales, 1972).
22. Ibid., pp. 140ff.
23. Yves Ullmo, *La Planification en France* (Paris, Dalloz, 1974) and John H. McArthur and Bruce R. Scott, *Industrial Planning in France* (Boston, Harvard University Press, 1969).
24. Lyn Krieger Mytelka, 'Crisis and Adjustment in the French Textile Industry', Working Paper, Carleton University, 1980.
25. Delanoë, op. cit., p. 15 and McArthur and Scott, op. cit., pp. 391-400.
26. *VIe Plan de développement économique et social 1971-1975* (Paris, Union Général d'Editions, 1971), pp. 317ff.
27. *Express*, No. 1352, 6-12 June 1977, pp. 48-50.
28. Ibid., p. 50.

3. The E.E.C. and the International Division of Labour

Since around 1973 the countries in the Third World have demanded a New International Economic Order. This demand has been expressed with increasing strength in international organizations, and one aspect has been summarized by Samir Amin as follows:

> To impose a rise in the real prices of raw materials exported by the Third World countries in order to acquire further resources which, together with the importing of advanced technologies, could finance a new stage of industrialization involving large-scale exports to the Centre of products manufactured in the Periphery with the advantage of favourable natural resources and abundant cheap labour — hence the demand for access to the markets of developed countries for these industrial products.[1]

This 'new stage of industrialization' has already experienced some progress in South East Asian and Latin American countries, but so far it has only been of marginal importance to the African Continent. Industrialization based on low-paid local manpower and production for export to the Western countries is a strategy already initiated by international capital, often in conjunction with local capital. A demand for a New International Economic Order is therefore not only in the interest of the peripheral countries themselves, but would also create new possibilities for international capital groups seeking new investment areas in a period of increased economic difficulties at home.

The Lomé Convention between the E.E.C. and now 56 developing countries in Africa, the Caribbean and the Pacific (the so-called A.C.P. countries) is sometimes characterized as one of the first institutionalized agreements to create a new international economic order gradually. The forerunners of the Lomé Convention were the Yaoundé Conventions, which were mainly aimed at relieving some of the economic burdens for France while still keeping the former colonies within the French sphere of interest. To what extent is the Lomé Convention a continuation of this? And which elements are entirely new, possibly contributing to a changing international situation such as the one outlined by Amin?

Some writers see the Lomé Convention as a contribution mainly to the construction of physical infrastructure and the improvement of agriculture, thereby facilitating the activities and profitability of international capital in the Periphery. Within this perspective, the Lomé Convention is seen as an instrument to cover some of the costs connected with the internationalization of capital. If this viewpoint is accepted, which national capital groups are then able to take advantage of the provisions of the Lomé Convention? At the same time, preferential trade agreements and the STABEX scheme contained in the Lomé Convention are seen as means to secure raw materials for Europe, an aspect very much brought into focus by the so-called oil crisis.

Other analysts take a very different view. They see the Lomé Convention as an instrument to channel finance to countries in severe need of funds necessary for economic development, while the trade liberalization measures and the STABEX scheme are seen as ways to improve the marketing of agricultural (and manufactured) products at relatively stable and predictable prices. In this view the Convention is directed exclusively at contributing to the economic development of the Associated countries. In what follows we will try to show that the Lomé Convention contains elements which can support both these views.

The Convention is a rather complex instrument which came into being at a time when those who shaped it still had the rather uncomplicated 1960s in mind, even if the oil crisis had just shaken some of its basic assumptions. The sudden increase in oil prices in 1973 forced a latent crisis situation to become manifest in the West European countries, and this, it can be argued, has entirely changed the relations with the peripheral countries from one of dependency to one of interdependency. Whether or not there is an actual shift with increased opportunities for some of the peripheral economies to engage in a broader industrialization policy, eventually leading to a self-sustained capitalist development, is, therefore, an important aspect to include in any analysis of the Lomé Convention.

Before doing this, however, a few remarks are necessary about the historical situation leading to the association to the E.E.C. of the French colonies in Africa.

The Historical Background

The existence of the so-called Franc Zone in the colonial period was one of the most influential facts in shaping the Implementation Convention by which the then French colonies in Africa were associated with the E.E.C. in

1958. Even after the independence of the African countries, the functioning of the Franc Zone was important for the content and organization of the subsequent Yaoundé Conventions.

The history of the Franc Zone goes back to the crisis in the 1930s when the French colonial empire established a trade and monetary system, isolated and excluded from world market competition. This was set up in order to serve France's own interests and to counteract the tendencies towards total breakdown of the multilateral foreign trade system. After World War II, the Franc Zone became institutionalized with the establishment in 1945 of two currencies, the colonial franc and the metropolitan franc, with a mutually fixed parity.[2] During the 1950s, measures were introduced to strengthen the financial ties between France and her African colonies, leading to a centralization of fiscal and monetary matters, but also eventually resulting in strict French control over other areas of the economic life of the colonies.[3] Development plans, mainly geared to building up the necessary infrastructure for extraction of raw materials, were imposed on the colonies. In order to improve the foreign currency earnings of France immediately after World War II, a productivity increase in the colonies in minerals and raw materials was assumed to be necessary. The development plans were intended to raise the productivity of labour by investment in physical and social infrastructure. $ 1.5 billion was set aside for this purpose, but by 1955 only just under half that amount had been spent. This was partly because of a general cut in state expenditure in France, but first and foremost it was due to a decline in private foreign investment in the colonies following improved investment opportunities at home. Around $ 1 billion was spent by France in her colonies between 1946 and 1958, the first year of the Implementing Convention.[4]

A system of customs duties, quantitative restrictions and restrictions on the issuing of import licences were other measures which contributed to discrimination against commodities from countries outside the Franc Zone. Other measures intended to strengthen the French position were a French monopoly on the transportation of goods between France and the colonies, and exclusive rights accorded to French trading firms.[5] But it was primarily a system of subsidization: exports of raw materials from the colonies were priced above world market prices, while at the same time exports of French manufactured products also had to be paid for at prices far above the competitive price level on the world market. Therefore, this system strongly contributed to keeping the colonies within the French sphere of influence. At the same time the not-very-competitive French manufacturing sector was subsidized by the colonies because of differences between the two excessive price levels: in 1957 the price for colonial raw materials exported to France was between 15 and 60% above the world market level, while the pricing of French exports were between 8 and 85% above.[6]

The rationale behind this system of trade preferences was that the colonies had to be paid above world market price levels if French industry was to succeed in finding markets for its non-competitive products. Ironically, this attitude substantially contributed to the slowing down of the necessary rationalization and automation of French industry, which later led to increased economic difficulties throughout the 1960s. While individual branches of French industry were able to gain surplus profits from their interaction with the colonies, the economic burden for France as a whole increased. The costs of the colonial administration were rising, partly because of the increased financial burden of carrying out the colonial development plans. But the primary reason behind the increased difficulties were the colonial wars in Indochina and Algeria. An extremely high rate of inflation as well as successive political crises led France to severe economic difficulties towards the end of the 1950s.

These economic difficulties had to be solved through an increase in productivity. Inside the new E.E.C. a larger market might be found, which could possibly absorb surplus production. At the same time, liberalization measures might contribute to a rise in the productivity of the member states through the intensified competitive situation. In France it was the most productive and competitive capital groups which supported the idea of a European Community; but the idea was resisted by those capital groups which had profited from the colonial adventure and the protection measures inside the Franc Zone. These firms had been prevented from a thorough rationalization, like the labour-intensive French textile industry, and the food products industry, which exported nearly 90% of its total exports to the colonies.[7] Indeed, around one-third of all French exports went to the colonies, and around 300,000 workers in the industrial labour force of 5 million worked directly for the colonial markets.[8]

At the time of the conclusion of the negotiations for a European Community, France was therefore in a difficult position. The closed exchange system of the Franc Zone and the consequent close ties of the colonies with the French market made the French capitals pressure the French Government to seek a successor to the colonial preferential system, which would not totally divert the colonies' exports away from the traditional mother country.

All this contributed to the conditions the French laid down for their involvement in the E.E.C.: basically, the establishment of an association agreement by which the French colonies would have preferential access to the broader European market. The French Government succeeded in letting the other European nations take the bait. She was also relieved of a great deal of her administrative expenditure, which then allowed for the building up of a French bilateral technical assistance scheme whereby more capital-intensive projects could be undertaken together with assistance in the cultural and educational field. The transferring of some of the economic burden took place under the first development fund of the E.E.C., the Implementing Convention, which to a large extent continued to finance the development plans of the colonies.[9] But the subsequent Yaoundé Conventions also very much favoured French interests.

The Lomé Convention between the nine member countries of the E.E.C. and 56 countries in Africa, the Caribbean and the Pacific came into force on 1 April 1976. As mentioned earlier, the Convention is described not only as a substantial improvement for the Associated countries, compared to the previous Yaoundé Conventions, but also as a model shaping future international co-operation agreements towards a more just and balanced world economic order.

In particular, administrators and politicians within the E.E.C. — such as Claude Cheysson, responsible for relations with the developing countries — emphasize this aspect. At the same time, however, he has observed that the Lomé Convention is not only advantageous for the Associated countries, but important for the industrialized countries as well: 'And while we are talking about our dependence on the Third World, let us not forget our own countries' need to recover their rate of growth and that our liberal society cannot develop, cannot take on its new form, unless it be in a state of growth: in the years ahead, the most probable engine of this growth is the opening of the Third World.'[10] Cheysson is also quoted as saying that the E.E.C. is almost completely without raw materials of its own and has limited economic elbowroom, which is why the E.E.C. *needs* the Third World.[11]

When dependency is defined as the ratio between imports and consumption, the E.E.C. dependency on external mineral resources varies from 70 to 100%.[12] For some strategic raw materials like copper, lead, zinc, bauxite and aluminium, and iron ore the dependency on supplies from developing countries varies from 22 to 37%.[13] Out of total exports from developing countries of these materials, Africa contributes 36%.[14]

In spite of intensive research within the E.E.C. countries and increased efforts to recycle raw materials, the E.E.C.'s dependency has been growing in recent years. An E.E.C. report concludes that it is necessary for Europe to have access 'to raw materials provision from Third World countries on satisfactory, mutual and lasting conditions'.[15] Other reports stress that for many of the strategically important raw materials the A.C.P. countries will in future be able to fulfil a substantial part of the E.E.C.'s requirements.[16]

It seems justified to interpret the Lomé Convention as an instrument of co-operation by which an advantageous trade arrangement and a scheme for the stabilization of Third World export earnings (STABEX) might bind resource-rich Africa closer to Europe. The consequence of this on a world scale is a vertical division of labour consisting of the axes U.S.A.-Latin America, Japan-South East Asia, and Western Europe-Africa. In this respect, the Lomé Convention might be seen as just another instrument contributing to a prolongation of the existing international division of labour.

The interdependency aspect stressed by Cheysson is probably among the most important factors to consider when talking about a new international economic order. Although the Periphery is heavily dependent on the Western countries, the so-called oil crisis and the international economic crisis have shown that peripheral countries, by virtue of their raw material resources, can reinforce crisis symptoms already latent in the Western world. In a situation like this, co-operation agreements like the Lomé Convention might contribute to a renewed growth in capital accumulation in the Centre.

Apart from these mainly economic facts which perhaps explain the content and form of the Lomé Convention, other factors may have contributed as well. The fact that certain concessions were granted to the A.C.P. countries is probably due both to these countries having acted as one bloc during the negotiations, and to the fact that very little was left of a common E.E.C. foreign policy apart from the attitude towards the Associated countries.

As a consequence of these economic and political factors, the Lomé Convention is a compromise which requires a more complex evaluation than the previous Yaoundé Conventions. The content of the previous conventions, and the way they arose from the specific historical situation in which France proceeded with her decolonization policy, has often led to the conclusion that these agreements were nothing other than instruments of neo-colonialism.

It is our view that the Lomé Convention must be evaluated not only in comparison and contrast to the previous conventions, but also in relation to the international division of labour. In the next section, therefore, we consider *whether the Lomé Convention contributes to a changed international situation improving the possibilities for capitalist development in the Periphery.*

The Association Agreements between the E.E.C. and the Developing Countries

The Early Association Agreements
The provisions for the Association of overseas countries and territories are found in the Treaty of Rome, Articles 131-6. Article 131 says that the aim of the Association is 'to further the economic and social development in these countries and territories and to establish close economic connnections between these countries and the Community'. These provisions were succeeded by others when the former French colonies obtained their political independence in the early 1960s. At first there were the Yaoundé Conventions I and II (1963 and 1969), which brought together 18 mostly former French colonies in an Association agreement, and later came the signing of the Lomé Convention in 1975.

Besides the Yaoundé Conventions, which embraced the francophone developing countries, another agreement with Tanzania, Kenya and Uganda was decided upon: this was the Arusha Convention. Both of these agreements consisted partly in the granting of mutual trade preferences and partly in the establishment of common institutions. However, financial assistance was given as part of the Yaoundé Conventions, while this was not the case with the Arusha Convention.

With regard especially to the countries under the Yaoundé Conventions, the E.E.C. insisted on the principle of reverse preferences; this led to intense criticism of the principles in the agreements, as it implied that the E.E.C. had achieved duty-free access to the economically weaker Associated countries. This, it was agreed, made it very much more difficult to establish local industries in the Associated countries and therefore tended to keep them in the position of exporters of raw materials and importers of manufactured products.

On the other hand, the reverse preferences meant that the Associated countries achieved duty-free access to the E.E.C. market, except for products covered by the Common Agricultural Policy. The Associated countries thus had a competitive advantage in the E.E.C. market compared to other developing countries. This advantage, however, has gradually been eroded in recent years by the lowering of E.E.C. tariffs on imports from other countries.

The total amount in financial assistance placed at the disposal of the Yaoundé countries through the European Development Fund was 581 million Units of Account for the Implementing Convention and 730 million and 900 million for the Yaoundé Conventions (1 U.A. in 1975 = US$1.21).[17] Comparing the amount of Community aid received by the 18 Associated countries with the overall amount of aid received by these countries during the period of the Yaoundé Conventions, the Community aid comes to 20%. When adding, however, the bilateral aid received from the then six members of the European Economic Community, the total Community aid, bilateral as well as multilateral, comes to 80% of the total aid received. This bilateral aid was very unequally distributed: 91% of the bilateral Community aid came from the major former colonial power France. The dominance of France within the E.E.C. in its early days had led to the conclusion that Community aid was mainly of a supplementary nature to the bilateral aid efforts of France.

The dominant French position is also reflected in the figures on delivery contracts obtained on Community aid projects. During the European Development Funds I-III (corresponding to the Implementing Convention and the subsequent Yaoundé Conventions), France and the Federal Republic of Germany each contributed about one-third of the funds required under the aid programmes. French industry obtained, however, between 41 and 53% of the total contracts, while Germany only got 7%, 20% and 12% under the three European Development Funds. The contracts obtained by the Associated countries varied from 27%, 15% and 20%.[18] However, a substantial number of these contracts went to firms in the Associated countries which were subsidiaries of French companies.

At the time of the Implementing Convention (in force from 1959) Community aid was very diffuse. No guidelines were worked out for aid projects, which were often selected from among proposals which the colonial administration happened to have on their shelves.[19] The main part of the funds were used for economic and social infrastructure — often large prestige projects.

As a result of the deficiencies of the Implementing Convention, a sharp criticism was raised from the former colonies, which negotiated the first Yaoundé Convention as independent countries. The way in which projects were implemented and administered was especially criticized, but so also was the fact that the majority of delivery contracts under the aid programme had fallen into French hands.[20]

The Yaoundé II Convention attempted to change this, and preferences for delivery contracts were given to companies registered in the Associated countries. But still, the majority of firms thus registered which had the size and experience to participate in tenders were in reality owned by French interests.

The majority of aid funds during European Development Funds I-III were used for the development of physical infrastructure (37%) and agricultural projects (30%), while only 5% on average was used for industrialization purposes.[21] This distribution of aid by sector seems to confirm the view that E.E.C. aid had the aim of covering part of the costs connected with the operation of international (French) capital in the Periphery, facilitating thereby the export of raw materials, mainly agricultural, rather than supporting an industrialization process.

Nevertheless, the Association agreements meant some *short-term benefits* for the African Associated countries. The enlarged E.E.C. market was now open to their traditional exports of raw materials and they received some aid, which was, of course, not only beneficial to international capital, but also contributed to the establishment of necessary infrastructure and agricultural diversification.

The Associated countries did not have much of a choice when deciding whether to sign the Conventions. Relations between France and her colonies had given them better preferential terms for their produce than could be obtained under the Conventions, but the risk of a direct setback in their conditions for exports to the European market made it imperative for them to enter the Yaoundé Convention. For the Associated countries the Conventions also gave opportunities to diversify economically so as to be somewhat less dependent on France.

The major drawback for the Associated African countries in the longer perspective was that their position in the international division of labour was not fundamentally altered. The Yaoundé Conventions maintained these countries as suppliers of raw materials, and contributed only very marginally to the industrialization which is the *sine qua non* for self-sustained economic development.[22]

The Lomé Convention: A New Era of Financial and Technical Co-operation?
The financial and technical co-operation made possible by the European Development Funds has been and still is one of the most important aspects of the co-operation between the E.E.C. and the Associated countries.

The amount set aside for European Development Fund IV under the Lomé Convention seems, at first, impressive: 3,000 million U.A. (1 Unit of Account in 1975 equalled US $1.21). Taking into consideration, however, that the number of Associated countries is now more than 50, the amount of aid *per capita* is more or less the same as it was at the time when the previous Yaoundé Convention went into operation. If inflation is taken into account as well, then the financial means at the disposal of the European Development Fund IV represent a decline of more than 25% in *per capita* transfers to the Associated countries.[23] It must also be remembered that the resources which are channelled through the European Development Fund may be deducted from the bilateral aid budgets of the E.E.C. countries.

In the negotiations, the Community did not question whether the amount demanded by the Associated countries — 8,000 million U.A. — was reasonable or not. The E.E.C. only insisted that for political reasons it was impossible to raise the amount of financial aid beyond 3,000 million.

This sum was distributed as follows: 430 million U.A. loans on especially favourable terms, 95 million U.A. 'risk willing' investment capital, and 375 million U.A. reserved for STABEX. Thus there remained 2,100 million U.A. which could be used as non-refundable aid.

The fourth European Development Fund attached to the Lomé Convention represents a substantial improvement compared to the former development funds regarding changes in the distribution of aid by sector and recipient countries and in the decision-making process. Throughout the history of the E.E.C. infrastructural projects have been predominant, but during recent years there has been a change, giving more emphasis to an increase in productivity and a diversification of production in agriculture. With the signing of the Lomé Convention, further changes were introduced; in particular, a special chapter on industrialization raises hopes that in future co-operative efforts will achieve more in this field.

The relatively rich countries like the Ivory Coast, Cameroun, Madagascar, Senegal, and Zaire received 53% of the total resources during the first three development funds. But this has been changed in the Lomé Convention, where priority now is given to the poorest Associated countries.

The lack of influence of the Associated countries over the administration of the Yaoundé Conventions had naturally also been criticized by these countries. This situation seems to be improved with the Lomé Convention. It is now stressed that the selection of projects is to take place as a result of co-operation between the representatives of the Commission and the A.C.P. country concerned, and that it is to be based on the development plans and priorities of the Associated countries. The developing countries thus have the opportunity to propose projects, and their bargaining position is strengthened as they can argue that the projects chosen should have priority in their development plans.

Another characteristic of the Lomé Convention is a strengthening of the negotiating power of the Associated countries. This is due to the fact that the developing countries know beforehand more or less the total amount they will receive in financial aid from the E.E.C. They can therefore choose only to present projects that correspond to the actual amount and thereby limit the influence of the Commission on the choice of projects to be included in each country's programme.[24]

Another point which the developing countries criticized in the former Yaoundé Conventions was the practice of tendering for actual projects; contracts had been given to European firms, particularly French ones. The Lomé Convention attempted to create 'equality in the conditions of participation in tenders and other means of getting access to contracts'.

The principal rule for contracts involving 'important complicated and technically difficult investigations' is that the Commission sets up a limited list of candidates from the member countries and/or A.C.P. countries. These candidates must fulfil certain qualifications, and the A.C.P. countries concerned can then choose whoever they want from among the companies on the list.

In principle, the E.E.C. procurement procedure is thus different from the well-known practice of tied aid so common in bilateral aid programmes. But it can be expected that, in practice, European firms or their subsidiaries registered as local A.C.P. firms will still dominate the delivery contracts. This point of view is supported by the fact that the Commission has introduced an unofficial principle, according to which the preliminary investigations and technical aid projects will be distributed among the E.E.C. member countries in accordance with the amount they have contributed to European Development Fund. This seems to indicate that the real controversy concerns the distribution of contracts *among the E.E.C. member countries*, and attempts by France's Community partners to reduce French dominance. The new procedure for tendering for contracts thus does not make any contribution to raising the present low degree of industrialization in the Associated countries.

A substantial change has occurred with the Lomé Convention, in that the former reverse preferences have been changed to unilateral preferences for the A.C.P. countries in the E.E.C. market. It has been calculated that free access to the E.E.C. market applies to 94% of the agricultural exports of the A.C.P. countries, while the remaining 6% are on favourable terms.[25] While the trade preferences in the Yaoundé Conventions discriminated against the non-Associated developing countries, the introduction of the General Scheme of Preferences in 1971 has been considered an improvement. Different studies have shown, however, that the introduction of this scheme has affected only 1.8% of total imports from the Yaoundé countries.[26]

The discrimination against third countries is true in the case of the Lomé Convention too, since the General Scheme of Preferences only covers relatively few agricultural commodities and does not cover at all primary products such as minerals, etc. The trade preference system in the Lomé Convention will thus still discriminate against non-Associated developing countries, partly as a result of the different groups of commodities in the two different kinds of trade preferences and partly as a result of the different sizes of tariffs and quantitative restrictions in the two systems.[27]

A consideration of how far these trade agreements can sustain a positive industrialization in the A.C.P. countries leads to the conclusion that nothing in the Convention hampers such development. But it should be remembered that the Associated countries have very little industrial development and that their exports of industrial products to the E.E.C. are still minimal. The value of the trade agreements can only be judged when the industrialization process has accelerated much further, since the willingness of the E.E.C. to give preferences in that kind of situation has still to be seen.

The STABEX Agreement

The most important innovation in the Lomé Convention is no doubt the Agreement on Stabilization of the Export Earnings (STABEX) of the A.C.P. countries. When the Lomé Convention is referred to as a model for future co-operation, it is mostly this particular scheme which is in mind.

The STABEX Agreement is, however, far from meeting the demands of the developing countries for the *indexation* of the prices of their export products. This particular issue led several times to a near breakdown of the negotiations because the developing countries insisted on this point. They stressed again and again that their primary goal was not to stabilize *export prices*, but to stabilize their *real purchasing power* in terms of trade with the E.E.C. The negotiators of the E.E.C. flatly rejected this demand, and a compromise was not reached until the Kingston negotiations in Jamaica in 1974, when the STABEX Agreement was finalized.

The Nigerian representative, E.D. Sanu, who was the chief negotiator of the A.C.P. countries in Kingston, opened the way for the compromise by stressing the reciprocity in the plan: in return for a commitment by the E.E.C. to keep the export earnings of the A.C.P. countries at an acceptable level, the developing countries would be willing to guarantee the provision of raw materials to Europe.[28]

The STABEX Agreement applies to twelve products and comprises the following conditions:

(1)   In order to ensure support for a product by STABEX, the export earnings of the product worldwide in the previous year should be at least 7.5% of the country's total earnings from exports (2.5% in the case of the least developed countries).

(2)   A reference level for the product is calculated as the average export earnings during the four years before the year in which the demand for support is made. If the export earnings in the year of application are at least 7.5% below the reference level (2.5% in the case of the least developed countries), then STABEX funds can be transferred in order to equalize the deficit. For five very poor countries, which traditionally only have small exports to the E.E.C., the reference level is calculated on the basis of the export to all destinations.

(3)   The repayment of STABEX funds takes place (except for the least developed countries) when 'the development of export earnings permits it'. In practice this means: when the quantity of exports as well as the unit value of the product exceeds the reference level.

(4)   For the five-year term of the Lomé Convention, 375 million U.A. have been reserved for this purpose, giving an annual average of 75 million U.A.

The estimates of the costs involved for the E.E.C. on account of the STABEX Agreement vary. In a report from the Commonwealth Secretariat[29] it is argued that the Agreement will lead to a net transfer of resources to the A.C.P. countries and thus augment the aid element in the Lomé Convention, since the transfers can be used freely by the recipients. In contrast to this,

David Wall[30] argues that, even on the basis of the period before the drastic increase in prices for raw materials in 1973, a 7.5% decrease among less than half the products involved would require a larger sum *in one year* than is allocated for the whole scheme over the five-year period.[31] In this, perhaps, hypothetical situation there is no guidance in the Lomé Convention on how to increase the funds in the Agreement. On the other hand, it is possible at any time for the Commission and the Ministerial Council *to reduce* the fund's allocated amounts.

There are other important modifications in the STABEX Agreement. The Commission has the authority to reject a transfer, if investigations have shown that the fall in export earnings is due to a deliberate trade policy of the A.C.P. government concerned which influences exports to the E.E.C. in a negative direction. In other words, if the developing country in its attempts to diversify its production, increases output meant for the home market or emphasizes markets other than the E.E.C., a transfer can be rejected.[32]

But the most important criticism of the STABEX Agreement is the fact that it does not take *inflation* into account. The reference level is calculated as the average of the export earnings of the last four years. Since inflation is high in most A.C.P. countries, this means that the real value of the transfer is considerably reduced. Although nominal export earnings, therefore, may be stabilized, the purchasing power of the developing countries in terms of real foreign exchange available will be reduced by price increases of their imports.

In conclusion, it should be said that the effects of STABEX are limited. The function of STABEX is to *reduce* the inconvenience of serious falls in export earnings caused by natural catastrophes like droughts, etc. STABEX compensates, but does not solve anything, as the Agreement is based on export *earnings* and not on changes in the demand for imports caused by increasing prices of imported goods.

Besides this, STABEX is an incentive for the A.C.P. countries to increase their trade with the E.E.C. Or conversely, STABEX punishes the countries which are not heavily involved in international trade, but are oriented to inter-regional trade. This is the case for most of the West African land-locked countries which have a rather large inter-regional trade with other African countries, but only few commodities covered by the STABEX Agreement.[33]

Industrial Co-operation

Industrial co-operation is discussed in a separate chapter of the Lomé Convention, and that is in itself an innovation. With the aim of preparing the path for industrial co-operation, a committee has been established (elected by the Ministerial Council). This committee at the same time has the task of supervising the newly created Centre for Industrial Development. This Centre should provide the A.C.P. countries with information, make industrialization forecasts, increase co-operation between investors and people responsible for industrialization policies, support education and research, facilitate the transfer of technology, etc. It is, however, still unclear which functions the Centre for Industrial Development will in the end perform. Some A.C.P. countries hope to see it develop into an 'exchange' for technology, while some E.E.C. countries would like to see it as the future agency of contact between governments of developing countries and private investors from the E.E.C.

The chapter in the Convention on industrial co-operation is characterized by intentions more than operational statements of how to further the industrialization process. No special funds are allocated to the Centre for Industrial Development, which means that resources for industrial projects have to be taken from the normal aid budget as has always been the case.

Apparently, an unofficial division of labour exists between the European Development Fund and the European Investment Bank, in that the Bank is concerned with industrial projects. This, however, has severe repercussions on the industrialization attempts of the Associated countries, as the European Investment Bank is financed through bonds and consequently follows a very restrictive lending policy since it is not able to sustain financial losses on its projects. Its criterion for lending out money is the rate of return on the investment — which has to be rather high in order to obtain support from the Bank. Considerations such as creating more even regional development, establishing industries with high intersectoral linkages, etc., do not enter the calculations of the Bank in giving loans.

The Ivory Coast and the E.E.C.

In comparison to the overall trade between the Associated countries and the European Economic Community, the Ivory Coast is in a remarkable position. The exports of the Associated countries to the E.E.C. declined between 1972 and 1977 (from 49% of total exports to 43%), while the corresponding figures for imports coming from the E.E.C. were 42% and 48% respectively.

While the trade balance between the A.C.P. countries as a whole and the E.E.C. has thus changed for the worse, the Ivory Coast has had a positive trade balance right from the time of independence (see Table 7).

Table 7. Ivory Coast's Imports from and Exports to the E.E.C., 1973-77 (Billion C.F.A. francs and % of Total Trade)

	1973	*1974*	*1975*	*1976*	*1977*
Exports to E.E.C. countries	120.2	192.8	146.4	247.7	317.3
E.E.C.'s share of total Ivory Coast exports (%)	62.9	66.0	57.6	61.5	60.0
Imports from E.E.C. countries	100.8	134.1	142.3	184.2	256.3
E.E.C.'s share of total Ivory Coast imports (%)	63.0	57.8	58.9	59.2	59.7

Source: *Europa Information*, September 1978, p. 9.

Not only is the Ivory Coast's trade balance with the E.E.C. positive, but the total share of the nine E.E.C. countries in the trade of the Ivory Coast is far larger than for the A.C.P. countries as a whole. France is still the major trading partner for the Ivory Coast: in 1977 43% of the Ivory Coast's total exports to the E.E.C. went to France, while France's share of the Ivory Coast's total E.E.C. imports was 66%.

That the Ivory Coast is of particular importance to the E.E.C. can be seen from an analysis showing E.E.C.-A.C.P. trade in 1977 in decreasing order of importance by country.[34] Apart from the clear dominance of Nigeria in this picture (not least because of the very large share of E.E.C. exports to the A.C.P. going to this country), two-thirds of E.E.C. imports from the A.C.P. in 1977 came from only eight countries, and Nigeria, the Ivory Coast and Zaire provided nearly half of all E.E.C. imports from the A.C.P. This picture is nearly identical on the export side where Nigeria and the Ivory Coast are again the two most important countries.

In other words, the countries relatively most well-off in Africa have the greatest integration in the world market penetration. It seems that the more 'open' (that is, the more export-oriented) an A.C.P. economy is, the higher its *per capita* G.N.P. Furthermore, with regard to E.E.C. aid, the Ivory Coast is – together with other relatively well-off African nations – in a favourable situation.[35] During 1960-74 the Ivory Coast received more than 25% of her total foreign aid from the European Development Fund and the European Investment Bank, making the E.E.C. the single most important foreign donor, closely followed by France.[36]

As stated in the Lomé Convention, it is the aim of this new Agreement to avoid favouring the relatively rich Associated countries with Community aid, but instead to give priority to the least developed countries. But the Ivory Coast has not felt any remarkable decline in the aid received.

When looking into the distribution of E.E.C. aid according to sectors, the Ivory Coast is also in a favourable position. Community aid going to industrialization purposes in the Ivory Coast is more than three times as high as the global figure, as of 31 December 1977. The major part of this came from aid under the Lomé Convention and aid from the European Investment Bank under the first development fund period (to agro-industrial projects in palm oil and textiles). This picture does seem to support the view that the Lomé Convention enables some countries to take advantage of industrial co-operation – and that these countries will probably be among the nations which are already relatively well-off. The Lomé Convention has been extremely important to the Ivory Coast in another respect. According to the Convention, the Ivory Coast has been able from 16 July 1975 to abolish the reverse trade preferences by ending the preferential treatment accorded to manufactured goods from the Community. The revenue arising from custom duties on imports was already twice as high in 1975 as foreseen and had reached 10.9 billion C.F.A francs by 31 October 1976. The amount coming from the introduction of customs duties is thus far from negligible.[37]

In conclusion, it might be said that, with regard to all the elements in

Community co-operation over the years, the Ivory Coast, together with a few other relatively well-off A.C.P. countries, has been in a position of advantage. The Ivory Coast has an intense trade with the Community; it has received substantial amounts of aid including for industrialization purposes; it has received substantial amounts in STABEX transfers and it has accrued large state revenues since abolishing the mutual preferential treatment of manufactured goods from the E.E.C. and Associated countries.

Conclusion

Like its predecessors, the Lomé Convention seems to be strengthening the already familiar international division of labour. Qualitatively speaking, the Lomé and the Yaoundé Conventions do not seem to differ with regard to the effects of their trade agreements and schemes of financial and technical co-operation. In both cases, they contribute to maintaining the position of the peripheral countries within the international division of labour as providers of raw materials to the Centre economy.

The new aspects of the Lomé Convention (the STABEX Scheme and the chapter on industrial co-operation) do not in our opinion contribute basically to new tendencies in the international division of labour. With regard to STABEX, it seems that the countries already most integrated in the world market are those which primarily benefit from the scheme, while for example the land-locked countries in West Africa, with a relatively substantial inter-regional trade and only a few exportable products, cannot take advantage of the scheme in the way in which for example the Ivory Coast has done.

It is our opinion that the Lomé Convention cannot *in itself* secure the creation of capitalist development processes. On the other hand, it might be foreseen that individual countries with favourable investment opportunities and an industrialization strategy geared towards exporting might be able to take advantage of the different offers contained in the Convention. The Lomé Convention together with other instruments of co-operation in the international system might, therefore, *in particular cases* contribute to a growing tendency of differentiation among the peripheral countries.

It is, therefore, our general conclusion that the Lomé Convention is not a model for a new international economic order, but rather has to be looked at in its historical perspective: as a partly modified but nevertheless continuous effort to preserve an already established international division of labour. This, however, does not — to repeat — exclude the possibility that a few relatively well-off peripheral economies can take advantage of the different elements in the Conventions in a development strategy combining the activities of international capital, the international donor agencies and the peripheral state. Whether such a combined effort actually leads to the establishment of a more mature capitalist development process, we will discuss in the following chapter.

As previously mentioned, the Lomé Convention was shaped during a period of continuous growth in the Western industrialized countries, and was signed shortly after the rash of enormous rises in the prices of raw materials, following the oil crisis. No wonder, therefore, that the Convention could only partially take into consideration aspects of a new international economic order. But the compromise reached in Kingston, Jamaica, was affected by the oil crisis in that, in exchange for certain concessions (relative to the terms of the previous Yaoundé Conventions) the A.C.P. countries did promise the E.E.C. an uninterrupted supply of raw materials.

The world economic crisis has deepened since then, and the Lomé II Convention was signed in late 1979. How has the crisis affected the structuring of Lomé II? On the one hand, the smaller and less competitive capital groups in Europe require protection from the nation state. On the other hand, the already internationalized and larger capital groups seek state and/or E.E.C. support in their penetration of the peripheral economies, with regard to both investment opportunities and expanded markets for commodities.

Particularly as regards the creation of an export-oriented industrialization in the Periphery, this conflict among different capital groups in the Centre came into the open in the negotiations leading up to Lomé II. The Commission suggested obligatory consultations between the Associated countries and the E.E.C. in cases where an A.C.P. country wished to engage in export-oriented industrialization measures. The suggestion was, however, reduced by the Ministerial Council to merely voluntary consultations. The Commission also suggested that observing the I.L.O. Convention on working conditions should be a precondition for having the right to export to the E.E.C. This — together with the human rights proposition of the E.E.C. — was flatly rejected.

While the Associated countries under the first Lomé Convention had free access, for example for their textile products, to the E.E.C. market, textiles were now grouped among the so-called sensitive products (i.e. those products which might pose a threat to the manufacturing process of certain Centre capital groups); and they were now included in the Multifibre Agreement. For a country like the Ivory Coast which, as a result of the provisions of the Lomé Convention on this point, had engaged in a large expansion of her textile industry (with the assistance, indeed, of the European Investment Bank), this implies severe difficulties. By 1980 the export of textiles have been constricted by a quota system far below the present exporting capacity, despite the fact that Ivorian textile exports to the E.E.C. market comprise only a tiny fraction of total Third World textile exports.

The present situation is, therefore, highly uncertain. On the one hand, import restrictions are being introduced on products which may be a threat to capital groups within the Community. On the other hand, the deepening of the crisis in itself may lead to certain types of capital seeking new and more profitable investment opportunities in the Periphery. Even the reverse process might take place, where industrialists might withdraw their investments from the Periphery and move back to the E.E.C. area, to countries like the United Kingdom with a large and relatively low-paid work force. The content of the Lomé II Convention is at the general level essentially a continuation of what is already in existence by virtue of Lomé I, even though it does contain measures stressing the present protectionist tendencies and relegates the longer-term hopes for a broader and partly export-oriented industrialization in the Periphery as a whole to the more distant future.

Notes

1. Samir Amin, 'Self-Reliance and the New International Economic Order', *Monthly Review*, July/August 1977, p. 11.
2. For aspects of the history of the Franc Zone, see Christian Uhlig, *Monetäre Integration bei wirtschaftlicher Abhängigkeit. Probleme einer währungspolitischen Strategie dargestellt am Beispiel der Franc-Zone* (Munich, Welforum Verlag, 1976).
3. Uhlig, op. cit., pp. 17-18 and 96-97 and Rainer Kühn, 'Afrika. Franc Zone, Währungsunion und Abhängigkeiten', Arbeiten aus der Abteilung Entwicklungsländerforschung No. 45, Forschungsinstitut der Friedrich Ebert Stiftung, Bonn, 1977, pp. 3-4.
4. Rainer Kühn, 'Voraussetzungen, Resultate und Perspektiven der Assozierung Afrikanischer Staaten an die EG', in J. Linhard and K. Voll (eds), *Weltmarkt und Entwicklungsländer* (Rheinstetten, Berliner Studien zur Internationale Politik, 1976), pp. 135 and 138.
5. Georges H. Lawson, 'La Côte d'Ivoire: 1960-1970. Croissance et diversification dans africanisation' in J. Esseks (ed), *l'Afrique de l'indépendance politique à l'indépendance économique* (Grenoble, 1975), p. 208.
6. Kühn, 1977, op. cit., p. 5.
7. Ibid.
8. Kühn, 1976, op. cit., p. 140.
9. Ibid., p. 141.
10. *The Courier*, No. 32, 1975, p. 12.
11. Ibid., p. XV.
12. 'Fællesskabets forsyning med råstoffer', *Bulletin for de europæiske Fællesskaber*, Supplement 1, 1975, p. 7 and 'Udvikling og råstoffer — aktuelle problemer', *Bulletin for de europæiske Fællesskaber*, No. 6, 1975, p. 43.
13. In particular the dependency is obvious in the case of tin, copper, and aluminium.
14. 'Udvikling og råstoffer', op. cit., p. 53.
15. 'Fællesskabets forsyning', op. cit., p. 6.
16. Huub Coppens, Gerrit Faber and Ed Lof, 'Security and Raw Material Provision, Development and the Lomé Convention', Paper delivered at the 8th International Colloquium of John F. Kennedy Institute, Center for International Studies, New York, 1975, p. 17.
17. *The Courier*, No. 36, 1976, p. 23.
18. *Fonds Européens de Développement* (Brussels, 1974), p. 87 and *Report from the Commission to the Council on the Results of Invitations to Tender*, Commission of the European Communities, COM (76) 167, Brussels, 1976, p. 4. Situation as of 31 December 1975.
19. *The Courier*, No. 36, 1976, p. 25.

20. Ibid., p. 26.
21. Ibid, p. 45.
22. See our article: H.S. Marcussen and J.E. Torp, 'Den internationale arbejdsdeling og Lomé samarbejdet (The International Division of Labour and the Lomé Co-operation)', *Forum for Utviklingsstudier*, No. 3-4, 1977.
23. David Wall, 'The E.E.C.-A.C.P. Lomé Convention. A Model for the New International Economic Order?' The Halifax Conference, Canada, 1975.
24. This financial policy is in contrast to that of the World Bank, where decisions are taken from project to project.
25. Quoted after Harry Stordel, 'Preference in the Lomé Convention and the Generalized System of Preferences and the World Trade System', Paper delivered at the 8th International Colloquium of John F. Kennedy Institute, Centre for International Studies, New York, 1975, p. 4.
26. Ibid., pp. 8 and 9.
27. For an analysis of the restrictions and their influence on the development perspective of the developing countries, see Ole Molgaard Andersen, 'EF's generelle toldpræferencer og deres betydning for lavindkomstlandene (The G.S.P. and its Importance for the Low Income Countries)', *Den Ny Verden*, No. 1, 1975-76.
28. *The Export Earnings Stabilization Scheme and the Lomé Convention* (London, Commonwealth Secretariat, General Section, Commodities Division, undated), p. 6.
29. Ibid.
30. Wall, op. cit.
31. Michel Dumas has calculated that for 1975 a 10% fall in the global demand for wood and iron alone would require the total amount of funds for that year: 75 million UA. Michel Dumas, 'Le Nouvel Ordre économique internationale', *Revue Tiers Monde*, No. 66, April-June 1976.
32. This problem has already arisen. With regard to the first STABEX transfer, parts of the British and German press criticized the transfer of STABEX funds to Congo and the Ivory Coast. The criticism was raised because of a resulting decline in the export earnings following nationalization in Congo and a larger amount of timber being produced in the Ivory Coast. The Commission has rejected the criticism as being unreasonable. *Telex Africa*, No. 63, pp. A4 and A5.
33. For a few of the countries traditionally not trading with the E.E.C. all their exports are included in the STABEX scheme. This goes for, among others, Swaziland (major trading partner being South Africa) and Guinea-Bissau (major trading partner being Portugal).
34. *The Courier*, No. 52, 1978, p. 50.
35. As has been previously mentioned, countries like the Ivory Coast, Cameroun, Madagascar, Senegal, and Zaire have during the first three development funds received 53% of the total Community aid.
36. *Aid of the European Community in Favour of the Ivory Coast between 1961 and 1974*, Delegation of the European Development Fund to the Republic of the Ivory Coast, 1975, p. 2.
37. Internal E.E.C. documents.

4. The Ivory Coast: Transcending Blocked Development?

In previous chapters, the considerable integration into the world market of the Ivory Coast has been stressed. In Chapter 2 aspects of the internationalization of capital were presented, emphasizing in particular French foreign investments in African and peripheral countries and in the Franc Zone. In Chapter 3 the close relationship between the Ivory Coast and the E.E.C. was described and analysed, both with regard to trade, where it was shown that the Ivory Coast has much closer links to the Community than the Associated countries generally, and to aid, where it was pointed out that the Ivory Coast together with a few other relatively well-off African nations has benefited most from the aid procedures and instruments in the Association conventions, notably the Lomé Convention.

With regard to all the major world market factors, the Ivory Coast occupies a unique role. Its integration into the world market has taken place continuously since independence in 1960. This means that internationalization of capital is an important theoretical concept to be understood in order to grasp the development conditions and prospects for the Ivory Coast. But this country's role in this international framework, where the agents of international capital can both support certain development processes and put restrictions on them, is only one part of the problem. The other side of the coin is the existence of relatively autonomous internal factors, of which the peripheral state is of utmost importance.

Since independence, the Ivory Coast has experienced a growth process which is sometimes called an economic miracle. In an African context, economic growth has only been faster in Nigeria with its oil and in Gabon with its mineral resources and oil. Since 1960 the annual growth rate of the Ivory Coast has been 19.7% – or 7.7% when adjusted for inflation.[1] The G.N.P.

IVORY COAST

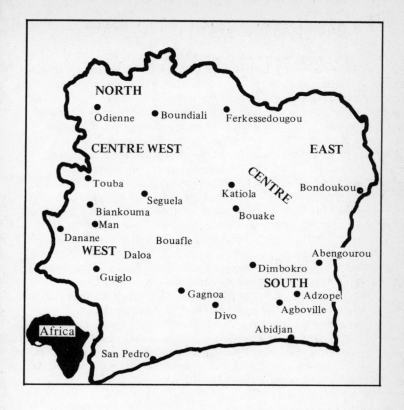

per capita is among African states only higher for Gabon and perhaps Zambia. In comparison with Kenya, for example, which has tried to pursue a liberal economic policy along similar lines to the Ivory Coast, the G.N.P. *per capita* was in 1978 U.S. $ 870 for the Ivory Coast against U.S. $ 330 for Kenya.[2]

Comparing the Ivory Coast with countries like Ghana, Cameroun, and Senegal which have neither mineral resources of any magnitude nor a population size much different, the growth process of the Ivory Coast is exceptionally fast. For the countries mentioned, the plan targets are for annual growth rates of 5%, while the corresponding figure for the Ivory Coast is 8%.[3]

The growth rate of the Ivory Coast since independence (from 1960 to 1973) has been around 3% higher than the average growth rate of the developing countries in general. The exceptional status of the Ivory Coast is even more apparent when countries benefiting from the exploitation of mineral resources like oil etc. are excluded. Not only has its growth process been remarkable, but it has also been very constant and regular.

Samir Amin's book *Le Développement du capitalisme en Côte d'Ivoire,*[4] which was published in 1967, is one of the more thorough analyses of Ivorian development. Amin's main conclusion is that the Ivory Coast is a prototype of 'growth without development', implying an export-oriented and externally generated growth process which results in the lack of any internal self-centred dynamics.[5] In his postscript to the second edition in 1971, he did not find that recent development trends in any way modified his analysis.

The problem of creating the 'self-centred dynamics' which Amin is talking about is certainly recognized by Ivorian planners. The former Minister of Planning, Mr. Diawara, said that the central development objective is to establish an irreversible growth process, gradually linking the economy together more and more firmly. This goal of reaching 'economic independence' is also expressed in plan documents, which state that the objective is to establish an integrated development process, self-sustained and modelled after the industrialized nations.[6]

But views on the means for obtaining this differ. The strategic conclusion of Samir Amin is that a mature capitalist development process can only take place through a break with the world market. But the development strategy of the Ivory Coast has been the obverse of this: to establish development through a high degree of integration into the world market.

While the factors conducive to world market integration have been analysed above, the influence of and effects of the internal dynamics in the Ivory Coast have not yet been dealt with. In this connection the role and activities of the peripheral state are crucial.

As has been previously discussed, the Ivorian state has been able to attract French investment into import substitution activities. This has also been the case with other countries in the Franc Zone. But it is a unique characteristic of the Ivory Coast that the investments are larger than in the other countries in the Franc Zone, and — more important — the Ivory Coast is the only country which has been able to attract large industrial plants producing commodities for export.

In an analysis made in 1971 of the motives for industrial enterprises to invest in the Ivory Coast,[7] 200 enterprises were included in a sample comprising 96% of total industrial turnover. In this study, three reasons for investment in the Ivory Coast were found to be decisive:
(1) the growth of the Ivorian market;
(2) political stability; and
(3) the liberal economic policy of the government.

For enterprises set up after the middle of the 1960s, the factors mentioned were of particular importance. Motives like 'keeping the market established through trade' — that is counteracting the effects of an Ivorian import-substitution industrialization — and the 'cost of labour', which are often considered important for foreign investment, were considered unimportant by most investors when deciding whether to invest in the Ivory Coast. It should be noted that the cost of labour is much higher than in the neighbouring countries, but still much lower than in Europe.

In the following, we shall try to describe in more detail some of the internal factors, relatively autonomous it is argued, with the hope of examining whether the Ivorian development prospect can be regarded as a step towards a more integrated capitalist development. Before doing this, however, the role of the Ivorian state must be briefly discussed.

The Role of the State in Ivorian Economic Development

Where there is no national bourgeoisie, the peripheral state is the main instrument capable of pursuing a capitalist-oriented development. By extracting an economic surplus from the agricultural sector, the state is in this situation the only institution able to accumulate funds which can be channelled into further productive investments, either in industry or agriculture (agro-industry), and possibly supported by international aid organizations and representatives of international capital as joint partners.

Concretely speaking, the extraction of economic surplus from the agricultural sector is in the Ivory Coast made through la Caisse (la Caisse de Stabilisation et de Soutien des Prix des Production Agricoles). The history of la Caisse goes back to colonial times, when it started in 1955 as two separate institutions dealing with price stabilisation for coffee and cocoa respectively. Later on, in 1962, the Ivory Coast decided to simplify matters by establishing a single institution jointly responsible for these two products. In 1968, la Caisse took on its present form, by becoming an institution generally responsible for the stabilization of prices for different agricultural products, which are at present coffee, cocoa, cotton, bananas, palm-oil products, copra, tobacco and cashew nuts.

The primary purpose of la Caisse is to guarantee a minimum price to the producers and to take care of the organisation of the selling of the products on the world market. The rather favourable world market prices for the different Ivorian agricultural products are the main reason behind the growing importance of la Caisse as the main provider of state revenue, which accrues from the difference between the price paid to the producers and the world market price.

The Caisse operates as follows: Each year a minimum buying price is decided, securing a guaranteed minimum income for the producers independent of world market price fluctuations. Secondly, an additional price is calculated representing all extra costs incurred between the point of collection and disembarkment. La Caisse guarantees the exporter this sales income (*valeur de réalisation*). If the actual selling price is above the guaranteed minimum, the exporter will have to refund la Caisse the surplus. If the opposite is the case, la Caisse will pay the difference up to the guaranteed minimum.

Previously, certain aspects of the above procedure were completely left to private initiative, but increasingly la Caisse is controlling a larger and larger part of the whole transaction. It is estimated that la Caisse is now selling three-quarters of all coffee exports, one-fifth of cocoa exports and all cotton exports.

La Caisse is in every instance trying to secure an agricultural product of the desired quality. Taking coffee, for example, la Caisse co-operates with the French Coffee and Cocoa Research Institute (the I.F.C.C., Institut francais du café et du cacao), and its regional research centres, which provide the varieties most adapted to ecological conditions in the region in question. Another Ivorian institution, the SATMACI (Société d'assistance technique pour la modernisation agricole de la Côte d'Ivoire), ensures that the seeds being delivered by I.F.C.C. are treated and cultivated according to the necessary prescriptions and with the required equipment and pesticides, insecticides etc.

Where la Caisse is not directly involved at the producer level, it still seeks to control the remaining links in the system. It sees to it that the buyers of the Product — the agents acting on behalf of the exporter — are paying the fixed price. For each season the buyer has to have a licence, which is only given if he is paying the minimum price, adheres to the rules regarding the treatment of the product, has a book-keeping system where every purchase is noted and registered etc. Furthermore, the buyer must be an inhabitant of the region in which he is dealing and not have been convicted of any 'disgraceful act'. The licence is issued by the prefect, and the buyers are obliged to buy up in total quantities.

The exporters, as well, are forced to fulfil certain requirements mainly regarding their financial reserves. In order to have a licence as an exporter, he must provide evidence as to having established a company with a capital of at least 30 million CFA francs and he must be able to raise a bank loan of not less than 15 million francs. Further, he must have an organization with the necessary administrative apparatus and technical competence. After the decision by the Minister of Agriculture at the start of every season, each exporter is given a buying quota (normally around 2%). In all there are around 30 exporters. Likewise the whole transportation system is subject to a wide range of regulations aimed at ensuring that the right quantities reach the right destinations in proper shape. A long list of information has to be filled in in order to secure the product, and control that the money is going to the right places.

If the whole system is working as prescribed — and nothing indicates that it is not — it seems that la Caisse has its finger on nearly every coffee bean in sight all the way from the direct producers to the principal importing nations, where la Caisse has established offices of its own (in Paris and New York). Compared to other marketing boards (e.g. Kenya) also established on the initiative of the colonial government, the Ivorian system exercises much more control, limiting the influence of the private business sphere to those functions defined and controlled by la Caisse, i.e. the state. With only slight modifications, the system operates in much the same manner for the other agricultural products, notably the cocoa, cotton and palm-oil (with regard to the latter product, we will return to the role of la Caisse later).

As mentioned above the income of la Caisse mainly originates from the price difference between the export cost and export price of the various agricultural products. But la Caisse also receives an income from various investments in manufacturing industry, like the textile factory Ets. R. Gonfreville in which it has a 30% share, the national agricultural development bank (B.N.D.A.) with 16.7%, the building societies, the Société africaine de cacao (25%), etc. According to *l'Agriculture Africaine*, the total revenue of la Caisse during the period 1963 to 1974 amounted to 205 billion C.F.A. francs, of which 29.35 billion went to the state's investment budget (B.S.I.E.), 39.7 billion for various projects and 25.8 billion in direct subventions to agriculture. For the year 1977, the contribution of la Caisse to the B.S.I.E. was 122 billion francs increasing to 167 billion in 1980.

Table 8. The Ivory Coast State Investment Budget (millions of C.F.A. francs)

Sources of Revenue	1977	1978	1979	1980
Domestic Resources				
Taxes	74,478	88,289	63,564	44,110
La Caisse	122,080	86,190	69,585	161,237
Sub-total	196,558	174,479	133,159	205,347
External Resources				
International Bodies	11,243	13,078	15,748	12,137
Government Institutions	4,982	5,138	11,888	11,470
Private Financial Institutions	22,591	35,867	39,498	43,410
Suppliers' credits	9,700	28,656	19,464	40,480
Sub-total	48,516	82,741	86,608	107,497
Total	245,074	257,220	219,767	312,844

Sources: *La Côte d'Ivoire en Chiffres 78-79, 79-80, 80-81* (Abidjan, Société Africaine d'Edition, 1979, '80, '81).

Taking the total income from the export of the principal agricultural products (coffee and cocoa) — that is combining the revenue accumulating in la Caisse as well as that going directly to the central government in the form of taxes — it emerges that the public sector took on average, in the period 1965-66 to 1974-75, 38% of the cocoa f.o.b. price and 31% of coffee. Around 50% of the f.o.b. price is the amount received by the direct producers, the cocoa and coffee farmers, while between 12% and 15% goes to the intermediaries, processors, traders and transporters.

In this period, la Caisse only had to pay out producers from its reserves three times. And with the favourable world market prices in most recent years, the earnings of la Caisse have sharply increased. Also contributing to its high earnings have been the time lags between changes in world market prices and the price adjustments to the producers, as well as a stockpiling policy which with rising world market prices has suddenly allowed for additional earnings.

Although the state may enter the scene primarily because of the absence of a coherent national bourgeoisie, it does not follow that the state in itself is acting in pure accordance with the rationality of the process of creating a national accumulation of capital, that is without reference to or influence from fractions of an embryonic national bourgeoisie. The state is, of course, an instrument to be understood in relation to underlying class relations.

As will be demonstrated in the subsequent sections of this chapter, one of the most remarkable features of the Ivorian economic development process is the active role played by the state. The share of Ivorian state capital in industrial investment has grown to 53% of total investments as of 1 October 1980.[8] The state is also actively involved in the promotion of growth in the agricultural sector.

But the state's activities in both industry and agriculture are closely linked with international capital. This touches upon another important function of the Ivorian state: that of attracting capital under favourable investment conditions. Already in 1959 a Code of Investment had been introduced; it is still in force and provides guarantees for foreign investors in a number of ways. According to one author,[9] the Ivory Coast was ten years ahead of other Third World countries in institutionalizing favourable terms for foreign capital. Among the measures are five years' exemption from customs duties, import and export facilities, free mobility of capital, provision of the necessary infrastructure, etc.[10]

Apart from this, state participation in key industries, its organization of the capital market, financial support for locally developed technological innovations, etc., are among the primary functions of the peripheral state in increasing the productivity of labour while at the same time keeping wages at a level acceptable to foreign investors. This can be done by way of a repressive state apparatus, where trade unions, strikes and other working class rights are suppressed.

Part of this is also the case with the Ivory Coast. Trade unions do exist, but they are entirely incorporated in the one-party system of political power.

Strikes are illegal. The labour force in industry seems to be quite disciplined. The labour force in agriculture, predominantly consisting of workers from Upper Volta, is exceptionally low paid — as will be discussed in the next section. While the Ivorian state officially pursues an income equalization policy, the lowest-paid jobs in industry and agriculture are reserved for proletarianized migrant workers from the neighbouring Sahel countries who act as a mobile army of reserve labour.

The transitional phase in which a coherent national bourgeoisie seems to be lacking partly explains the active role of the state, and partly explains the eagerness with which the state seeks to promote a stratum of entrepreneurs. This policy is officially exposed both in the development plan for 1976-80 and in many of the presidential speeches as well as in governmental publications. The creation of a rural bourgeoisie owning at least 15 hectares each is also the explicit target in agriculture. The effort on the part of the state to persuade Ivorians to invest their savings in industry, and thereby diminish state intervention, is another example of this.

This transitional phase without clearly defined classes does not imply that class interests and conflicts do not greatly influence the activities of the state. Although many of the Ivorian plantation owners who played an important role in the process of decolonization are still of great importance in shaping Ivorian development, they are clearly but gradually losing ground. The most significant fact about the present stage is, therefore, that economic development has not yet been carried so far that the different social groups and classes have been structurally and solidly founded within Ivorian society. In the absence of coherent classes with a material basis, one might suggest that the administrative bureaucracy is developing into a class in itself, ruling and governing the state apparatus. At least, that is the result of one recent investigation.[11]

Agriculture in the Ivory Coast is carried on mainly by small subsistence farmers (although the social situation is fairly uncrystallized with only a small layer of wealthy plantation owners and some large-scale plantations initiated by the state). The question arises whether this situation is irreversible. The state may officially want to create entrepreneurs in agriculture, but its own activities in themselves limit these opportunities, simply because enormous areas are used for state-supported projects. Also contributing to this halt in the development of entrepreneurs is the land question, where the state still has not found a solution to the question of private ownership. No formal land registration is in operation.

In the light of this, Ikonikoff and Sigal[12] conclude that the embryo of a national bourgeoisie is at present amongst people who are active in commerce and industry. However, the substantial increases in farm income following the rather high world market prices of Ivorian agricultural export products do suggest the possibility of the emergence of a rural bourgeoisie. In our study of palm oil production, we describe the use of technology together with increasing social differentiation in agriculture, which may develop into some class constellations between the bureaucracy and the (embryonic) bourgeoisie, controlling the state apparatus. Finally, the autonomous national development factors, notably the state, do not make it easy to draw conclusions as to the possible existence and power of a 'comprador bourgeoisie'.

No doubt, the situation is complex. And this complexity is not least brought about by the favourable national and international development conditions in recent years, from which nearly every layer of Ivorians have profited (together with international capital, of course). The drastic rise in inflation in recent years may easily change the whole picture completely, resulting in different social strata emerging to fight for their interests. That profound changes may be developing is illustrated by the case of palm oil to which we shall turn in a moment.

The Agricultural Development of the Ivory Coast

In his analysis of Ivorian agricultural development, Samir Amin[13] concluded that:
(1)   the export orientation of the agricultural sector will in the future create an increasing need for imported foodstuffs, creating a heavy drain on financial resources;
(2)   the growth in agricultural production has so far been carried out by extending the cultivated area rather than by intensifying production by means of the introduction of machinery and new varieties of crop;
(3)   agriculture is still dominated by a few products, and diversification is needed;
(4)   an agro-industry combining agricultural and industrial development is missing.

Let us now analyse the recent agricultural development trends in the light of these conclusions.

Although the agricultural sector is still the backbone of the Ivorian economy, its relative economic importance has decreased since independence. The primary sector's contribution to G.D.P. was 47% in 1960, but only 25% in 1978.[14] While the average annual growth rate in the primary sector since independence has been 8%, the corresponding figures for the secondary and tertiary sectors are 14% and 12% respectively. However, agriculture still contributes two-thirds of the export earnings of the country, and two-thirds of the population derive their income from agricultural activities.

Agricultural production has increased ever since independence, in both foodstuffs and agricultural export products. It has been calculated that the provision of calories *per capita* per day has increased to 2,654 in 1974,[15] making the food situation relatively satisfactory, apart from a lack of vitamins and animal protein.[16] For many of the food products such as yams, maize, manioc, and taro, the production figures in 1975 were far ahead of the amounts expected for 1980, as presented in the Development Plan 1971-75. However, this development has not entirely reduced the importation of food products. But the share of food products in total imports did decrease from 14% in 1973 to 11% in 1974, and was in 1976 reduced to around 8%.[17]

Ivorian agriculture is still predominantly export-oriented. Coffee, cocoa and timber are the most important export products, although their relative importance is decreasing, due to diversification and local processing. The growth in production of export products has made the Ivory Coast the third largest coffee producer in the world (after Brazil and Colombia) and the largest cocoa producer, overtaking Ghana.

Attempts at diversification have resulted in a variety of products, some of which are increasingly important. Among these are palm oil (the Ivory Coast being the world's third largest exporter after Malaysia and Indonesia), cotton (the second producer in Africa after Chad), coconuts (largest producer in the world), rubber (sixth largest in the world), pineapples (a yearly growth rate during the last 15 years of 17.5%, and the world's largest exporter of tinned pineapple), and bananas, avocados, tobacco, etc.

Although uncultivated arable land still exists in the Western region, there is a growing pressure on the land in the highly fertile areas of the Centre and South, where export production is concentrated. This has, together with the shortage of manpower (around 80% of labourers are migrant workers coming mainly from Upper Volta), forced the state now to concentrate on a policy of intensifying production on the existing acreage. While growth in output until 1970 took place mainly by increasing the area of individual plots under cultivation, in recent years an intensification has taken place in certain regions of production, using highly sophisticated machinery and new high-yielding varieties of crops. In certain cases new types of machinery adapted to the special conditions in the Ivory Coast have also been invented, and efforts to further mechanize have been made in French research institutes supported by Ivorian state capital. Such research institutes are situated all over francophone Africa as branches of the mother institute in Paris and supported by the French state. The research done has produced new high-yielding varieties in all fields and has resulted in certain cases in exports of seeds from the Ivory Coast to other tropical countries.

The local processing of agricultural products has been a primary goal in the development plans. 20% of cocoa production is now manufactured locally.

The direct foreign influence on agricultural production has been reduced to a great extent. In the case of coffee and cocoa production, European plantations amounted to 9% of total production in 1950, but only 0.7% in 1965 and nil today. In forestry foreign capital is still predominant, and also in the production of bananas where 100 major European planters own half the cultivated land. Large-scale farms are particularly a feature of banana production. European capital also has a certain, although minor, role in palm oil and rubber plantations.

In conclusion, it must be said that with regard to agriculture in the Ivory Coast, the pessimistic forecasts of Samir Amin have not been fulfilled. The emphasis on production for export has not prevented a growth in food production, attempts at diversification are widespread, production is becoming intensified to a greater and greater extent, and the build-up of agro-industries is far from minimal.

In order to reach a firmer conclusion regarding the problem of systematic capitalist development in the Ivory Coast, however, we will now look at palm oil production as a specific example of an attempt at diversification, intensification and the establishment of agro-industries.

Palm Oil Production as a Case Study

Introduction

Apart from presenting the organization and structure of the so-called SODEPALM plantations, it is also our intention to look into the specific role of technology in development. The combination of a centrally located factory, a nucleus estate (the industrial plantations) and outgrowers (the village plantations), where the factory and industrial plantations secure the economic viability of the system (supplemented by the production on the part of the smallholders), has implied the use of modern technology. This development of the productive forces, which right from the start has been judged as the necessary precondition for the economic viability of the system, has been further accentuated in the course of the subsequent years, mainly due to the shortage of manpower in the rural sector. And it is this development which is considered to be the key factor in a qualitatively new trend towards the establishment of capitalist relations of production in agriculture. The role of technology in palm oil production in the Ivory Coast will, therefore, be given detailed treatment in this chapter before we conclude with an analysis of the socio-economic consequences for the smallholders attached to the system.

We will first present the palm oil production in its world market context and then look more closely into the specific conditions and results of the introduction of new high-yielding varieties in the Ivory Coast since 1963. After that, we will describe the role of international capital and the large donor organizations, and their effects not least in contributing to an enlarged state revenue. The technology used, SODEPALM's effort to invent new technological devices and the role of SODEPALM as an exporter of technological expertise will also be touched upon. Finally, the socio-economic consequences of this way of organizing and controlling the production process will be discussed.

Palm Oil Production in its World Market Context

The market for vegetable oil has been growing in recent years, mainly due to an increased demand in West European countries. The different types of vegetable oil contribute increasingly to the export earnings of several developing countries. World market prices rose rather favourably in the beginning of the 1970s. The vegetable oil market reached a record high price in 1974, gradually declining again in 1975 and the beginning of 1976, while a new peak — although still below the record level — was reached in 1977 with still rather good prospects for 1978.[18]

After soy-bean oil (with around one-third of the world market) and sun-flower oil, palm oil is the most important vegetable oil product, presently contributing 12% of the total production of vegetable oil,[19] and this share is growing. Among the reasons for this increase is the fact that, with the right technology, the output of oil per hectare is far higher for palm oil than for other vegetable oils. At the same time the content of free fatty acids is at a level guaranteeing competitive quality.[20]

Traditionally African countries like Nigeria, Benin (formerly Dahomey), Zaire etc. were the world's main palm oil producing countries. In general, the African countries' contribution has dwindled — with the Ivory Coast as the only exception — resulting in a shift to Malaysia and Indonesia as the centre of gravity of the world's palm oil production.

The stagnation in African production is connected to the failure to plant new trees or to develop high-yielding varieties, together with the lack of use of modern technology in plant breeding and protection. The growing internal demand for vegetable oil in the African countries, which cannot be met any more by local production, may, of course, change this picture in the near future.

More important than the production as such is the quantity of palm oil exported. The major world exporting countries are Malaysia, Indonesia, and the Ivory Coast. The rather drastic increase in the total quantity exported is due to a considerable improvement in palm oil quality, which has led to the much improved position of palm oil among the other vegetable oil products. Palm oil has consequently become the second most important exported vege-table oil (after soy-bean oil) with a world market share of 25% (including palm kernel oil).[21]

The most common use of palm oil is as a raw material for the production of vegetable salad oil, margarine and soap, and this kind of oil is increasingly used for other industrial purposes. In the food industry it is used for the manufacture of ice-cream (nearly all ice-cream production in the United Kingdom is based on palm oil), cocoa and chocolate products, pasta, biscuits and pastry and other manufactured foods in which the more expensive butter fat can be substituted by palm oil. In this respect palm oil also has an advan-tage due to its natural colour, not needing artificial colouring.

Within the medical and pharmaceutical industry, palm oil has shown new possibilities. It has a growing importance as a softener in the steel and tin industry, as a binder linking synthetic fibres and natural cotton fibres, as a detergent in the manufacture of washing powder, etc.

Another aspect contributing to the increasing importance of palm oil is the fact that the new high-yielding varieties of palm trees can be harvested all year round with only minor seasonal variations. If the palm trees are suitably treated with fertilizers, pesticides, insecticides, etc., they will mature in about 3 to 4 years to give a high and relatively constant yield which facilitates precise calculations of future harvests.

The major importers of palm oil are the Western industrialized countries.

The E.E.C. countries take more than half the total quantity exported (with the United Kingdom as the primary importer followed by the Federal Republic of Germany and the Netherlands).

The Development of Palm Oil Production in the Ivory Coast

The history of palm oil production in the Ivory Coast dates back to the beginning of the century when primarily small units of production were established. In 1912 a plantation of about 2,000 hectares was created at Grand Drewin. Other small and medium-sized plantations were created in subsequent years, but the world economic crisis in 1929 ruined the majority of them.[22]

The French research organization IRHO (Institut de Recherche pour les Huiles et les Oléagineux) took over the 2,000 hectares plantation at Grand Drewin together with an oil factory, and later added the first West African large-scale plantation (10,000 hectares) on a concession basis at Mopoyem. An experimental research station including an oil factory and the later establishment of another oil factory at Mopoyem made IRHO one of the more influential non-Ivorian palm oil growers. The capacity and output of the IRHO-owned activities are today, however, still marginal compared to the output of the oil factories created by SODEPALM.

Another palm oil producer in the Ivory Coast is the Société des Plantations et Huileries de Côte d'Ivoire owned by the Blohorn group. The gradual increase in the production and capacity of the Blohorn-owned factories in the Ivory Coast has been closely connected to the development of the *Plan Palmier,* initiated by the Ivorian state. The total hectarage of oil palms grown by private foreign investors is, however, only small compared to the development in the state-owned plantations which has taken place since 1963.

The *Plan Palmier* was decided upon in 1961 and gradually brought into effect from 1963. That year a special institution, the SODEPALM (Société d'Etat pour le Développement et l'Exploitation du Palmier à Huile en Côte d'Ivoire), was created and put in charge of the establishment of 32,000 hectares of plantations, both as estates and run by outgrowers.

With the *Plan Palmier*, a tremendous increase in the hectarage used for oil palms has taken place. This is largely due to the increase initiated in the state plan, resulting in a total area of 81,000 hectares towards the end of 1975.[23] Out of this total, only around 10,000 hectares is privately owned plantations not within the scope of the *Plan Palmier*.

The extension in hectarage used for oil palms has been followed by an impressive increase in production and export of palm oil. The number of fruits harvested has more than doubled in the period 1965-76, while the oil produced has increased from 17,600 to 145,000 tons. Of the total amount of palm oil produced, around two-thirds is exported and the remainder is sold locally to the Blohorn group for further manufacturing.

Palm oil's share of the total value of the Ivory Coast's exports was only around 2% in 1973, but increased to 4% in 1975. Palm oil is still of relatively marginal importance as an export, but the planned future extensions of the hectarage used for oil palms together with the fact that the existing plantations will show their maximum yield within the next 5 to 10 years may very well change this pattern fundamentally.[24] According to E.E.C. estimates the palm oil scheme has so far already demonstrated its profitability.

In the last seven years (that is up to the end of 1975) the state has received in dividends, taxes and contributions to the Caisse a total of 50.55 million U.A. According to other information[25] the annual state income from the activities of SODEPALM was estimated in 1974 to be around 8 billion C.F.A. francs (equivalent to around 30 million U.A.), gradually increasing to between 10 and 20 billion C.F.A. francs annually, when the plantations reach their maximum output. The results of SODEPALM up to 1975 have been remarkable, also when compared to the total amount of investment, which towards the end of that year amounted to 137.8 million U.A. The export of SODE-PALM crude palm oil, which amounted to 43 million U.A. in 1975, has also implied a net earning of foreign exchange, and the increased local manufacture of palm oil has of course eliminated any import costs for vegetable oil products.

The industrial subsidiary of SODEPALM, PALMINDUSTRIE (in charge of ten palm oil factories), also demonstrates the growing economic importance of palm oil activities in the Ivory Coast. In 1977 PALMINDUSTRIE was second in the Ivory Coast in terms of cumulated investments, fifth in terms of industrial turnover, fourth in export earnings and number eight in the number of industrially employed workers.[26]

The activities of SODEPALM are also geographically widespread. At present the estate plantations and outgrowers' schemes cover a nearly continuous distance over 400 km from Ghana in the east to the River Sassandra in the west.

Foreign Aid and the Establishment of Palm Oil Production

The Ivory Coast has always been reliant on foreign aid. This dependency, however, has been replaced in recent years by an increased borrowing in the international money markets, in particular the Eurodollar market. But with regard to the public investment programme, international aid still plays a crucial role: from 1960 to 1972, 40% of public investment was financed from international aid sources and for the period 1973-74 this share was 60%.[27] Originally grants predominated, but loans now contribute the majority share, around 50-60% of the requirements for the public sector investment programme.[28]

For the period 1972-74, aid from the European Development Fund comprised 17% of the total aid received, but when loans by the European Investment Bank are included, total E.E.C. aid contributed 28% of the total aid received. This made the E.E.C. the single most important donor for the Ivory Coast — followed by France with 23%, the World Bank (16%), the International Development Agency (14%), while the United Nations Development Programme (U.N.D.P.) played only a marginal role. In the most recent years the World Bank, the European Investment Bank and the African Development

Bank have taken the dominant role as donors of international aid to the Ivory Coast.[29]

Compared to aid to other recipients among the Associated countries, the E.E.C. aid to the Ivory Coast has always been substantial, especially in the case of the activities of the European Investment Bank. Under the Yaoundé II Convention the contribution of the European Investment Bank (primarily aimed at the establishment of large and very modern textile factories) was no less than 44% of the total aid budget of the Bank.

The major part of E.E.C. aid has been directed towards the establishment of palm oil production and cotton-growing and textile manufacturing. By the end of 1975 the E.E.C. had contributed a total of 50.3 million U.A. to the Ivorian state's *Plan Palmier*, making palm oil production in the Ivory Coast the single most important aid project of the E.E.C. and one which received around 35% of the total Community aid to the Ivory Coast.

The Organization of Palm Oil Production
The cultivation of oil palms requires rather large capital inputs: expenses for fertilizers, insecticides and pesticides, for the necessary mechanization, etc. This implies that only large farms of between 5,000 and 7,000 hectares can be operated economically in a rational manner. The large capital input is closely connected to the development of new high-yielding varieties. But when the technologically developed inputs are used as prescribed, an increase in output from 300 kg to 3.5 tons of oil per hectare is likely on fields with selected oil palm varieties.

To get this extremely high output per hectare, a relatively skilled work force is also required. The harvesting of the fruits (which takes place almost continuously throughout the year) has to be done with extreme care, as the use of wrong techniques can prevent new fruits from maturing. At the same time the quantity and quality of the oil produced is dependent on a fast and reliable transportation of the fruits to the factories. The development of fatty acids takes place after harvesting and bruising the fruit may increase the fatty acid content, which has to be kept at around 5%.[30]

It is Yves Pehaut's opinion[31] that the French-initiated research institute IRHO is the main source of inspiration for the organizational set-up of the SODEPALM plantations. IRHO experiences[32] show the difficulties of running a palm oil factory entirely on the basis of voluntary deliveries from independent smallholders. IRHO is also the site of the experiments with new high-yielding varieties, and has supplied all the palm trees planted under the *Plan Palmier*.[33]

The organizational structure chosen by SODEPALM is one in which a well-organized system of highly mechanized, state-owned industrial plantations in combination with surrounding privately owned small-scale plantations guarantees a reliable and continuous provision of raw materials to a centrally located factory.

So far ten such organizational centres have been built. A centrally located factory and well-equipped social infrastructure (primary and secondary schools, a health centre, housing facilities free of charge for the salaried workers employed on the estate plantations, local market place, supermarket, church and mosque, etc.) constitute the core of the system. Around the factory are situated the privately owned small-scale plantations, easily accessible by a widespread network of roads by which the newly harvested fruits can be brought to the factory.

The economic viability that is secured mainly through these estate plantations gives at the same time the basis for the means of production for the smallholders, which they probably would never have had the chance of procuring by their own efforts. The organizational structure of SODEPALM therefore transcends well-known barriers to productivity increases in an agricultural system based on smallholders.

A smallholder can be attached to the SODEPALM system if his farmland is situated within 20 km of the factory, if his farm is easily reached by road, and if his land is in a condition suitable for the growing of oil palms. When these conditions are met, as judged by the SODEPALM experts, the smallholder may be invited to join the system. SODEPALM will support future growing of selected oil palms by giving cash rewards to peasants who change from coffee or cocoa to oil palms. Credit facilities which secure the smallholder an acceptable income during the first three to four years until the trees are mature enough to yield are among the means for keeping the peasants as growers. In return, the smallholder is contractually obliged to grow only the selected varieties offered by the SODEPALM technicians, to follow any advice on the use of fertilizers etc. given them, to deliver the harvested products once a week to the factory (the factory will provide lorries, which will collect the fruits regularly) and to accept the deduction from monthly pay of gradually increasing interest on the credits received.[34]

The price paid for produce delivered to the factory is fixed by the state. From 1963 the price was fixed at 4 C.F.A. francs per kg. In 1974 it was doubled to 8 per kg after growing dissatisfaction among the smallholders and increased efforts to sell the produce on the local market instead of delivering it to the factory. Another increase in price took place in 1977, and it has been kept constant at 10 francs since then. Once more the smallholders have reacted to a producer price considered to be out of line with the rate of inflation, and the result has been SODEPALM's worst crisis ever. Unfavourable climatic conditions (irregular and short periods of rainfall), peasants neglecting their trees when they reach a height where harvesting is increasingly difficult, a marked tendency for the peasants either to sell the fruits on the local market or to sell whole palm-trees intended for the production of palm wine, has led to a catastrophic decline in SODEPALM's production results for the years since 1977. The state has not yet (as of Spring 1981) decided on a necessary increase in the producer price; this is an illustration of the difficult balancing act between the maximization of state revenue by extracting the greatest possible surplus from the agricultural sector, and the ostensible social objective of improving living conditions for the direct producers.

About 12,600 persons are employed on the estate plantations. The workers mainly come from the drought-ridden Sahel states, primarily Upper Volta (around 80% of the total work force). Upper Volta has until recently been seen as an immense and nearly inexhaustible labour reserve for Ivorian agriculture, but in recent years the Ivory Coast has nevertheless experienced a serious shortage of labour which has badly affected the output of several of her agricultural products. More and more workers from Upper Volta have either returned home or sought employment opportunities elsewhere (as far away as Gabon) because of the extremely low wages within Ivorian agriculture. The guaranteed minimum wage for an agricultural labourer has until recently been 240 C.F.A. francs a day, while the guaranteed minimum wage in industry is 736. According to E.E.C. estimates, the minimum wage in agriculture, where the foreign manpower is absolutely predominant, is on the edge of the minimum level of subsistence.

Apart from the 12,600 labourers on the estate plantations, the SODE-PALM system includes 7,500 smallholders (the outgrowers' plantations) who in turn employ around 7,000 labourers (also mainly from Upper Volta). In all it is estimated that around 140,000 people derive their main source of income from the activities of the SODEPALM system.

In the first two agreements with the Ivory Coast, the European Development Fund stated as a condition for granting the funds to set up the ambitious *Plan Palmier* that the combination of estate plantations and outgrowers' plantations was to be replaced eventually by the smallholders taking over cultivation of the estate plantations, adding the latter to their individual holdings. This, however, has never been accomplished. According to sources within the SODEPALM administration, the reason is a fear that the profitability of the whole system might be forfeited if it was to depend only on the smallholders. One might add that the contractual system binding the smallholders to SODEPALM at least for the period until the loans have been repaid, and the very tight control over production and output, might eliminate part of this fear. In any case, SODEPALM is presently considering a scheme to build two new factories to the north of the existing palm oil belt, the basis of which is to be production by small-scale farms only, indicating that after more than 15 years of operation the farmers have really experienced a sense of entrepreneurship.[35]

While the European Development Fund at least formally seemed to seek a social objective, the efforts of the European Investment Bank and the World Bank have continuously been to secure the economic viability of the system. The institutional set-up reflects this influence.

The European Investment Bank made it a further condition of their decision to participate in the SODEPALM projects that private capital should be represented as well, as the Bank refused to deal solely with the state as main organizer and shareholder.[36] The World Bank and the French donor organization, C.C.C.E., agreed to this in order to secure a maximum economic efficiency. As a direct consequence of these demands, two subsidiary institutions of SODEPALM were created, namely PALMIVOIRE and PALMINDUSTRIE, both with European (mainly French) minority capital, while SODEPALM remained entirely Ivorian state-owned. This resulted in a unique situation where the European Investment Bank and the World Bank negotiated support directly with PALMIVOIRE and PALMINDUSTRIE without the active participation of the Ivorian state, which confined itself to problems of the solvency of the mother organization, SODEPALM. This lack — or partial lack — of state control over very large-scale and important development projects was 'counterbalanced' by an 'extremely detailed and efficient control' on the part of the donor organizations.[37]

It seems fair to conclude not only that there were conflicting interests between the two E.E.C. aid organizations, but also that the economic objective of the projects weighed heavier. At the same time, as we will see, this institutional set-up paved the way for one French investor in particular: Blohorn.

As mentioned, SODEPALM is 100% state-owned, acting as the administrative mother organization, which formally owns the estate plantations and gives technical advice to the smallholders. The state also has 69% of the shares in PALMINDUSTRIE which is the institution owning the industrial infrastructure, primarily the oil factories and storage facilities. In PALMIVOIRE the share of the state is 61% and this body runs the estate plantations and the factories with their storage facilities and provides additional funds for further investment. Among the private investors in PALMINDUSTRIE and PALMIVOIRE are the Blohorn group, originally with 18% of the shares in the former and 39% in the latter.[38] More recent information, however, indicates that the Blohorn group's holding has diminished to only 6% in PALMINDUSTRIE. The influence of the group is also revealed by the fact that M. André Blohorn, its Managing Director, is Vice-President of SODEPALM as well as of PALMINDUSTRIE and is a board member of PALMIVOIRE.[39]

In June 1976 the Ivorian Government took a decisive step to change the institutional set-up completely (most likely after consultations with the international donor agencies). The Ivorian state now judged that SODEPALM itself had the technical expertise to secure the smooth running of the system, and at the same time wanted to get hold of the eventually substantial dividends paid to the private investors. After buying up the shares, the state decided to eliminate PALMIVOIRE in an effort to rationalize the administration. Instead of SODEPALM marketing the products, the Caisse took on that responsibility (creating offices in the more important European cities and the U.S.A.) and licensed out some of the marketing rights to a Belgian company (a Unilever subsidiary).

A further institutional restructuring took place in late 1977 following a ministerial reshuffle which involved among others the Minister of Agriculture. SODEPALM, which over a decade had evolved into a near autonomous body, itself deciding (in conjunction with the international aid organizations) on its future investment policy and reserving funds for this, thereby depriving the Caisse of some of its income,[40] was put under much tighter controls and placed under the supervision of the new Minister of Agriculture.

SODEPALM, however, has been until recently one of the Ivory Coast's truly successful institutions (in contrast to other SODEs like SODERIZ and SODHEVEA, which were dissolved following the reshuffle), and it has now taken over the planning and supervision of all agricultural production in the coastal belt, not only oil palm and coconut production but also products like cassava, rice, bananas and pineapples. This means that the state has tightened its control over the SODEs and that a much more integrated agricultural strategy has appeared, gradually eliminating the previous overlap in planning and administration, which was formerly done separately for each product.[41]

The Role of International Capital in Palm Oil Production
In the previous sections we tried to identify the main agents which have contributed to the economically very successful establishment in the Ivory Coast of large oil palm plantations (estate and outgrowers' plantations) and the ten factories — surrounded by the social and physical infrastructure — which treat the harvested products. These agents have been the international aid organizations, the European Development Fund and European Investment Bank, followed by the World Bank and the French C.C.C.E., the Ivorian state itself, and international capital, here represented by the Blohorn group.

While the state-owned SODEPALM and its subsidiary run the estate plantations and carry out the initial refining of the palm fruits into crude vegetable oil, the final manufacturing process of around 40% of the crude oil into vegetable oil and derived products takes place within the Blohorn factories, situated in the industrial zone of Vridi at Abidjan. Blohorn's oil and soap factory was created in 1932. Later on in 1954 the P.H.C.I. (Plantations et Huileries de Côte d'Ivoire) was established — together with an oil factory running from 1967 — with 17% of the shares owned by the Ivorian state and the remainder by Blohorn. The plantations were intended to provide crude oil for the factories of the Blohorn group, which expanded from 1960 onwards.[42]

Already in 1960 the production of the Blohorn factories was far from minimal. Until 1968, however, Blohorn's main problem was to secure a continuous supply of raw materials in a situation where the Ivory Coast was net importer of vegetable oil products. No wonder, therefore, that Blohorn strongly favoured the grandiose *Plan Palmier* and took an active part in its development. In fact, the whole expansion process of Blohorn throughout the 1960s and 1970s can only be understood in terms of an agreement between Blohorn and the Ivorian state regarding the provision of the necessary raw materials for his factories.

The major expansion of the Blohorn factories was started in 1969 and the new complex was inaugurated in 1974 by the President of the Republic, Félix Houphouët-Boigny. This complex is considered to be the world's largest and most modern integrated fat processing plant, which apart from the refinery plant also includes a chemical and a packing plant.[43]

The expansion of the Blohorn factories has also allowed for an increase in exports. In 1970, 467 tons of refined vegetable oil were exported; in 1976, 13,410 tons. The export of glycerine expanded fourfold in the same period.[44]

As of 1 January 1974 the Blohorn cumulated investments were around

7 billion C.F.A. francs.[45] — making Blohorn the seventh largest industrial investor in the Ivory Coast in 1977, the fourth in turnover, ninth in exports and seventh in number employed.[46]

The Blohorn group has been able to establish production processes and plants by joining a national division of labour, in which the Ivorian state provides Blohorn with the necessary input of raw materials. The fast growth of the Blohorn factories also implies that Blohorn has been able to expand into a range of products not directly connected to palm oil. For example, Blohorn is together with the large French firm Nobel Bozel engaged in a silicate processing plant, and the two latest established societies in technological research and education seem to indicate a new range of activities taking advantage of the overall favourable climate for investment in the Ivory Coast.[47]

With the planned extensions of the hectarage used for oil palms, one might have expected that SODEPALM itself would sooner or later engage in refinery activities, competing with Blohorn. But according to sources within the SODEPALM administration, that is not at all envisaged. Blohorn will continue to have a virtual monopoly on refining, and SODEPALM will instead engage in the production of vegetable oil based on palm kernels. Recently, an immense factory has been built at Vridi (financially supported by the European Investment Bank) aimed at the production of palm kernel oil.

Figure 2 gives an outline of the palm oil production process *in toto*. It shows how the division of labour is managed, while at the same time the unique integrational aspect of the process is indicated together with the rather wide range of products stemming from the growing of oil palms.

The production process is exceptional in the way that there is practically no production waste. The normal waste products are either used as fuel in the factories, making these nearly self-sufficient in energy, or they are used as fodder for the cattle, which are increasingly being bred under the palm-trees (where they eat the parasitic plants living on the trees and other weeds, thus doing part of the labourers' normal job, while also helping to improve the local supply of animal protein).

The figure also shows, however, the system's dependence on a continuous flow of raw materials, in part explaining the necessity of having large nucleus estate plantations running on purely capitalist lines and employing wage labour with no other source of income than selling their labour. Also the need for a highly mechanized and centralized management (with the state acting as 'capitalist', that is extracting the surplus value from the employed labour force), thereby securing the economic viability of the whole set-up. The system implies also the necessity to control the attached smallholders to the extent that their formal private ownership of their means of production is reduced to purely formal ownership plus rights of use over the land, and with all other factors of production centrally controlled by SODEPALM, which acts as the institution responsible for the extraction of an economic surplus from this part of the agricultural sector.

85

86

Figure 2 The palm oil production process

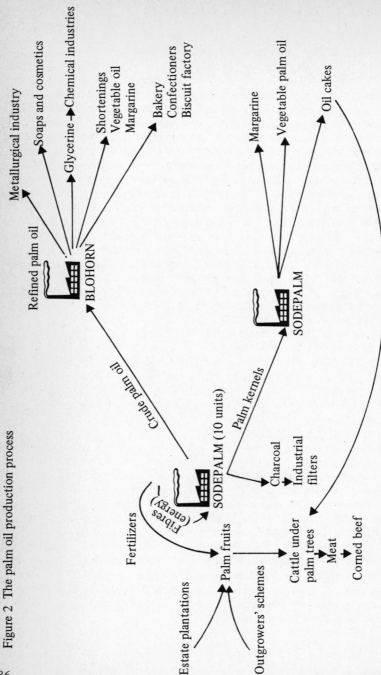

Source: Victor Amagou and G.L. Gleizes, 'Le groupe SODEPALM et l'agro-industrie du palmier a huile en Cote d'Ivoire', *Economies et Societes*, Series A.G., No. 13, 1976, p. 1498.

The Role of Technology in Palm Oil Production

When describing the role of technology and innovations in the development of palm oil production in the Ivory Coast, it might be fruitful to distinguish between three different levels of adaptation. First, there is the technological development connected with the growing of selected varieties of oil palms, and the mechanical and other equipment used on the estate and outgrowers' plantations, etc. Secondly, there are the technological aspects related to the running and development of the SODEPALM factories. Thirdly, there is the role of technology in the final processing stage, at the Blohorn factories.

Technology in the Plantations

As previously mentioned, IRHO is the research institute mainly responsible for the experimental plant breeding which eventually leads to the delivery of selected varieties of palm trees to SODEPALM. By cross-breeding varieties from South East Asia with local varieties, and experimentally adapting fertilizers, new varieties have been successfully developed. These have an oil content of 90% (as against 50-60% for the traditional ones) and a free fatty acid content of around 4% (as against 20-30%).[48]

On the best land in the Ivory Coast, output figures of 3,000-3,200 kg per hectare have been achieved — equalling the output of South East Asian countries. The new varieties have the further advantage of maturing after a period of only three and a half years.

Technology in the SODEPALM Factories

The consultant and engineering unit within the SODEPALM organization has worked in close collaboration with the French Bertin group, a consultant engineering firm, according to an agreement signed in 1975 between Bertin and SODEPALM.[49]

One of the main results of the technological effort has been the development of an oil factory which processes the palm kernels of SODEPALM. This factory, situated in the industrial area of Abidjan, is able initially to process 100,000 tons of oil per year, and began operating at the beginning of 1977. Another innovation has been the establishment of a factory at Jacqueville which processes coconuts.[50] Behind the development of the factory at Jacqueville lies a technological innovation resulting in a completely mechanized and automated production process, which is unique. Until this innovation the processing of coconuts all over the world had involved initial treatment by hand, and the total processing operation had thus been enormously labour-intensive.

Another remarkable invention made by the joint SODEPALM-Bertin unit is the development of a machine which plucks cassava tubes. This invention has been awarded a prize at the 'Innovation 1976' international exhibition in Paris — the first prize ever awarded within this field to a developing country.

SODEPALM's major role outside the Ivory Coast has been as exporters of technological know-how to neighbouring Liberia. Drawing on the experience of the Ivory Coast, SODEPALM was asked in March 1976 to sell a turn-key oil palm project comprising 10,000 hectares of estate plantations plus 6,000 hectares of smallholders' plantations in palm oil as well as 6,000 hectares in coconuts. In other words, these projects are to be organized precisely along the lines of the Ivory Coast. During the initial phase SODEPALM will act as manager, until Liberians have been trained to take over. With this *Plan Palmier* of their own the Liberians have succeeded in securing the necessary funds from the European Development Fund.[51] Asked about future technological co-operation agreements with other foreign countries, the Director-General of SODEPALM answered positively.

SODEPALM has thus developed a rather exceptional status in the African context with regard to technological innovations. It also seems to be extraordinary that the Ivorian state has been able to export turn-key palm oil projects — an activity which is usually handled by large and very competitive world-market-oriented Western companies.[52]

Technology in the Blohorn Refineries

The French Blohorn group has also established consulting and engineering design organizations, although on a much smaller scale than SODEPALM. 70% of the work of the Blohorn development institute consists of preliminary research and design, while the remainder is supervision of work and projects adopted. In particular, it is the objective of the institute to rationalize the purchase of machinery and equipment by designing purpose-built machines. Also the creation of the unit is the result of bad experiences with international consultancy and engineering firms, which are 'not directly interested in the ultimate profitability of a project and very rarely give you the best process' and which 'very often charge a percentage of the total capital investment, [which means that] they tend to over-equip plant with production machinery which could frequently be replaced quite easily by other machines that are just as efficient and much cheaper'.[53]

Concluding Remarks

In conclusion, the SODEPALM organization represents a unique example of the establishment of a very large and complex production process, including the production of raw materials. It has come about mainly due to the interaction between three factors: the international aid organizations, notably the European Development Fund and the European Investment Bank, international capital (the Blohorn group), and the Ivorian state.

Within this complicated system of production, each of these seems to profit. The aid organizations get a satisfactory rate of return on their investments — and their activities, especially re the E.E.C. aid, are clearly also to the advantage of international capital in cheapening their investments.[54] And the advantages to Blohorn seem obvious; the division of labour between the group and the Ivorian state has developed favourably for Blohorn, securing a basis for continuous and extended investments. As for the Ivorian state, the system has resulted in an accumulation of revenue in the Caisse, because of the difference between the price paid to the producers and the price obtained on the world market. This revenue has made it possible for the state to invest in increasing output in agriculture and in manufacturing.

One crucial factor in this triangle of co-operation has been the technological development of the productive forces, which has contributed fundamentally to this capitalist success story. Without the use of technology — selected palm varieties developed with scientific knowledge in IRHO, and specially invented machinery and production processes — the story would probably have been completely different. The experience of growing oil palms in, for example, Benin or Nigeria might tell another story.

We must now turn to another important aspect — the consequences of this production for the ultimate producers: the smallholders.

Socio-Economic Consequences of Smallholders' Attachment to SODEPALM

As described in the previous section, it can be argued that the smallholders are very much like wage earners in a purely capitalist system, in spite of their private ownership of the land (their means of production). What remains to be investigated is to what extent the smallholders can be regarded as small or medium-sized capitalist farmers. To what extent do they hire wage labour on a permanent and/or seasonal basis? And to what extent do they use the modern technology promoted by the SODEPALM? Also do they invest in this type of agriculture purely from a profit motive? And what trends in the development of land distribution can be observed? A development towards greater inequality might mean that a process of proletarianization is going on.

When dealing with these types of problem, however, one runs into difficulties regarding the nature of the material available. It has not been possible for us to carry out field work for long enough to gain really reliable information on these matters. We are thus forced to rely on available socio-economic surveys, which have been carried out with objectives different from those sketched out above. This will naturally put a question-mark against the validity of our conclusions.

The literature regarding the socio-economic consequences of the introduction of new oil palm varieties is limited. But at least surveys have been carried out in the 1950s, 1960s and 1970s, which gives us a much more diachronic view than is normally the case with such surveys.

The Socio-Economic Study of the Adioukrou Palm Oil Growers, 1954-55
During 1954 and 1955 an ethnological and sociological survey was done in the Dabou coastal region of the Ivory Coast.[55] The objective was to investigate the technical and social factors which might have been responsible for the failure of a palm oil project.

In 1950 a palm oil factory was built in Adioukrou with a planned production of 4,000 tons of oil per year (corresponding to an annual supply of 40,000 tons of palm fruits). The factory, however, was never able to work at full capacity due to a failure of supply from the peasants, and this led to the closing down of the factory.

The raw materials supply was based on voluntary deliveries from individual farmers scattered throughout the area. The results of this study probably had a certain impact on the actual organization of the estate/outgrowers' scheme later brought in under the SODEPALM system.

In the Adioukrou area, the indigenous oil palm trees are collectively owned, with a complicated system for the distribution of revenue from the sale of the produce on the local markets. What is important here, however, is that, because of the completely new scheme of collection, manufacturing, and sale resulting from the establishment of the palm oil factory, some of the villagers were deprived of their cash income. This was particularly true of the matrilineal side of the combined patri- and matrilineal society. Previously, the women had been responsible for the collection of the palm fruit (with youngsters in the village acting as 'climbers'); they were also responsible for the artisan-like processing of the fruit into oil and for its sale on the markets. By means of this money income the continued existence of the matrilineal system was secured, i.e. money was available for the hereditary transfer of wealth according to the rules of the combined matri- and patrilineal system. But the establishment of the palm oil factory meant that the palm fruit would now be collected daily by trucks from the factory, and technical means for the renovation of the palm trees as well as their protection against plant diseases etc. could be provided. So the factory caused not just major technical change, but a socio-economic transformation as well. The farmers reacted by keeping back the palm fruits from the organized factory collection, and instead delivering to the local market, where occasionally a higher price even than the factory buying price was obtained.

For a long time the oil palm fruits had been the most important source of monetary income — besides contributing essentially to the nutrition of the villagers. The complicated system of division of the monetary income not only secured the matrilineal society but also gave the old and the young an income, which together formed the basis of savings in the village. Part of the money was used for ceremonial festivities and buying expensive clothes. But to maintain a person's social status and prove the riches he had acquired, it was not enough to save; the money income had also to be invested, to be transferred into capital.

Particularly among the young generation, it became more and more common to use savings for investment, rather than for ceremonies. Investments in trading firms and shops and in houses to let were considered safe. Extending the plantations and employing a greater labour force was also possible, but this kind of investment was mainly considered by the planters who had moved to the cities as a consequence of their investments there. The sale of land was prohibited, and making money in that way was not widespread, although the village chief could lend out land for a fixed sum.

The authors of the survey assert that Adioukrou society had passed beyond the level of simple accumulation, but it was not clear whether it was on its way towards a broader accumulation where cash income would be used for productive investment such as the modernization of agricultural production through the use of modern techniques.

However, a few examples are mentioned which show tendencies in this direction. The proximity of the major cities of Dabou and Abidjan facilitated the process, and also influenced the consumption pattern. According to the survey, imported goods had an important place in the budget of Adioukrou households, and although everyday consumption was still based almost entirely on the local production of foodstuffs, the buying of luxury consumer goods such as French bread, canned food, and wine occasionally took place. Other consumer goods such as metal beds, tables and chairs, cameras, and gramophones were also rapidly spreading.

Clearly, a rather rapid development seemed to be on its way in that part of the economy which was directed towards the market. The consequence of this was more a change in lifestyle and consumption patterns, rather than a fundamental change in production techniques enabling cumulative productive investments to take place. Whether the successful introduction of a production system like the SODEPALM example might change this will be discussed in the following section.

The Socio-Economic Studies Made by SEDES, 1967-68 and 1975

The most thorough socio-economic analysis so far of the growing of the new high-yielding oil palm trees is the study undertaken in 1967 and 1968 by the French Société d'Etudes pour le Développement Economique et Social (SEDES).[56] The analysis combined a complete enquiry in which all farmers were questioned regarding socio-demographic characteristics, a more limited enquiry investigating a sample of SODEPALM growers, and a sociological enquiry based on intensive interviewing of a sub-sample of the SODEPALM growers. The results of the study were presented in reports published in 1968 aimed at describing the farmers attached to the SODEPALM system, their motivations, and their attitudes towards problems arising.

One of the most interesting findings regarding the occupational background of the farmers attached to SODEPALM was the relatively large group of farmers who pursued an occupation other than farming as their main means of subsistence. Around one-sixth of all farmers had their main occupation as civil servants, technicians and lower level employees, artisans and traders and transporters (listed in order of importance).[57]

Not surprisingly, the number of 'non-agricultural' farmers varied according to the proximity to Abidjan; those village plantations nearest to Abidjan were the ones most favoured by investment from this particular type of farmer. 42% of non-agriculturalists were living in urban or semi-urban areas. The majority of farmers (around four-fifths of the total), however, had their origins in the villages where their plantations were. It seems that the original members of the village community exercised their rights on the use of inherited land. But apart from this an investment motive did seem to be present. This was underlined by the fact that the number of non-agriculturalists was at least three times that of non-agricultural planters in the total South East region, and that the mean area of these planters was far greater than the overall mean area (6 hectares against 3.6 hectares).

This rather strong minority of non-agriculturalists influenced the survey results in a number of ways. Because of this group the number of planters with a certain education was larger than in the agricultural population at large. Around three-quarters of the planters proper were described as being illiterate, which, however, was a far lower proportion than for the remaining agricultural population. This relatively high level of education led the survey to conclude that this factor could in the future facilitate a transition towards increased mechanization and modernization in agriculture.

Palm oil growers have much larger farms than the average Ivorian farmer described in the previous section. A typical farmer in the southern region only had 2-3 hectares — maybe a little more — while the farmers attached to the SODEPALM system have a total area of around 11 hectares (of which typically 4 hectares is for palm oil, 3 for coffee, 3 for cocoa and 1 for other products).

The growing of oil palms is particularly attractive to the large plantation owners. According to the survey,[58] 20% of the large plantations (more than 20 hectares) were attached to the SODEPALM system, by as early as 1966. The period under study is too short, however, to draw any definitive conclusions as to whether there is a trend among the farmers attached to the scheme generally to increase their land under cultivation.

Another interesting point is that the primary motive given for being attached to the system was the regular monthly income it provided in contrast to the uncertain income derived from cocoa and coffee, which, in any case, was available only during a very short period of the year.

The introduction of the high-yielding varieties of palm trees would seem to imply a much greater use of hired labour, either on a monthly or on a contractual basis. The situation before the introduction of the new varieties was that the majority of the work was done by the family (around three-quarters of the total), but the new palm varieties have completely changed this picture. The two most labour-intensive processes in the cultivation of oil palms, land clearance and maintenance, are now done by hired labourers on 90% of the hectarage.

The report concludes that the introduction of the selected palm tree varieties does not constitute a completely new pattern within Ivorian agriculture, but has accentuated tendencies already existing. Among these tendencies is a predominance of rather large farmers, which means that the financial potential of oil palm growing may very well increase still further the rural inequalities already present.

A follow-up analysis was made by SEDES in 1975.[59] Its scope was, however, limited by the sample analysed: only 65 planters were studied, among whom were 33 adherents and 32 non-adherents to the SODEPALM system. Compared to the 1967-68 survey, the average hectarage was slightly smaller than previously: around 8 hectares, as against 10 hectares in the earlier study.

But this was probably due to a certain over-representation in the sample of young farmers who have been particularly attracted to SODEPALM in recent years.

Big limitations on the possibilities of extending the area of land under cultivation was another aspect dealt with in the 1975 follow-up analysis. Particularly in the regions covered by the enquiry, the growing pressure on land already seemed to present real difficulties. With the parcelling out of land to family members and consequently the creation of plots too small to keep the farmers in business, the whole situation of these people will be at risk and their semi-proletarianized situation will become overt. The increased pressure on land together with the process of monetarization is judged by the report to be among the primary reasons for a growing rural inequality.

With regard to the use of manpower, the report largely confirms the findings of the 1967-68 survey. Of the SODEPALM farmers, 32 out of 33 mentioned that they used paid labour in various parts of the cultivation process.

A disrupted balance between the production of foodstuffs (and so relative self-sufficiency in this respect) and the production of cash crops is an aspect often touched upon by writers dealing with commercialization of peripheral agriculture.[60] The priority given to perennial crops — in particular palm oil production — and the relative scarcity of land naturally increase this problem. In the 1975 survey, however, only a few examples are given of this situation, although the report clearly foresees problems in future with the increased scarcity of land. The widespread use of labourers aggravates the problem further, as the agricultural labourers, apart from their cash income, are also given food, thereby increasing the actual size of the households. The 1975 survey gives a few examples of farmers who are already being forced to secure their means of subsistence outside their holdings, while others increasingly have to buy rice and bread, etc., on the market. Still, the majority of farmers declare themselves self-sufficient in the provision of foodstuffs.

The cash income derived from the growing of cash crops, oil palms being particularly attractive, leads to a higher and higher consumption of manufactured products, as well as the establishment in the villages of basic social infrastructure such as schools, electricity, dispensaries and maternity clinics, etc. The survey does not say anything about the actual use of the surplus generated from the cultivation of coffee, cocoa, and palm oil. It only mentions that the building of a concrete house with a corrugated iron roof is a favourite investment, but says nothing about whether any surplus goes back into agriculture in the form of modernized equipment aimed at a higher productivity.

The report expresses the opinion that these successful combined industrial/ village plantation schemes provide an example that might be followed by other similar schemes, since the farmers have expressed themselves willing to grow selected varieties of other crops and are generally willing to consider new methods of cultivation.

As previously mentioned, the very limited sample included in the 1975 enquiry certainly reduces the validity of the findings. Nevertheless, certain of the conclusions seem to confirm the 1967-68 survey, particularly with regard to the effects of the monetarization process resulting from the growing of perennial crops, notably oil palm. These effects include tendencies towards inequality and a growing pressure on the land, which together lead to a rather unstable socio-economic situation.

The ORSTOM Investigation in the Eloka Area

With the purpose of studying the effects of the establishment of a SODE-PALM agro-industrial complex on the socio-economic situation of the villagers, the French research institute ORSTOM (Office de la Recherche Scientifique et Technique Outre-Mer) carried out a study over a 12-month period in 1972-73.[61] Among the agro-industrial complexes — at that time nine in all — the Eloka estate/outgrowers scheme was selected for an exhaustive investigation in which all except three villagers were interviewed.

One of the most interesting findings of this study is revealed in the breakdown of the attached villagers by occupational background. As will be recalled from the SEDES study discussed above, the overall percentage of villagers who in 1967 had a source of income other than agriculture was 16%, while the 1975 study of the Eloka area shows that no fewer than 41% of the planters interviewed declare that they have incomes from sources outside agriculture. Among these are 17% so-called 'absentee farmers', i.e. people having their permanent place of residence outside the Eloka region. This high figure is probably the result of both the specific development of plantation owners investing in agriculture rather than other sectors (a trend which has manifested itself particularly during the past years) and also the geographical proximity of the two major cities, Abidjan and Bingerville.

The plantation owners residing in urban areas are generally younger, better educated and have a larger hectarage under cultivation. Their professional background and secure monthly salaries give this stratum a very stable social position. Among the persons in this group are two Ministers, the mother-in-law of the President of the Republic, an adviser to the Minister of the Interior, two heads of groups within SODEPALM, and other civil servants like army personnel, economists, customs officers, etc.

Taking the Minister of Agriculture as an example, he is in possession of around 31 hectares of oil palm plantations, an area which has gradually increased from 1967 to 1971. According to the survey, he is planning to enlarge his hectarage further, making it around 100 hectares of oil palm trees. Besides, he has invested in coconut and cocoa plantations, and is also the owner of a village plantation of around 100 hectares. The Minister has made contracts with IRHO and SODEPALM concerning the maintenance of his farm land, and he has engaged five labourers. The productivity of his land is much higher than that of the ordinary village plantation owners, although it is still not fully comparable to the productivity of the industrial plantations run by SODE-PALM. The case of the Minister of Agriculture is not a typical case, although it is — according to the author — one which is becoming more common.

The semi-urban village plantation owners comprise a little more than a quarter of the total. Their main activities are also outside the rural setting, and apart from two or three civil servants they are a homogeneous group of independent workers in the tertiary sector. Their engagement in business life outside agriculture makes them a rather frequent 'absentee' group, although not as markedly so as with the former group of farmers we have just discussed. The average hectarage of land in this group is well above the average. Among the farmers is a relative of the President's mother-in-law, who owns 12 hectares of palm trees together with around 20 hectares for coconuts and food products like manioc, yams, and vegetables. The main occupation of this plantation owner is as a quack-doctor, although he has also invested in a car which frequently functions as a taxi. He is following the SATMACI courses on better farming techniques on television — and employs nine labourers together with five or six of his wives.

The third group consists of true village plantation owners — 57% of the total — who are entirely dependent on their agricultural activities. Compared to the other groups, this group of farmers is older and has a lower hectarage. They engage on average 1.5 land labourers (corresponding to one labourer per 3 hectares) on a *permanent* basis, a figure much higher than in the surveys previously mentioned.

One of the major findings is that the cultivation of oil palm trees is much less advantageous for the smaller farmers than was foreseen by SODEPALM. Not only is the cash income derived from farms smaller than 7 hectares on the edge of the profitability margin, but there is also a tendency for the cultivation of perennial crops like palm trees to take place at the expense of food crops, forcing the plantation owner increasingly to buy his food on the market.

Although it is not possible to characterize a stratum of villagers as a 'rural bourgeoisie', the speed of change in the system is evident. Plantation owners under a certain minimum hectarage (judged by the author of the survey to be 7 hectarage) increasingly risk being proletarianized in a situation where the large plantation owners become bigger to the detriment of the smaller farmers.

It was the conclusion of the SEDES surveys that SODEPALM is only intervening in a situation which is already subject to change, and that farmers' experience of growing other cash crops like coffee and cocoa has developed a clear awareness among them about what can be gained from the greater circulation of money. In contrast, the ORSTOM study believes that the changes brought about by SODEPALM's introduction of new high-yielding varieties have affected many farmers very brutally.

The proximity to the capital, Abidjan, from where 50% of the investments in village plantations derive, is probably a fact which aggravates the unequalization process that may result in greater tendencies towards proletarianization in the future. In any case, the presence of the rather strong minority of 'absentees' who choose to invest in agriculture among other possible investment opportunities, clearly introduces the mechanism of the appropriation of land rights through commercial transactions rather than through the traditional hereditary means. The land seems increasingly to become an individual property right rather than a collective one.[62]

We also have to see what the regular — and in a number of cases fairly substantial — money income is used for. During one year (1972-73), the author of the ORSTOM study followed the consumption pattern of selected farmers' families. Very few examples of reinvestment in better farming implements and machinery were found. Most of the cash income went into improvements in housing, investment in greater land area or an increased consumption of commodities. Nearly every use of cash income for productivity purposes took the form of hiring more labourers rather than buying machinery. Practically no money was saved.

One has to bear in mind that the validity of these results is much restricted by the extremely limited number of families studied. The fact that SODE-PALM is often able to provide the necessary technical improvements in the cultivation process may nevertheless be one of the reasons for the farmers' limited interest in investing themselves in higher productivity through modern technology.

The results of the ORSTOM study seem not to diverge from the previous surveys. The new cash crops introduced in already monetarized areas seem to develop increasing investment opportunities for urban residents who most often have some other source of income. Cash crop production as an investment opportunity seems to stimulate individual rather than collective ownership of land, and the semi-industrial cultivation pattern on the larger holdings provides a relatively high productivity and profitability, thereby increasing rural inequality. For the smaller farmers, the cultivation of cash crops seems to reduce the area used for food growing, resulting in an increased orientation towards the market for the provision of foodstuffs.

Concluding Remarks on Socio-Economic Effects

The results of the SEDES and ORSTOM surveys over time indicate that, in the areas where cash crops and monetarization are introduced rather early, the impact of the SODEPALM system on the village plantation owners has been one of furthering a latent process toward greater inequality. The already relatively well-off farmers are being favoured to the detriment of the small-holders, creating an increased danger of proletarianization in the near future. This process is also very much influenced by increased pressure on the land as a consequence of population growth.[63]

The studies in the areas strongly affected by the proximity to Abidjan have also revealed clear tendencies towards greater investments in oil palm trees for the sole motive of investing in order to get a profit. The rather big minority of 'absentee farmers' in the ORSTOM study substantiates this. And these generally large farms are run on a semi-industrial basis, i.e. in a way very similar to the cultivation pattern on the industrial plantations surrounding the SODEPALM factory, a pattern which we have in the previous section labelled as capitalist relations of production.

However, it is still hard to identify a stratum which might be called a rural bourgeoisie. But the imminence of increased proletarianization, the widespread use of permanent labourers on a monthly wage basis, the tendency to invest in oil palm plantations purely from a profit motive, and the growing inequality in land distribution, are all in favour of the notion of a 'rural bourgeoisie'. The continued predominance of smallholders and their consumption pattern geared towards extending the land under cultivation, improving their housing, securing the education of their children and other dependants, covering part of their subsistence through the buying of foodstuffs and manufactured products on the market, rather than investing the surplus in modern technology which might further an extended accumulation process, are factors which might underline the mobility in the situation, but which we still regard as being only the preconditions for a more profound capitalization process.

Industrial Development in the Ivory Coast, 1960-76

In his book *Le Développement du capitalisme en Côte d'Ivoire*[64] Samir Amin points at two main characteristics of the industrial development in the Ivory Coast: its unintegrated structure and the dominance of foreign capital. He argues that, in spite of rapid economic growth at the moment, there is a great danger that continued growth will be blocked. This is because of the difficulties of continuing an import substitution strategy within the limited market of the Ivory Coast, and the dependence on foreign companies which may lead to a substantial outflow of capital and thereby to balance-of-payments difficulties.

We shall analyse the industrial development that has taken place during the ten years since Samir Amin wrote his book. We shall concentrate on the main points of his analysis just mentioned, and also on whether the forces Amin emphasized as endangering the prospects for self-centred growth have developed, or whether other forces have counteracted them. In addition, we shall look at the social effects of industrial development such as the ownership of capital, employment, the composition of the labour force, and the wage structure. Finally, we shall discuss the role of the Ivorian state in the industrial development.

The Main Tendencies in Industrial Development

In 1950, the total industrial sector consisted of two small canneries, some soap factories, two factories producing beer and mineral water, a spinning-mill, and some saw-mills. Today a varied industrial sector exists, consisting of 442 enterprises in 1974, and 705 in 1980.[65] The turnover of Ivorian industry has increased rapidly, from 13 billion C.F.A. francs in 1960 to 650 billion in 1978-9 (the corresponding indexes: 1960 = 100; 1978-79 = 5,000).[66]

Industrial exports have increased dramatically in the last few years, going from 41 billion francs in 1972 to 203 billion in 1978-9, although the share of total industrial production meant for export has stayed static — 31% in 1972 to 31% in 1978-79. In other words, the share of industrial production sold in the local market was 69% in 1978-79.[67]

The share of national production in total domestic sales of manufactured goods has increased from 25% in 1960 and 31% in 1970 to 40% in 1974. The share is, however, considerably larger for food and beverages (where it is more than 50%) than for processed goods (less than 30%). The market share is particularly low in sectors like chemicals, transport equipment, and machinery, where it is about 10-15%. Accumulated investments have also increased considerably, from 47 billion francs in 1967 to 460 billion in 1979.

The Economic Structure of Industrial Production

Linkage Effects

In order to examine the hypothesis that the industrial sector has an unintegrated economic structure, we shall look into the linkage effects of the sector. Linkage effects are the ability of the industrial system to spread development through the purchase of inputs. We distinguish between purchase of inputs according to: (1) geographical origin; (2) type of commodities; (3) type of purchasing industry. Only direct inputs will be dealt with, i.e. inputs which form a part of the product, while other inputs, such as energy, maintenance, transport and insurance, will be left out.

The distribution of purchase of inputs for the industrial sector as a whole, and for selected industrial subsectors, is shown in Table 9.

Table 9 Purchase of Inputs in the Industrial Sector (%)

	1961	1966	1971	1976
1. The Industrial Sector				
Share of imports	56	63	58	46
Share of local inputs:	44	37	42	54
from the primary sector	19	19	25	29
from the secondary sector	25	18	17	25
2. Branches of Manufacturing				
Share of imports				
Timber	5	4	7	6
Food and beverages	62	45	28	21
Textile	58	49	63	51
Chemicals	57	86	79	62

Source: Jean Chevassu and Alain Valette, *Les relations intermédiaires dans le secteur industriel ivoirien* (Abidjan, ORSTOM Sciences humaines, 1975), Table 3 and *Les Comptes de la Nation 1971*, Ministère du Plan, Direction des Etudes de Développement, Abidjan, and *Centrale de Bilans 1976* (Abidjan, Ministère de l'économie, des finance et du plan).

As appears from Table 9 more than 50% of inputs purchased by the industrial sector in the period 1961-71 took place abroad. This indicates that the sector was relatively unintegrated with the rest of the economy and tied to imports. Only during the last few years has this pattern changed. The figures for 1976 suggest higher consumption of local inputs, in particular as a result of the large investments in import-substituting industry undertaken by the Ivorian Government in the early 1970s.

Among the inputs bought locally, a large share comes from the primary sector, mostly agriculture. In 1966, 1971 and 1976 more than half of the inputs bought locally came from the agricultural sector.[68] This shows one of the main characteristics of Ivorian industry, its close interrelationship with agricultural development. On the other hand, the relatively modest amount of purchasing between industrial sectors is an indication of a weak inter-sectoral relationship within manufacturing although it is definitely on the increase. A thorough analysis of the industrial sector undertaken in 1971[69] shows that Ivorian industry bought only 25% of its industrial inputs from Ivorian firms, the rest being imported from other countries. The missing inter-industrial relationship is further emphasized by the fact that the local purchases consisted primarily of packaging material.

Finally, Table 9 shows there is a marked difference between the different industrial sectors in their reliance on imported inputs. They can be grouped into three categories:

(1) timber, packaging material, certain kinds of food and beverage production — in these subsectors practically all inputs are bought locally;
(2) textiles, most food and beverage production — here more or less half the inputs are bought locally; and
(3) chemicals, building materials, electrical industry — here most inputs are imported.

Thus, it is a characteristic of Ivorian industry that one part concentrates on processing agricultural raw materials, another on assembling and minor processing activities of imported inputs.

In conclusion, it can be said that inter-industrial relationships have been very weak. Nevertheless, there is now a tendency to an increase in inter-industrial relationships, and it appears that there are important linkage effects between industry and agriculture.

The Role of Abidjan in Industrial Development
In 1971, 75% of all industrial enterprises were situated in Abidjan.[70] These firms produced 70% of total industrial turnover and represented 60% of all industrial investments. Nevertheless, only 22% of industrial inputs came from Abidjan, while 26% came from other parts of the country. In addition to this, only 14% of the semi-processed goods purchased came from Abidjan. A large part of these semi-processed inputs consisted of packaging materials made of plastics, metal, and cardboard.[71]

This leads to the conclusion that, in spite of the existence of a large metropolis with more than 500,000 inhabitants and three-quarters of all industrial enterprises, it is not possible to speak of an industrial milieu, if we understand by this term the geographically concentrated existence of economic and technological exchanges and other interconnections between industrial units. Instead we see a new type of 'dualism': an agricultural sector tied to the industrial sector, but only limited linkages between the industrial enterprises themselves.

Sub-contracting

The degree of sub-contracting is an important measure of inter-industrial connection. In an analysis of 200 industrial enterprises in Abidjan, Chevassu and Valette observed[72] that sub-contracting in *production* was very limited and existed only in printing, smithery, and joinery. In all cases referred to, it was sub-contracting by specialization. In no cases was sub-contracting caused by lack of production capacity.

Concerning sub-contracting in maintenance and repair, the two authors found that most work was done by the companies themselves employing personnel on a permanent basis instead of using sub-contractors. A government report[73] on sub-contracting draws the same conclusions, but adds that much bitterness exists among Ivorian firms and craftsmen against European firms for not buying their services. In an attempt to find the reason, the European companies were asked to give their comments to the African sub-contractors and craftsmen. Most European enterprises replied that deadlines were not respected and work was not done properly.

Conclusion

We have found two types of industry in the Ivory Coast:
(1) agro-industrial firms characterized by rapid growth, a variegated output and a predominant export orientation; they have a large share of the domestic market
(2) industries manufacturing goods for the local market by assembling imported inputs; they only have a small part of the domestic market.

Textiles and palm oil are the most important products made by the agro-industrial firms, and they are thus good examples of the connection between agriculture and industry. But it should be stressed that food processing and textile production are quite simple production processes, while other types of industry can be much more complicated.

The Ivory Coast has thus in the 1960s passed through an easy phase in its import substitution policy, and is now faced with much more difficult groups of commodities, where increased research and development activities will be necessary, and where the underdeveloped state of relationships between industrial branches may be an obstacle to further progress in industrialization.

It is the policy of the Ivorian Government to continue the import substitution strategy and extend it into new areas, while at the same time the government has emphasized its confidence in foreign capital as the best tool to realize this aim. Ivorianization of the industrial sector is only a long-term and indirect goal, in spite of the fact that a large group of skilled local artisans seems to exist, within several sectors.[74]

The Social Structure of Industrial Production

The Owners of Capital

The Ivorian state has taken an increasingly active role in industrial development by participating with equity share capital. Its share of total capital has grown from 10% in 1967, to 18% in 1971, 27% in 1976, 33% in 1978, and 53% in 1980.

There exists no clearcut government policy on participation with share capital in industrial development. But the state has made the largest investments in industrial sectors like chemicals, food and beverages, and textiles. More than 80% of the capital furnished by the state is used in enterprises processing products from the agricultural sector, notably rubber, palm oil, and textiles.

It is worth emphasizing that an increasing percentage of the investments made by the state is financed by the Caisse, the marketing board for all cash crops in the Ivory Coast. In 1973 and 1974 the surplus extracted in this way from the agricultural sector financed one-third of the state investments in industrial development, and in 1980 the Caisse's contribution made up more than 50% of the state's investment budget.

Private Ivorian capital only represents a very small percentage of total industrial share capital. In 1971 it was 3%, increasing to 11% in 1980.[75] It should be noted that three-quarters of the capital invested in 1971 was placed in five enterprises.

An analysis made of the industrialists in the Ivory Coast in 1971[76] showed that only approximately 300 investors existed in the Ivory Coast. They were primarily civil servants, big farmers, and traders. The genuine entrepreneurs were a very limited group. In this study, which covered 96% of total industrial turnover, only five Ivorian entrepreneurs were found. The Ivorian bourgeoisie is thus not an industrial bourgeoisie, but is rather engaged in agriculture, trade and real estate. In spite of much rhetoric, the state does not support the development of privately owned Ivorian industry, but co-operates with foreign capital in all areas.

There is a clear long-term decline in the dominance of specifically French capital, however, from 91% of total capital in 1961 to 52% in 1974, 34% in 1978, and an estimated 21% in 1980. A distinction must be made between two kinds of French enterprises:
(1) French capital from France, i.e. having its dominant interests in France, and making a direct investment abroad (75%)
(2) French capital from the Ivory Coast, i.e. having its dominant interests in the Ivory Coast, and the Frenchmen involved having lived in the Ivory Coast before the investment was made (25%). There is a large group of Frenchmen living in the Ivory Coast, the estimates varying from 50,000 to 70,000. The largest French industrial group is the Blohorn group already mentioned, a family firm which manufactures fats, notably palm oil.

Among capital groups from France, the three dominant industrial investors are the large trading companies like C.F.A.O. and S.C.O.A., which are also well-known in other West African countries, the banks which besides their industrial investments have created local banks in the Ivory Coast, and finally genuine industrial enterprises which represent 30% of total share capital.

Wage Earners and the Wage Structure

Of the 71,000 wage earners employed in Ivorian industry in 1980 75% were Ivorians, 22% other Africans, and 3% non-Africans. This represents an increase in the proportion of Ivorians, which had been 58% in 1971, and a decline for other Africans (38% in 1971). There seems to be a tendency towards increased employment of Ivorian wage earners in the less skilled occupations, while the higher positions are completely occupied by non-Africans.

A study of the industrial wage structure in 1971 showed that:[77]

(1) Ivorians received 42% of total salaries, but represented 58% of the work force — receiving an annual average income of 254,000 C.F.A. francs each;

(2) Other Africans received 22% of total wages, but represented 38% of the work force — receiving an annual average income of 201,000 francs;

(3) Non-Africans received 37% of the wage bill, but represented only 5% of the work force, receiving an annual average income of 2,760,000 francs each (more than ten times the income received by Africans).

Conclusion

French capital is not dominant in the industrial sector any more, since its dominance has been decreasing while the Ivorian Government has — at least — so far — been capable of channelling foreign investment into sectors given priority in national development by offering very favourable economic conditions. In contrast to the situation in the 1960s, the Ivorian state is now the most dynamic factor in industrial development, controlling 53% of total capital invested in industry. No domestic industrial bourgeoisie has developed in the Ivory Coast, so that industrial development is dependent on managerial and technological expertise from abroad.

This finding is in contrast with the analysis made by Samir Amin, who considered Ivorian state apparatus to be completely dependent on foreign economic and political interests, and controlled by a 'comprador bourgeoisie'.

The share of domestic financial resources devoted to industrial investment has been on the increase, especially due to the Caisse's extraction of a surplus from the agricultural sector. As has been indicated above, this surplus has been on the increase in absolute terms and in recent years in relative terms as well.

The financial terms have hardened on loans from abroad obtained recently by the Ivory Coast. As a result of the rapid increase in G.N.P. *per capita*, some important multilateral aid donors have tended to give a lower priority to the Ivory Coast. This development has been strengthened by a tendency for the capital/output ratio to increase on investments. The tougher terms of finance and the increase in the necessary size of investments have created difficulties for the government in its effort to continue a development strategy based on rapid economic growth.

The recent industrial development in the Ivory Coast has not prevented a continuation of the overall rapid economic growth process, as was predicted by Samir Amin. On the other hand, a number of recently emerged factors, which might endanger the continuance of the progress must be taken into consideration. In order to get a more detailed insight into the mechanisms favouring or putting constraints on such a development, we will in the following section look at the textile sector which has been the most dynamic branch of Ivorian industrial development.

The Ivorian Textile Industry

In major studies of the textile industry in the Ivory Coast published in 1973 and 1975,[78] the main conclusion was that French trading companies established textile factories in the Ivory Coast immediately after independence in order to keep control of the local market. In this interpretation, the first ten years of the post-colonial period led to a situation where the Ivorian textile sector was split into two parts: the export of the raw material, cotton, to France, where it was processed into cloth; and the import of the finished commodity, cloth, to the Ivory Coast. Here it only obtained its last finishing with the printing of patterns. In other words, these studies concluded that Samir Amin was right in his conclusion that the economic development of the Ivory Coast was blocked.

Let us see whether this conclusion is correct, by analysing the economic structure of the textile sector in the whole period 1960-78. We shall analyse the impact of Ivorian state intervention on the social and economic structure of the Ivorian textile industry. From this we hope to be able to assess the interrelationship between the autonomous factors in Ivorian development and the present tendencies in the internationalization of French capital, as they were presented in Chapter 2.

The Economic Structure of the Textile Industry
An outline of the structure of production in any textile industry can be found in Table 10. This model enables us to analyse whether the Ivorian textile industry is split up in different subsectors, or whether it is by now characterized by a coherent production structure.

Before the era of colonization, cotton was widely grown in West Africa, in most cases together with food crops. The cotton was utilized by traditional weavers, and this type of handicraft was widespread in the areas which later became Nigeria, Senegal, and the Ivory Coast. Some sources consider that weaving was the most dynamic occupation in these areas before colonization.[79] The colonial penetration reoriented production towards the needs of the European colonial power, where cotton was manufactured into cloth and resold

Table 10 The Textile Production Process

Type of Operation	Operation	Stage of Operation
cultivation	cotton growing	primary
preparation	cotton ginning	primary
assembly	spinning	intermediary
	weaving	
	knitting	
	bleaching	
	printing	
transforming	dyeing	
	napping	
decomposition	cutting	manufacturing
	sewing	
assembly	selling	

Source: Bonnie Campbell, 'The Social, Political and Economic Consequences of French Private Investments in the Ivory Coast, 1960-70'. Ph.D. thesis, University of Sussex, 1973, p. 37.

in the colonies (and elsewhere). The result was a severe setback for traditional industry, although the indigenous techniques of cultivation were maintained.

In other parts of French West Africa, cotton was produced with the intention of exporting it raw to France, but this was never the case in the Ivory Coast. Here all cotton was processed by CITEC (Compagnie de l'Industrie Textile Cotonnière), the overseas agent for the French Boussac Company, which sold the cotton lint to Ets. R. Gonfreville, which produced yarn for the local artisans and the local market. So although cotton cultivation and traditional weaving were widespread in the Ivory Coast, this area had no importance as a supplier of cotton to France during the colonial period. The importance of the Ivory Coast was, therefore, primarily as a secure market for textiles from France.

The Ivorian Textile Sector, 1960-78

Cotton Production
Food crops like maize and groundnuts are traditionally cultivated together with cotton. But in 1960 the Allen type of cotton, to be grown in separate fields, was introduced. The Allen variety may yield ten times as much as mono, the traditional variety, and its fibres have some important physical characteristics, including greater power of resistance, uniformity, and fineness. Its rapid distribution was due to C.F.D.T. (Compagnie Francaise pour le Développement des Fibres Textiles) and I.R.C.T. (Institut de Recherche sur les Cotons et Textiles).

Table 11 The Development of Cotton Production, 1960-61 to 1975-76.

	Area (ha)	*Production of Allen Variety (tons)*	*Production of Mono Variety (tons)*	*Total Production of Cotton Fibre (tons)*
1960-61	137	69	5,500	—
1962-63	1,278	765	11,000	290
1964-65	6,408	5,533	4,900	3,224
1966-67	23,810	22,036	3,000	8,689
1968-69	48,139	41,737	2,500	16,799
1970-71	35,867	29,316	2,000	11,653
1972-73	56,500	52,798	1,000	20,900
1974-75	58,653	59,938	—	23,400
1975-76	65,474	64,000	—	25,280

Source: *L'Industrie textile en Côte d'Ivoire*, op. cit., p. 6, and Robert Lagiere, *Le Cotonnier* (Paris, Maisonneuve et Larose, 1966), Table XXXVI, p. 188.

Cotton Ginning
In all, there exist five companies which gin cotton, namely three C.I.D.T. enterprises in Bouaké, Boundiali, and Mankono and two Escarre enterprises in Korhogo. The five enterprises process the total Ivorian cotton crop, which, as shown in Table 11, has increased from 6,000 tons in 1960-61 to 64,000 tons in 1975-76. Production is expected to increase to 90,000 tons in 1980.[80]
This cotton is processed into 25,000 tons of fibre.[81] From this, 14,000 tons are absorbed by local industry, while the remaining 11,000 tons of fibre are exported, especially to France and Japan. The establishment of three large spinning-and-weaving factories (namely UTEXI, COTIVO and ERG II) since 1974 has, however, completely changed the structure of the market, since the three factories already absorb 15,000 tons of cotton fibre and will consume 30,000 tons by 1980.

Textiles, 1964-70: Simple Import Substitution
In the period 1964-70 four pattern-printing factories were established.[82] ICODI (Impression sur Tissus de Côte d'Ivoire) started production in 1964; UNIWAX (Société UNIWAX) started in 1970, SOTEXI (Société Industrielle Textile de Côte d'Ivoire) and ERG (Ets. R. Gonfreville) started in 1969. In terms of production, the pattern-printing factories must be considered a great success, ensuring a major breakthrough in import substitution in terms of printed cloth.
ICODI has traditionally sold 80% of its output on the local market and 20% in Niger, Mali, Madagascar, and Benin. But in 1975 a major increase in production was accompanied by an increase in exports to neighbouring countries, so the ratio of home market sales to sales to neighbouring countries

fell from 55% to 45%.

UNIWAX only produces for the local market, as part of an agreement with the Ivorian Government for a 10-year monopoly ending in 1977.

In 1973 SOTEXI sold 80% of its production on the domestic market, while 20% was sold to the neighbouring countries. This pattern changed, however, in 1975, when nearly the whole of the production was sold on the domestic market. The reason for this was that similar factories now exist in the neighbouring countries.

In the case of Gonfreville no exact information exists about the pattern-printing department, only overall figures for the factory as a whole. In 1976, 59% of turnover was sold on the Ivorian market, 28% in neighbouring countries, and 12% in Europe.

ICODI was started by the three trading companies C.F.C.I., C.F.A.O. and S.C.O.A. in 1964 in co-operation with Ets. Schaeffer. UNIWAX has the trading company C.F.C.I. as the main shareholder, and Gonfreville has OPTORG, the trading company, as the largest investor with 13% of share capital. This means that the four major colonial trading companies all have made important investments in the textile industry in this period. So the trading companies adjusted themselves to the new situation at independence in the early 1960s and invested in the last part of the production process — pattern-printing — directed towards the Ivorian market and the neighbouring countries. A major reason for this development was the Yaoundé Convention which opened up the formerly closed French market for competition.

Textiles, 1971-74: Partial Integration of the Industry
Three of the four factories established in this period process cotton fibre: UTEXI (Union Industrielle et Textile de Côte d'Ivoire), which was founded in 1972 and began production in 1975; COTIVO (la Cotonnière Ivoirienne), which was also established in 1972 and began production in 1976-77; and Gonfreville, which established a spinning-and-weaving department in 1974 (ERG I), which was extended in 1978 (ERG II). Finally, there is a spinning-and-weaving factory for synthetic fibres, SOCITAS (Société Ivoirienne de Textiles Artificiels), which started production in 1969, after being founded in 1966.

The establishment of these enterprises involved a strong geographical decentralization of textile production, since they were all situated outside the industrial area of Abidjan: UTEXI in Dimbokro, COTIVO in Agboville and Gonfreville in Bouaké.

Besides these factories, there have been plans to establish other factories, plans which never materialized. For instance, for some time, the French textile company Agache-Willot considered the possibility of establishing a project competitive to SOTEXI by opening a spinning-and-weaving factory for cotton fibre and synthetic fibre at Agboville with an annual capacity of 4,000 tons. But the establishment of COTIVO stopped this initiative. There are also plans for the existing factories to extend their capacity. This is the case for UTEXI, COTIVO and SOCITAS, while Gonfreville is considering the possibility of setting up a completely new unit for spinning and weaving.

Since these factories involve an intermediary production process, the question of backward linkages arises. Generally, there are very strong backward linkages in this type of production. The provision of cotton fibre for ERG I and II, UTEXI and COTIVO will in 1979 demand 30% more raw cotton than was harvested in 1975-76. It is thus characteristic of the textile sector that domestic linkages will increase.

The establishment of the four spinning-and-weaving factories has profoundly changed the economic structure of the Ivorian textile industry, since the processing of cotton fibre is now done in the country itself. This contradicts the conclusions presented in the study referred to above of the textile sector in the period 1960-70. We shall later return to the general implications of this for the dynamics of the textile sector.

Half the production has been sold to the local processing factories ICODI and UNIWAX, and in the last few years also to Blue Bell Côte d'Ivoire and SOTEXI. The other 50% has been directed towards exports for Western Europe.

In recent years, however, problems have occurred both in sales on the local market and in exports to the E.E.C. The director of UTEXI, M. Paul Pascal, reported in an interview in *Afrique Industrie* in December 1977 that, from 1976 to 1977, demand for UTEXI products fell by 40-45% on the Ivorian market.[83] He saw the reason for this first of all in inflation, which had led to a situation in which many Ivorians had to restrict their purchases of textile commodities and concentrate on essential consumer goods. At the same time, UTEXI had encountered increasing problems on the export market. The background for this was explained by M. Paul Pascal:

> However, the high consumption markets to which we export have not lived up to our expectations. Consumption, especially in France, is controlled and relations between the producing countries and the consuming countries are very difficult. This is amply illustrated both by the problems which emerge when it comes to signing the multifibre agreement and by the rigid quotas on textile imports fixed by the E.E.C. Although we are below the '1%' threshold and represent no real threat to the E.E.C. countries' own industries, the articles we produce continue to be classified as 'very sensitive' or 'sensitive'.

There is a further problem in that the Ivory Coast is not competitive in terms of wages with the South East Asian countries, and has therefore attempted to obtain low production costs by constructing very large factories in order to achieve the advantages of large-scale operations.

It is the judgement of Paul Pascal that in order for UTEXI and the other spinning-and-weaving companies to expand, there would need to be at least an annual growth rate in the E.E.C. of 4%, while the actual growth rate is only expected to be 1-2%.

This question was discussed in more detail in Chapter 2, and the findings clearly present the contradictory nature of present developments in the Ivorian textile industry: the establishment of an integrated industry oriented towards the European market, accompanied by the closure of this very market to Ivorian textile products.

Textiles, 1975-78: Integrated and Export Industry
Besides the seven spinning, weaving, dyeing and printing units already mentioned, there existed in 1975 a second group of factories processing textiles, tied to supplies from the first group. Ten of these constituted the clothing industry: five producing lingerie while the other five produced various items of clothing.

Among the factories which produced clothing, the only two companies which were established before 1970 were Gonfreville and les Ets. Michel (TREFOR). Generally, ready-made clothing is the least developed part of the Ivorian textile industry. In 1972 there were only seven enterprises which could be called genuinely industrial. This number increased substantially in 1977, when a further eight industrial or semi-industrial enterprises had an important export capacity.[84]

While many new enterprises have been established in the last few years, many have also disappeared. Among the clothing industries oriented towards exports, some of the important old firms have stopped their activities since 1975. Also some new companies have stopped production.

There is a certain amount of specialization in the clothing industry. Gonfreville has a solid position among 'classical articles of a tropical nature' like trousers, shirts, shorts, and light vests. Sicofem produces the same kind of commodities as Gonfreville, but with more emphasis on women's wear. The same is the case for Akwaba and Mafrico, which also produce a series of articles for children. In children's wear, the company la Manufacture Ivoirienne de Confection Enfantine (MICE) is the most important, both in terms of specialization and size.

It is likely that the development of MICE and Blue Bell Côte d'Ivoire will lead to a regrouping of the Ivorian clothing industry, resulting eventually in a concentration of production in rather fewer firms. It is for example evident that the companies Michel and Mafrico, which both produce working clothes, will be engaged in fierce competition with the products from the new company Blue Bell Côte d'Ivoire. Generally, the minor clothing firms with an invested capital of below 100 million francs will have to specialize in 'niches' not covered by the large clothing factories.

Lingerie production exists, but is not very significant compared to total consumption, because of imports from South East Asia. This situation is typical of other countries in Africa. There is only one enterprise in this particular sector which produces all the usual types of lingerie, namely la Société Africaine de Bonneterie (SAB).

The Ivorian clothing industry has in the past few years passed through a difficult transition period, from a situation characterized by approximately fifteen minor ready-made clothing and lingerie producers, to a situation where a few very large companies dominate.

In a study of the Ivorian textile industry,[85] a number of reasons have been put forward to explain this crisis, which has been especially serious in the ready-made for wear industry. It is argued in the study that:

(1) there was fierce competition from cloth smuggled into the Ivory Coast and processed by 'underground' tailors;

(2) the markets of the neighbouring countries were closed because of the development of clothing factories there;

(3) some enterprises had hoarded raw material in order to benefit from their status as *'enterprise prioritaire'* and thereby profited from tariff protection and other duties.

It is reported that some of these problems have been solved after the establishment of an association of textile producers (FITEXHA), and by efforts of the Government to reduce competition from imported clothing, by increasing tariffs on imports and making them more difficult. But in spite of the fact that these predominantly internal contradictions in the clothing industry may have been solved, major problems have emerged with the E.E.C. decision to introduce quotas for the Ivory Coast's exports. In 1977-78 total exports from the textile sector were valued 17,454 million C.F.A. of which 25% went to France. In a major effort to get access to new markets, 40% of total textile exports were directed towards the neighbouring countries of the Ivory Coast. However, the exports to these countries consist of raw cloth sold at very low prices, which implies that this type of export only reinforces the present crisis in the strategy of export orientation of the textile industry.

Conclusion: The Economic Structure of the Ivorian Textile Industry
Table 12 shows the structure of the three groups which dominate the Ivorian textile industry. If the cotton growing and cotton ginning undertaken by C.I.D.T. are added, they involve *all* stages of production in the cotton industry, as set out in Table 10.

Table 12 The Three Dominant Groups in the Ivorian Textile Industry

	Group 1	Group 2	Group 3
Pattern-printing	Gonfreville (1959)	ICODI (1964)	UNIWAX (1970) SOTEXI (1967)
Spinning-and-weaving	Gonfreville (1921, 1965, 1974)	COTIVO (1976)	UTEXI (1974)
Clothing manufacture	Gonfreville (1967)	Blue Bell Côte d'Ivoire (1975)	

Note: Besides these major groups, there exist other textile companies, especially in clothing. Figures in ( ) = year of initiating production.

In contrast to the findings of earlier studies which considered the Ivorian textile industry to be split into different subsectors, each subject to the French trading companies, we find that the Ivorian textile industry now has a coherent production structure involving all aspects of the industry except the production of textile machinery.

However, we have thereby only made a structural assessment of the industry and have not considered the dynamics which led to the emergence of this situation. We shall therefore in the following two sections relate the impact of Ivorian state intervention to the present tendencies in the internationalization of capital.

The Ownership of Capital in the Ivorian Textile Industry

Earlier we observed that the Ivorian state had taken an increasingly active and dominant role in industrial development by supplying share capital. There exists, however, no clearcut government policy on participation with share capital in industrial development. But the state has made its largest investments in sectors like chemicals, food and beverages, and textiles. More than 80% of the capital furnished by the state is employed in enterprises using products from agriculture, including textiles.

We have also observed that, while French capital still dominated Ivorian industry in 1971, there has been a tendency towards long-term decline in French dominance. Summarizing the distribution of total industrial share capital in 1977, the Ivorian state accounted for 33% and French capital for 36%, making the two almost equal in size; but Ivorian state capital was clearly on the increase, and French capital on the decline.

Turning to the textile industry, total share capital has increased from 11,421 million C.F.A. francs in 1975 to 16,457 million in 1979. Table 13 shows the distribution of capital between the major groups within the textile sector.

It appears from Table 13 that, in all three major textile groups, and also in the sector as a whole, the state is of major importance in supplying capital. However, it is also clear that the state in all cases participates as a minority group. Secondly, it can be seen that three different types of national capital dominate the three groups, namely Japanese, U.S. and French capital, together with a fourth element either consisting of the old French trading companies or private Ivorians.

In conclusion, although the large French textile groups invest in the Ivorian textile industry, they do it in co-operation with the Ivorian state *and* with trading companies or groups of people with a long-established presence in the country.

The Intervention of the Ivorian State

In 1959 *le Code des Investissements* was introduced, laying down the conditions for foreign private investment in the Ivory Coast. It is the opinion of serveral observers[86] that this law sets out the most favourable conditions for foreign investors among all the investment codes of African countries. It was also introduced ten years before similar laws in other African countries.

Table 13 Distribution of Share Capital in Ivorian Textile Industry, 1 January 1976 (%).

	Ivorian State	Private Ivorians	French Capital	French Trading Cos.	Non-French Capital
ICODI	33.0	–	8.3	38.7	15.2
SOTEXI	20.0	–	5.0	30.0	30.0
ERG	32.8	23.1	10.0	10.0	(10.0)[a]
Total %, 1 October 1977	22.9	15.4	32.0		(29.6)[b]
Total millions of francs 1 October 1977	3,330	2,238	4,653		4,305

Notes: a. Capital supplied by a multilateral finance organization.
b. Lumping together private capital as well as capital supplied by state institutions.
Sources: L 'Industrie ivorienne en 1977(Abidjan, Chambre d'Industrie de Côte d'Ivoire, 1978), and Société générale de Banques en Côte d'Ivoire, *Industrie textile en Côte d'Ivoire* (Abidjan, April 1976).

The law stipulates the conditions for a company to obtain status as a 'priority enterprise' (*enterprise prioritaire*), thus securing exemption from taxes for five years and tariffs for ten years. For some of the priority enterprises, there is also the opportunity to obtain other privileges through signing an 'establishment agreement' with the Government.

The Code has been crucial for the development of the Ivory Coast's industrial sector. In 1974 there were 350 enterprises in the modern sector, and among these 97 had obtained status as priority enterprises, while more than 20 had signed establishment agreements with the Government.[87]

In what follows, we shall, first, outline the investment law, and, secondly, analyse its concrete application in relation to foreign capital groups investing in the textile sector. This will be done through a case study of the investment conditions obtained by the American textile company Blue Bell, when investing in the textile factory Blue Bell Côte d'Ivoire in 1974.

The Law Regulating Private Foreign Investment[88]
The following categories of undertaking are eligible to become priority enterprises: real estate, industrial crops and related processing industries, industrial preparation or processing by mechanical or chemical means of local vegetable and animal products, manufacture and assembly of goods and articles for mass consumption, extractive industries, and power generation. Undertakings may be recognized as priority enterprises if they fulfil the following requirements:

(1)   they contribute to the implementation of the economic and social development plans in accordance with the provisions of the decree granting approval;

(2)   they make investments which are of particular importance to the development of the country;

(3)   they have been established since April 1958, or since then have effected considerable extensions (approval in such cases shall be granted only in respect of the extensions).

All approved priority enterprises benefit from tax exemption or relief. Those which are particularly important may be permitted by a specific law to participate in a long-term tax scheme and conclude establishment agreements with the Government.

The long-term tax scheme is intended to ensure that all or part of the taxes to which an approved priority enterprise is liable shall remain constant for a period not exceeding 25 years, except in certain cases where the ordinary period of up to five years, which is allowed for initial installations, may be added. For the duration of a long-term tax scheme agreement, no changes may be made in the rules on which the assessment and collection of taxes are based nor in the rates fixed by the scheme for the undertaking concerned. During the same period no taxes or duties of any kind resulting from a law subsequent to the date of commencement of the long-term tax scheme will be applicable to the undertaking concerned. In the event of amendment of the general tax law, any enterprise participating in a long-term tax scheme may ask to benefit from the new provisions. Finally, the act institutes establishment agreements, which lay down the conditions of the establishment and activities of enterprises enjoying the long-term tax scheme.

The Case of Blue Bell Côte d'Ivoire

The establishment agreement of 1974 between the Ivorian Government and Blue Bell Côte d'Ivoire seems to be representative of the conditions laid down in the agreements the Ivorian Government enters into with foreign investors in textiles. The agreement concerns a capital investment of 180 million francs in a limited company, which will produce work and leisure clothes, especially blue jeans.

In the establishment agreement, which is in force for a 25-year period, Blue Bell Côte d'Ivoire obliges itself to:

(1)   Increase production gradually until it reaches 468,000 pieces of clothing a year;

(2)   Undertake the necessary replacements, rationalization and enlargement of the investment;

(3)   Export 80% of the output at world market prices;

(4)   Extend the domestically available range of textiles and create 910 new jobs;

(5)   Buy cotton fabric from COTIVO, and buy other domestically available raw materials when they are competitive internationally.

In return, the Ivorian Government secures the company a number of privileges:

(1)   to have the land on which the factory is built free of charge (and the Government undertakes to construct some training facilities in order to train Ivorians to take over the jobs of expatriate staff);

(2)   to buy industrial equipment necessary for the construction and running of the factory;

(3)   to buy raw materials not available on the domestic market;

(4)   to pay dividends to foreign stock owners in Blue Bell Côte d'Ivoire;

(5)   to transfer every month 50% of the salaries of expatriate staff to their homeland.

By Statutory Instrument of November 1969, the Government of the Ivory Coast also guarantees:

(1)   compensation in case of voluntary or forced liquidation of Blue Bell Côte d'Ivoire;

(2)   the possibility of sale of shares both domestically and abroad;

(3)   the availability of state loans in order to pay mortgage and interests on loans obtained in other countries.

Besides these privileges spelled out in the establishment agreement, Blue Bell Côte d'Ivoire enjoys a number of exemptions from taxes and tariffs as a result of being a priority enterprise. These include exemptions from tariffs on imports of industrial equipment, purchase taxes on trade with domestic suppliers, duties on imports of raw materials and means of production, all lasting for ten years, and exemption from income tax for five years.

Further, the Government has guaranteed that no other company will be allowed to produce blue jeans for a five-year period. The contract also stipulates that modifications are only possible with the consent of both parties and that laws of the host country will not apply as far as they are contrary to the agreement. It seems clear why foreign capital is attracted by investment conditions in the Ivory Coast!

In a comparative study of investment conditions in Zaire, Senegal and the Ivory Coast,[89] it was concluded that the conditions offered to foreign investors by the Ivory Coast in terms of security for the capital invested was not only far greater than in the other two countries, but also far in excess of the normal guarantees laid down by international law for foreign investors.

Conclusion: The Dynamics of the Ivorian Textile Industry

The textile industry of the Ivory Coast is clearly dominant among those of the other West African countries (see Table 14). Why is this, when they all are part of the same external framework? This question can be answered along two different lines.

First of all, we have seen that the Ivorian state has been able to attract foreign capital in the textile sector, in spite of the fact that wages for industrial workers in the Ivory Coast are considerably higher than in other West African countries. This underlines the importance of the Ivorian investment laws; it is also a reflection of the creation of general favourable conditions of production, which is a necessity in order to have a broader process of

Table 14. Investments and Turnover in West African Textile Industries,* 1975

	Investments (Millions of francs)	%	Turnover (Millions of francs)	%
Benin	5,877	9.7	2,409	3.8
Cameroun	5,500	9.0	6,200	9.7
Central African Republic	2,600	4.3	1,300	2.0
Chad	2,018	3.3	2,600	4.1
Congo	2,175	3.6	1,900	3.0
Gabon	633	1.0	1,667	2.6
Ivory Coast	22,517	37.0	23,780	37.0
Mali	6,357	10.5	3,875	6.1
Niger	2,333	3.8	1,807	2.8
Senegal	6,683	11.0	11,933	18.7
Togo	2,793	4.6	3,700	5.6
Upper Volta	1,353	2.2	2,722	4.3
Total	*60,857*	*100.0*	*63,893*	*100.0*

Notes: * By textile industry is understood in this table spinning, weaving and printing of cotton material.
Source: *Bulletin de l'Afrique Noire*, No. 880, 15 September 1976, pp. 17163-9, and No. 881, 22 September 1976, pp. 17182-8.

industrial development. The pattern of development in the textile sector thus seems to be a combination of the internationalization of capital, where the Centre capital groups are searching for favourable investment opportunities in the Periphery, and of the intervention of the Ivorian state to create these conditions.

Secondly, we have seen that to characterize the Ivorian textile sector as an example of blocked development, in accordance with the evaluation of Samir Amin, clearly does not describe the present situation correctly. This sector now represents an integrated production process, embodying all stages of operation. It should be stressed, however, that this success story has been achieved under special conditions. In the concluding section, therefore, we shall assess the overall dynamics of the present trends in this process more carefully.

Concluding Remarks: Extended Reproduction of Capital

The new situation following the international economic crisis has led to new perspectives for development in the Periphery, which in certain cases may break with the 'blocked accumulation of capital' described by Samir Amin.

The state is the most dynamic factor in Ivorian economic development. Although foreign influence in terms of direct investment and the degree of export orientation continues to be substantial, the role of the state is increasingly dominant in internal investment. These activities of the state are often related to and combined with foreign investment. The state's predominance in the internal dynamics is furthered by the absence of an industrial bourgeoisie of any importance. The existing bourgeoisie consists of a mixture of an agrarian bourgeoisie, persons engaged in trading activities and civil servants, but none of these groups is yet solidly founded enough in the Ivorian economy to act as a coherent class. Some writers suggest that the bureaucracy is developing into a class in itself, while others stress the creation of a rural bourgeoisie as the most dynamic class factor in the future.

As a result of this process in the *industrial* development of the Ivory Coast, tendencies towards transcending blocked development in Samir Amin's sense do seem to exist. The industrial sector seems to be connected both to agricultural development and to the internal market, although linkage effects among the various industrial branches are still weak but on the increase. However, it should be stressed that the Ivory Coast has, so far, passed through an easy phase in its import substitution policy and is now faced with much more difficult groups of commodities to be produced. This situation has been worsened by the tougher terms for borrowing money and by a tendency for the capital/output ratio on investments to increase. These factors will make it more difficult for the state to continue its development strategy based on rapid economic growth.

In the same way, agricultural development has generally consisted of attempts at pursuing a policy like the one recommended by Samir Amin. The preconditions for the establishment of self-centred dynamics like diversification, intensification, establishment of agro-industries, and industries geared to the demands of the agricultural sector have successfully been accomplished in this sector. Certain constraints on this development may, however, occur in the future. The foreign manpower on which the agricultural sector is totally dependent is one of the main constraints. Others are the world market prospects for Ivorian export products, the need for an intensified effort in technological development, the rural exodus accentuated by regional imbalances, increased social inequalities, etc.

Finally, let us try and interpret these observations from the perspective of Centre capital as well as peripheral capital.

Seen from the Centre, the role of this type of peripheral social formation is, on the one hand, to supply agricultural raw materials (in the case of the Ivory Coast cocoa, coffee and timber), but also, on the other hand, through the national accumulation process to supply the industrial sector with locally accumulated capital, which is used to supply — among other things — capital for projects in which foreign capital is interested. This makes it possible for foreign capital to take out even higher profits than before, since capital supplied by the state will be cheaper, presumably, than if capital has to be obtained through the international capital markets.

Seen from the perspective of the peripheral social formation, it is an important innovation that possibilities of a national accumulation process now exist by virtue of the extracted surplus from the agricultural sector via the state's marketing board. It is particularly important, in assessing the process, to take into consideration that a major part of the state accumulated surplus derives from the difference in buying prices (from the peasants) and selling prices on the world market. In other words, favourable world market prices for major exportable products are crucial factors. In its diversification policy, however, the Ivorian state has at the same time introduced new high-yielding varieties (in cotton, palm oil, rubber, etc.) within a new organizational set-up. This new combination may in the long run be able to secure a continued extraction of surplus from the agricultural sector, even if world market conditions for the major (and most common) export commodities should deteriorate.

The surplus extracted through this process from the agricultural sector has so far primarily been used by the state for investment in industrial enterprises owned by foreign capital, or in joint ventures of state and foreign capital. In other words, the possibility of a national capital accumulation process through a linkage between agriculture and industry has not led to a nationally owned or managed industrial sector, although it has made it possible for the Ivorian state to attract foreign investment. For the peripheral social formation these investments have the advantage of creating access to industrial know-how, technology, and capital within areas given priority in national development, and perhaps making it feasible later on to develop production in new sectors such as the capital goods sector.

In conclusion, we thus observe that the changing historical conditions for capital accumulation in Western Europe in the 1970s have led to new ways in which peripheral capital in its reproduction is embodied in the reproduction of the Centre capital.

Concretely speaking, this process has led to a situation in some peripheral social formations where the situation of blocked capital accumulation has been replaced by extended reproduction of capital.

Whether this nationally based accumulation process in the periphery can continue is still very much dependent on the future conditions of capital accumulation in the Centre. However, the fact that this process of accumulation is organized under the control of the peripheral state does represent some autonomous factors. These might therefore — in spite of possible unfavourable changes in the internationalization of capital as seen from the interests of peripheral national capital — contribute to a process of continuous national capital accumulation.

Instead of Samir Amin's perspective of 'self-centred' or 'autonomous and self-reliant' development, we thus see the present tendencies in the internationalization of capital and the role of the peripheral state, as contributing to an extended reproduction of capital internationally, transcending the situation of the blocked capital accumulation in the Periphery.

The extent to which the Ivorian example is representative may be limited.

But in comparison to other Third World countries, the Ivory Coast does show some important features in the present tendency towards an increased differentiation within the Third World.

Notes

1. The World Bank, *Ivory Coast: A Basic Economic Report* (New York, February 1978).
2. The World Bank, *World Development Report, 1980* (New York, June 1980).
3. Jean Chevassu and Alain Valette, 'Les Modalités et le contenu de la croissance industrielle de la Côte d'Ivoire', *Cahiers ORSTOM, Sciences humaines*, Vol. XIV, No. 1, 1977, p. 28.
4. Samir Amin, *Le Développement du capitalisme en Côte d'Ivoire*, 2nd edn (Paris, Editions de Minuit, 1971). (First published 1967.)
5. A discussion of what is meant by 'self-centred development' can be found in a number of books written by Samir Amin, notably *Le Développement inégal* (Paris, Les Editions de Minuit, 1973) and *L'Accumulation à l'échelle mondiale* (Paris, Editions Anthropos, 1970). In particular his model of self-centred accumulation is discussed in Amin, 'Le Modéle théorique d'accumulation', *Revue Tiers Monde*, No. 52, October-December 1972.
   Briefly, for Samir Amin, a self-centred economic structure implies the creation of the preconditions for the realization of an autonomous defined development strategy in the peripheral countries. In practice this means the establishment of an economic structure in which the combination of sectors ties a production of means of production with consumer goods. This is in contradiction to the present situation characterized by an export-oriented economic structure combined with light industry, which serves the demand of the wealthy few for luxury consumer goods. In agriculture, development should be intensified and diversified. Instead of increasing the area of land cultivated, productivity should be raised by means of intensification, which utilizes locally produced insecticides, pesticides, fertilizers and agricultural machinery. At the same time agricultural production should be diversified, not towards the introduction of new export commodities, but towards the demand of the local market. In industry development should be directed towards the agricultural sector, partly in the form of production of agricultural machinery and partly in the form of processing raw materials from the agricultural sector. Besides of this a heavy and more capital- and technology-intensive industry should be established directed towards the regional market.
6. Chevassu and Valette, op. cit., p. 28.
7. Jean Chevassu and Alain Valette, *Les Industriels de la Côte d'Ivoire, qui et pourquoi?* (Abidjan, ORSTOM, Sciences humaines, 1975).
8. *L'Industire ivoirienne en 1979* (Abidjan, Chambre d'Industrie de Côte d'Ivoire, May 1980). The share of *private* Ivorian capital in total

industrial investment has grown to 12%, leaving 55% of total industrial investment in the hands of foreign capital, which is a remarkable reduction over time of the role of foreign capital.

9. Jacqueline Dutheil de la Rochère, *L'Etat et le développement économique de la Côte d'Ivoire* (Paris, Pédone, 1976), p. 295.
10. See the 'Code of Investment of the Ivory Coast', in *How to Do Business in Ivory Coast* (Abidjan, Société africaine d'Edition, 1979).
11. Moises Ikonikoff and Silvia Sigal, *L'Etat relais: un modèle de développement sociétés peripheriques? Le cas de la Côte d'Ivoire* (Paris, I.E.D.E.S., undated).
12. Ibid.
13. Amin, 1971, op. cit.
14. *La Côte d'Ivoire en chiffres, 1978-79*, p. 38.
15. Eurostat, A.C.P., *Statistical Yearbook 1970-76* (Luxembourg, 1977), p. 231.
16. The development in the most recent years seems to have changed the picture somewhat, resulting first and foremost in an increased importation of rice and beef.
17. It is not an easy task to calculate the share of food products in total imports as the residual category 'Divers' is the single most important factor in the importation pattern. It seems, however, that food products in total imports in 1979 once more has passed well over 10%. *La Côte d'Ivoire en chiffres, 1980-81*.
18. Banque Centrale des Etats de l'Afrique de l'Ouest, *Statistiques, économiques et monétaires,* No. 260, April 1978, pp. 23-9. Later price developments have been fluctuating at a lower level than expected (partly as a result of the international economic crisis and the generally falling demand), resulting in a decline in the price in real terms.
19. Hans H. Walker, 'Entwicklung, wirtschaftliche Bedeutung und Zukunft von Palmöl und Palmkernelöl in Rahmen des Weltmarktes an Ölen und Fetten', *Zeitschrift für ausländische Landwirtschaft,* Vol. 16, No. 2, April-June 1977, p. 129.
20. UNIDO, *Technical and Economic Aspects of the Oil Palm Fruit Processing Industry* (New York, U.N., 1974).
21. Walker, op. cit., p. 131.
22. Anne-Marie Pillet-Schwartz, 'Capitalisme d'état et développement rural en Côte d'Ivoire'. Ph.D. thesis, University of Paris, 1973, p. 19.
23. *Bulletin de l'Afrique noire*, No. 891, 1976, p. 17387. The total area in 1978 reached 100,000 hectares. *La Côte d'Ivoire en chiffres, 1980-81*, p. 142.
24. This optimism was justified in relation to the development in production until 1978. A drastic decline in production has taken place in recent years putting a question-mark against the whole organizational principle. This will be further discussed in Chapter V.
25. Victor Amagou and G.L. Gleizes, 'Le Groupe SODEPALM et l'agro-industrie du palmier à huile en Côte d'Ivoire, *Economies et Sociétés,* Series A.G., No. 13, 1976, pp. 1504-5.
26. *L'Industrie ivoirienne en 1977, statistiques industrielles du 1.10.1976 au 30.9.1977* (Abidjan, Chambre d'Industrie de Côte d'Ivoire, 1978).
27. *La Côte d'Ivoire en chiffres, 1977-78*, p. 77.

28.   'Investments in the Ivory Coast', *Marchés tropicaux*, Special Number, 24 October 1975, p. 61.
29.   *La Côte d'Ivoire en chiffres, 1977-78*, p. 77.
30.   UNIDO, op. cit., p. 4.
31.   Yves Pehaut, 'Les Oléagineux dans les pays d'Afrique occidentale associés en Marché Commun'. Thesis, University of Lille III, 1974, p. 1051.
32.   Marguerite Dupire and Jean-Louis Bontillier, *Le Pays Adioukrou et sa palmeraie. Etude socio-économique* (Paris, L'Homme d'Outre-Mer, ORSTOM, 1958).
33.   Amagou and Gleizes, op. cit., p. 1487.
34.   SEDES, *Etude socio-économique des plantations villageoises de palmier à huile*, pp. 277-9.
35.   This sense of 'entrepreneurship' might easily be eroded by the state failing to keep the prices paid the producers at an acceptable level.
36.   De la Rochère, op. cit., p. 265. This information is confirmed by Pillet-Schwartz, op. cit.
37.   De la Rochère, op. cit., p. 266.
38.   'L'Industrie africaine 1975', *Bulletin de l'Afrique Noire*, Special Number, p. 18.
39.   SODEPALM, *Rapport annuel* (various years). M. André Blohorn is also Honourable President of the Chambre d'Industrie in the Ivory Coast, and his Director, M. Joseph Aka-Anghui is the first Vice-President of the Chambre d'Industrie.
40.   Critics spoke of SODEPALM as having developed into a 'state in the state'.
41.   A very large number of Ivorian peasants are growers of several products like cocoa, coffee and oil palm, which created a lot of confusion when several state societies were in charge of for example providing fertilizers.
42.   Pehaut, op. cit., p. 1155 and Pillet-Schwartz, op. cit., p. 26.
43.   'L'Industrie africaine 1975', op. cit., p. 18 and *Marchés tropicaux*, 30 September 1977, p. 2666.
44.   *Marchés tropicaux*, 30 September 1977, p. 2666.
45.   'Investments in the Ivory Coast', op. cit., p. 82.
46.   Chambre d'Industrie de Côte d'Ivoire, 1977-78.
47.   *Afrique Agriculture*, No. 7, March 1976, p. 38 and No. 35, July 1978, p. 61.
48.   'L'historique du développement de la culture du palmier à huile en Afrique, *Afrique Agriculture*, No. 7, March 1976, p. 24.
49.   *Development of Local Engineering Capabilities for Industry. Case Study of the Ivory Coast*. O.E.C.D. Development Centre, Industry and Technology, Occasional Paper No. 20, February 1978, p. 4.
50.   *Afrique Agriculture*, No. 35, July 1978, p. 63.
51.   Corresponding agreements have been established with the Ivorian SATMACI regarding the coffee and cocoa development in Liberia. *Fraternité Matin*, Agri 77, May 1977, p. 10.
52.   Administrators within SODEPALM attribute the success of the organization partly to the many foreign experts, mainly French, who in the Ivory Coast have practised precisely the same planning and management principles that were successful in the French development plans in the

1960s. It was — as will be recalled from earlier — the intention of these plans to create a planning framework and develop techniques which might further the restructuring of the French economy, making it more internationally competitive.

53. 'Development of Local . . .', op. cit., pp. 12 and 14.
54. According to M. André Blohorn he himself was the man responsible not only for working out the Plan Palmier, but also having the Community take the bait. Both the European Development Fund and the World Bank were not very eager to join the project because of the then over-production and low world market price of vegetable oils, but Blohorn and the Ivorian Government representatives convinced them of the long-term profitability of oil palm projects. *Afrique Agriculture*, No. 7, March 1976, p. 36.
55. Dupire and Boutillier, op. cit.
56. Michel Pescay, *Etude socio-économique des plantations villageoises de palmier à huile* (Paris, SEDES and SODEPALM, 1968).
57. Ibid., Rapport de Synthèse, p. 11.
58. Ibid., pp. 25-7.
59. J.F. Drevet, *Enquête socio-économique dans les plantations villageoises de Basse Côte d'Ivoire* (Paris, SEDES and SODEPALM, 1975).
60. See for example M.L. Mazoyer, 'Développement de la production et transformation agricole marchande d'une formation agraire en Côte d'Ivoire', in Samir Amin (ed), *L'Agriculture africaine et le capitalisme* (Paris, Editions Anthropos, 1975).
61. Pillet-Schwartz, op. cit.
62. Ibid., p. 190.
63. The figures available from the recent population census seem to show an extremely high population growth rate of between 3.6 and 4%.
64. Amin, 1971, op. cit.
65. This figure reached 620 in 1979. *L'Industrie ivoirienne en 1979*, op. cit.
66. For 1978/79 the figure is 650 and the index 5,000.
67. Industrial exports reached 203 billion F C.F.A. in 1978/79 while the repartition of the industrial production meant for export increased slightly to 31%.
68. In 1978/79 58% of the total raw materials industrially manufactured was Ivorian in origin.
69. Jean Chevassu and Alain Valette, *Les Relations intermédiares dans le secteur industriel ivoirien* (Abidjan, ORSTOM, Sciences humaines, 1975).
70. A certain, although minor, decentralization has taken place as is indicated by the fact that only 66% of all industrial enterprises were situated in Abidjan in 1978/79. *L'Industrie ivoirienne en 1979*, op. cit.
71. Chevassu and Valette, *Les Relations . . .*, op. cit.
72. Ibid.
73. *Etudes sur la sous-traitance en vue de la création d'une bourse de sous-traitance à Abidjan* (Abidjan, SIGES, 1970).
74. See the discussion in 'Le Marché de l'habillement et de la confection, 1973-74', *Analyse de marchés*, No. 8, 1975.
75. The increase from 1978 to 1980 is primarily due to large investments

in agro-industries related to sugar and coffee.

76. Chevassu and Valette, *Les Industriels* . . ., op. cit.
77. Jean Chevassu and Alain Valette, *Les revenues distribués par les activités industrielles en Côte d'Ivoire* (Abidjan, ORSTOM, Sciences humaines, 1975).
78. Bonnie Campbell, 'The Social, Political and Economic Consequences of French Private Investments in the Ivory Coast 1960-70. A Case Study of Cotton and Textile Production'. Ph.D. Thesis, University of Sussex, 1973 and Bonnie Campbell, 'Neo-Colonialism, Economic Dependence and Political Change: A Case Study of Cotton and Textile Production in the Ivory Coast 1960-70', *Review of African Political Economy*, No. 2, 1975, pp. 36-54.
79. *L'Industrie ivoirienne en 1977*, op. cit.
80. In 1978-79 production reached 115,000 tons. *La Côte d'Ivoire en chiffres, 1980-81*, p. 154.
81. 46,000 tons in 1978-79.
82. For the following information, see *Marchés tropicaux*, 30 September 1977, pp. 2670-78.
83. *Afrique Industrie*, No. 152, 15 December 1977, p. 54.
84. For a detailed listing of these 15 companies by name, production capacity and type of specialization, see *Marchés tropicaux*, 30 September 1977.
85. Société générale de Banques en Côte d'Ivoire, *Industrie textile en Côte d'Ivoire* (Abidjan, April 1976).
86. De la Rochère, op. cit., p. 295 and Günter Wiedensohler, 'Westafrikanische Staaten als Vertragspartner ausländischer Privatunternehmen', *Afrika Spectrum*, No. 2, 1977, p. 159.
87. De la Rochère, op. cit., p. 311.
88. For a full presentation of the law, see *Private Investments in the Ivory Coast: Investment Law* (Abidjan, Ministry of Finance, Economic Affairs and the Plan, undated).
89. Günten Wiedensohler, *op. cit.*, p. 158ff.

5. The Socio-Economic Consequences of Economic Development in the Ivory Coast

In the previous chapters we have again and again emphasized the role of the Ivorian state in economic development as one of the more important characteristics of the growth process pursued since independence in 1960. This is true both of industry, with the increasing share of state investments in total industrial investments modifying the role of foreign capital while at the same time continuously seeking to attract international capital, and — not least — of agriculture, where the state has succeeded in extracting an economic surplus over the years, enabling it to expand its economic interventionist measures. The state seems thus to have established a material basis for its own continued reproduction and to have established itself as a relatively autonomous factor vis-à-vis external forces in its creation of the preconditions for an extended production and reproduction process, i.e. a process of capital accumulation.

This relative success of state policy pursued has been furthered by a number of favourable conditions, of which many have been mentioned above: a relatively favourable development in world market prices for exportable products, favourable natural and geographical conditions for agricultural production, the availability of a vast reserve army of labour in the drought-ridden Sahel states, etc. The combination of these favourable conditions has greatly eased the delicate balancing act of the state: to extract an economic surplus from the agricultural sector under conditions where international capital and international aid organizations are also getting a share of the cake, without squeezing the peasants to an extent where they simply give up production for the market in an increasingly deteriorating situation.

This special and perhaps unique situation of the Ivory Coast naturally raises a number of questions, of which the more important are: What happens in a much less favourable economic environment like the one we are presently experiencing with a world economic crisis heavily constraining the economies of most Third World countries? How is the balancing act of the Ivorian state affected by increasing international and national economic difficulties? At a more general level: What are the socio-economic consequences for the different groups and classes of the Ivorian population under the development policy being pursued? What are the political preconditions of the policy carried out? What is the class nature of the Ivorian state?

Social Differentiation in the Ivory Coast

The liberal economic thinking that prevailed in the 1950s and 1960s, according to which rapid economic growth was the unquestioned development goal for the developing countries at large, has since then been continuously criticized. The 'trickle-down' effect has not proved itself to be the more or less automatic result, as expected, of an economic growth policy emphasizing openness towards the world market and privileges granted to foreign capital. Growth and equity are not necessarily identical as increased social differentiation has often been the common effect of the growth policies pursued in nearly every Third World country.

The Ivory Coast has successfully achieved an ambitious growth rate of 7% annually in real terms during the period 1950-75. According to World Bank sources, the country seems also to have escaped this social differentiation trap: 'Income distribution calculations show a distribution similar to, or more equitable than, those found in comparable countries. Farm price policies and regional investment plans not only show an active concern with equity but also indicate that growth and equity are to a large extent consistent.'[1]

When looking into the distribution of income among various groups of people and different economic sectors, one has to bear in mind the very special and extensive use the Ivory Coast is making of foreign manpower. The number of primarily French expatriates has for some time been above the pre-independence level, the estimates — as previously mentioned — varying between 50,000 and 70,000,[2] to which has to be added about 100,000 Lebanese and Syrians. These groups occupy the top levels of income, while the lowest-paid groups are the unskilled immigrant workers from neighbouring countries, estimated to constitute almost 30% of the population.[3]

According to World Bank figures, this group of 'Other Africans' is most numerous in the primary sector, even increasing as a proportion between 1971 and 1974.[4] What is even more remarkable is the fact that non-Africans have very high earnings, ranging from twenty times the average African wage in the primary sector to ten times that in the secondary sector and five times that in the tertiary sector. As mentioned by the World Bank, 'Non-Africans usually cost, in money terms, two to three times as much as Africans in the same job classification. The cost of expatriates is high indeed, and contracts of some U.S. $50,000 a man-year — excluding costs of housing, car, and other fringe benefits — are not exceptional.'[5]

Nevertheless, the World Bank concludes on the basis of an estimate of the distribution of the national income of the Ivory Coast in 1973-74 that, in international terms, the Ivory Coast is placed in the category of 'low inequality'.[6] Although not specifying the basis of the comparisons between the present estimate and one conducted in 1970 by Hollis Chenery *et al.*,[7] the World Bank further concludes that the situation has even improved over the years.

Other aspects are presented in the Ivorian Agricultural Census, the result of which was published in 1976. The World Bank estimates are very rough, not least because of the limited data available. The lack of appropriate data is, however, a more general bias, which also affects discussions of rural differentiation patterns such as the distribution of land, consumption and investment opportunities, etc. It is also impossible to discern any significant trend as only one Agricultural Census has ever been carried out. Another difficulty with the agricultural statistics is that they only include holdings of up to 99 hectares, although according to the Census data itself a significant number of holdings (550 in all) were over 100 hectares.

Abdoulaye Sawadogo, the former Minister of Agriculture, is devoting a short chapter in his book[8] to trying to answer the question whether in the Ivory Coast a stratum of rich and wealthy plantation owners has developed. Although not substantiating his argument with statistics, it is his opinion that the Ivory Coast rural scene is predominantly one of smallholders possessing 2 to 3 hectares of land.

With holdings of more than 100 hectares excluded from agricultural statistics, Sawadogo is obviously right in stressing the smallholder nature of Ivorian agriculture. According to the Census data, 60% of holdings are below 5 hectares, 27% between 5 and 10 hectares, and 13% above 10 hectares.[9] Not surprisingly, the number of permanent labourers employed varies according to farm size, e.g. the larger the farm size the more people employed (an average of 3.2 for holdings of 20 hectares and more and 7.5 for holdings between 50 and 100 hectares). On the 27,588 holdings in southern Ivory Coast,[10] 71,955 permanent labourers were employed and 260,803 temporary labourers, indicating that the use of employees in agriculture is quite widespread even for the smaller farmers, and the process of capitalization quite advanced. Other information as to consumption and investment patterns seems to confirm this view.[11]

The more detailed picture of the composition of agricultural income from the sale of cash crops and food crops, and the percentage of total income which is represented by subsistence, is not covered by the Agricultural Census. Eddy Lee, however, does present some estimates.[12] From the information available, it seems that more than two-thirds of the total income of farms below 2 hectares is in the form of subsistence, and this percentage declines sharply with increasing farm size. Only 15% of total income is derived from cash crops for farms below 2 hectares (and an equal percentage from sales of food crops), while 82% of total income stems from the sale of cash crops in the case of the largest farms. This rather profound social differentiation is illustrated by the fact that farms of over 20 hectares have a cash income 35 times larger than the income of farms below 2 hectares, while the range in total income (that is including the imputed value of food consumption) between these two groups of farms is 12.3.

Differences in farm income and other aspects of social differentiation are among the facts substantiating Eddy Lee's argument that the Ivorian rural scene is much more marked by social inequalities than the analysis of, for example, the World Bank seemed to show.

Eddy Lee is thus heavily criticizing the conclusions drawn by the World Bank regarding the relatively low inequality of the Ivory Coast compared to other Third World countries, and the basis on which these conclusions were made. The inconclusiveness of the data is shown by the fact that no household surveys have ever been carried out and the World Bank estimate was derived from average *per capita* income figures in the 24 departments into which the Ivory Coast is divided, ignoring income differences between households within each department 'and, if anything, yields information only on interdepartmental differences in income'. Lee concludes his criticism by mentioning that:

> It is totally invalid to treat a measure of overall inequality derived from this procedure as being equivalent to the size-distribution of household incomes and to use it for comparisons with the size-distribution of household incomes in other countries. Equally baseless is the attempt to compare these figures with an earlier estimate in 1970, derived on a totally different basis, and to draw conclusions to the effect that the distribution of incomes had improved.[13]

But Lee is also trying to refute the conclusions drawn, by looking at the development of rural incomes when inflation is taken into consideration. The figures for gross revenue per hectare at current prices in cocoa and coffee production show an annual increase of 7 and 5% respectively for the period in question.[14] In an effort to deflate the increase in gross revenues, Lee uses the not very reliable Abidjan consumer price index for the 'African family', as no rural cost-of-living index exists. His argument is that, although there may be great differences between the rural and urban costs of living, 'it is likely that the magnitude and direction of *change* in cost-of-living indices cannot be greatly at variance. Since a very high proportion of the consumption of urban Africans would consist of rural-supplied food items, this would constitute a link between movements in urban and rural price indices.'[15] As no precise information is available as to the composition of the two existing price indices (the urban Abidjan indices for the European and African family type), this is certainly — as is admitted by Lee — a very rough deflator. But the development in the two indices are very similar with regard to the yearly increase,[16] possibly reflecting to a large extent the price developments on imported goods primarily sold on the urban market.

Using the Abidjan cost of living index for the African family as deflator thus probably implies an inflation rate on rural incomes higher than exists in reality and leads to a somewhat exaggerated conclusion:

> The rate of increase of gross revenue per hectare for cocoa drops to three per cent per annum, while it becomes insignificant in the case of coffee. Thus in comparison to the *real* rates of growth of over seven per cent per annum of GDP and the value of total exports, our proxy for real producer incomes shows that these gains have been inadequately transmitted to producers in the case of cocoa and hardly at all in the case of coffee.[17]

Lee adds that his conclusion does not imply that the low growth in producer incomes rules out the possibility that incomes have increased either because new land was acquired or because more land was devoted to cocoa and coffee.

Lee also tackles another aspect of social differentiation in Ivorian agriculture, namely the standard of living of the 177,318 permanent labourers, comprising 10.5% of the total employed labour force in agriculture. The daily wage rate of the permanent labourers was held constant at 156 C.F.A. francs (the minimum wage) for the entire period 1956-72; it was increased slightly in 1973 to 160 francs and in 1974 and 1975 to 200, ending up at 250 in 1976. Lee makes two points about this. First, as previously mentioned, the Agricultural Census does not include the large-scale coffee and cocoa farms of over 100 hectares. These farms are exempted from minimum wage legislation, and in 1968 it was estimated that one-sixth of agricultural wage employees worked on them. Secondly, 'it is also likely that these minimum wages represent actual or even maximum wages in view of the labour supply situation and are not fictitous legislative figures which are below the market wage.'[18]

By using the Abidjan consumer price index, Lee constructs a real wage index showing that this group of labourers have experienced a steady reduction in their standard of living throughout the period. This picture of a steadily deteriorating situation for the poorest segment of the Ivorian economy is confirmed by other sources like the E.E.C., who state that:

> Certain information and statistics suggest that the very low wages in agriculture have begun to encourage some of the latter to return to Upper Volta. The poverty of farm workers (mainly foreign) has become increasingly obvious in the last two years (that is, the years prior to 1976), especially on the agro-industrial plantations where the guaranteed wage remains abnormally low (240 C.F.A. francs a day) while the general guaranteed minimum wage is 736 francs a day.[19]

But at the same time the World Bank has found that 'during the 1970-76 period, non-agricultural minimum wages increased from three times to about four times agricultural minimum wages', resulting in a situation where the

Government wage policy has certainly favoured 'Ivorian producers of export crops or import-replacing crops' at the expense of their employees. Summarizing the general effect of the wage policy of the Government, the Bank goes on to say that:

> Wages have been raised, but farm wages have been raised much less than non-farm wages. The policy has benefited Ivorian producers of export products and the large Ivorian- and government-owned plantations employing foreign African labour . . . . Wage differences within the farm sector appear to have increased.
>
> Non-farm wages have increased more than farm wages. This has primarily benefited Ivorians, who are the majority in non-farm wage employment . . . .
>
> The difference between Ivorian and other African wages, at least in money terms, seems to have increased, but government policies have been clearly geared to improving income distribution for Ivorians.[20]

This apparent redistribution of income from non-Ivorian African workers and labourers in agriculture to that tiny minority of Ivorians and the Ivorian state who own the large plantations totally dependent on foreign manpower can only be explained by the fact that the seasonal migrant workers from the Sahel states, temporarily entering wage employment in the south, experience the situation as an improvement compared to the one they have just come from. But this seems to have changed. Recently the Ivory Coast has experienced increasing difficulties in attracting the necessary foreign manpower; they are preferring to seek new job opportunities as far away as Gabon. Shortage of this manpower has been claimed as one of the major reasons for the poor harvests in for example the production of bananas, oil palms and pineapples. The situation has not been improved by the recent increase in the minimum daily wage; and the large plantations are sending their lorries on veritable 'raids' to the northern parts of the country picking up anyone seemingly without employment.

One aspect of the social differentiation pattern in Ivorian agriculture is the increasing polarization between the (mainly) non-Ivorian African labourers and the Ivorian farmers. This point is emphasized by Lee:

> Labourers in agriculture were estimated to earn an average of 6,100 C.F.A. francs per month in 1974, whereas the figures on total earnings per farm for 1978 show that, even after allowing for the intervening inflation, average earnings in the smallest farms (below 2 hectares) would be almost twice as high. Earnings per farm in farms over 200 hectares would be more than 20 times greater than the average wage of labourers.[21]

Another aspect of the social differentiation pattern is the one which is gradually developing among the Ivorian farmers themselves. On this, however, information is scarce.

Samir Amin concluded that, mainly due to the colonial system of forced labour and the dominance of French plantation owners, no real bourgeoisie developed among Ivorian planters up to 1950.[22] Whether a rural bourgeoisie, however, was only embryonic around 1950, it is the conclusion of many other writers that it soon developed thereafter — perhaps partly as a result of the abolition of the forced labour system in 1947. For example, Osendé Afana[23] believes that during the 1950s there came into being a stratum of important Ivorian planters in possession of abundant agricultural holdings and material wealth. Their wealth was founded on the export of coffee and cocoa, now much facilitated by the building of the deep sea harbour of Abidjan and the construction of the Vridi canal in 1950. According to Afana (who, unfortunately, does not give any exact figures to substantiate his argument), it was estimated that around the time of independence this stratum had reached the number of 8-10,000 members, owning plantations ranging from 10 to 12 hectares and employing at least 5 labourers each. Representatives of this new indigenous planter bourgeoisie, having succeeded in getting a higher education (in France), have throughout the post-independence period formed the basis of the Ivorian state and have so far been the persons guaranteeing the continuity of Ivorian political life. It is Samir Amin's estimate (and he also does not give any information as to the sources for his estimates) that by 1965 the stratum of relatively rich planters consisted of about 20,000 people, exploiting around one-quarter of the total land and employing two-thirds of all wage labour.[24]

According to the Agricultural Census, the top 11% of landholders operated 34.3% of total cultivated land in 1973-74. Lee suggests a rural bourgeoisie consisting of farmers owning more than 10 hectares, thus concluding that their numbers have increased to over 60,000:

> The average of the 89% of total holdings which were less than 10 hectares in size was 3.8 hectares, whereas the average size of the top 11% of holdings was 15.5 hectares. There were 20,000 holdings of between 15 to 40 hectares in size, almost 400 of between 40 to 100 hectares in size and, as mentioned earlier, 550 holdings of over 100 hectares which were not included in the statistics of the agricultural sector.[25]

To Lee, this development seems to confirm that social differentiation in Ivorian agriculture had proceeded 'to a very substantial degree since the introduction of cash cropping'. This development in social differentiation might largely be correlated with household size, thus reducing the validity of the argument. Although this correlation exists, the 'average farm size increases by an overwhelmingly larger proportion than average family size . . .'[26]

The relatively egalitarian social structure of the Ivorian rural sector — and the community at large — which the World Bank describes is thus probably an exaggeration. Increasing social differentiation has proceeded during recent years, if the various studies are to be believed. This, however, does not necessarily imply that the World Bank is not right in judging the social structure of the Ivory Coast to be more equitable than other countries in Africa by international standards. Moreover, the Ivorian state has to a great extent succeeded in avoiding the most overt symptoms of poverty, which the policy of rapid growth might according to the theory have involved. The absence of a marked and significant process of proletarianization in Ivorian agriculture at present is, however, only to be understood in relation to the precondition of Ivorian economic development: the existence of a vast reservoir of foreign manpower, mainly from the Sahel states, who come from a situation of pure misery and are willing to work on the plantations in the Ivory Coast at a cost barely enough to keep themselves alive. One cannot deny that at the roots of the Ivorian 'economic miracle' lie *also* the indirect transfer of values from the Sahel states. It is these countries which have covered the 'reproduction costs' of the manpower used by the Ivory Coast by investment in physical infrastructure, education, social infrastructure like hospitals and medical centres etc. In this way, value is transferred to the economies in the south, not only the Ivory Coast, but also countries like Ghana, Nigeria, Togo etc.

In the last two Ivory Coast development plans it has been a primary goal to reduce *regional inequality* by putting emphasis on investments in physical infrastructure in the Northern region, stressing the introduction of new cash crops such as for example cotton (the Allen variety), soy beans, horticultural products, sugar and beef cattle, all intended to increase the incomes of the poorest in the ecologically disadvantaged areas and thereby to reduce the strong trend of migration to the cities.

Not least in its heavy investments in sugar production the state has shown its readiness to direct substantial resources to the northern region, but still it is the more favoured regions in the south which have received the lion's share of public investment programmes. As appears from the investment programme for 1975-77,[27] the Abidjan area is allocated 30% of total investment, the southern and centre regions the major part of the remainder while the northern region is only allocated around 18% of the total. In spite of the Government's efforts to decentralize investment, the regional imbalances are still fundamental — and seemingly increasing over time. The coastal and forest belt south of Bouaké is still the economically dominant area in the Ivory Coast, and as can be seen in Table 15 the regional disparities in agricultural cash income have increased from 1971-73 to 1975. While the average income in the south for 1971-73 was around four times that of the north, this disparity increased to five times in 1975.

The Ivorian Economy under Current Harsh World Market Conditions

As has been mentioned previously, part of the explanation for the relative success of the Ivory Coast has been the rather favourable world market prices during the 1960s and 1970s for its major export products like timber, cocoa

Table 15 Agricultural Cash incomes, 1971-73 and 1975 (C.F.A. francs *per capita*)

	Average for 1971-73	*1975*
South East	21,105	32,400
South West	8,810	12,000
Centre	13,770	21,340
Centre West	19,170	30,500
Total South	*16,310*	*25,000*
Greater North	4,970	6,000
Centre North	4,210	5,000
Total North	*4,640*	*5,500*
Total Ivory Coast	*14,000*	*21,000*

Source: Daniel Bollinger, *Le Marketing en Afrique* (Abidjan, CEDA, 1977), p. 71.

and coffee. That the Ivory Coast presently is going through an economically very difficult time can be illustrated by its growth rate of only 2% for 1980, and probably zero for 1981, increasing balance of payments difficulties (which a recent I.M.F. loan of $ 589 million is intended to alleviate), heavy borrowing on the private lending market bringing external debts to a critical point, etc.[28] Major strikes of oil off the coast east of Abidjan may soon alter this bleak picture, as the country expects to be self-sufficient in oil in 1983, and a net exporter thereafter. But basically the fall in export revenues resulting from the drop in world market prices has shown the vulnerability to external forces of the Ivorian economy.

Previously, we have discussed the difficult balancing act of the state in extracting the surplus from the agricultural sector while not squeezing the farmers to an extent where they simply drop out of production for the market. This process took place amid rather good economic circumstances on the world market, which were its major precondition. But our palm oil case also illustrates the volatility of the whole organizational set-up when it is faced with increased economic difficulties abroad and at home — and with falling world market prices for vegetable oils.

The difficulties for the peasants attached to the SODEPALM system started in 1976 and got worse in the subsequent years. Two main factors caused this spiralling down of the previously well-known success story of Ivorian agriculture: climatic conditions, primarily lack of rain, created in 1976 and 1977 a production output below forecasts, eventually leading to an output in 1979 of only 53.2% of the targets; in addition, there were falling world market prices in real terms for the major vegetable oils. The price paid the producers had been held at 4 C.F.A. francs per kg of harvested oil palm fruits from 1965 to 1974, when it was doubled to 8 francs per kg. On

1 October 1977 the price per kg was further increased to 10 — but has not been increased since in spite of increases in the cost of living (an inflation rate at a very high level which has only recently been brought down to around 12% for 1980) and in the cost of labour.[29]

The peasants have responded to this situation in a number of ways, causing even further reductions in output, and threatening the profitability of the whole SODEPALM system, as the fall in supplies to the factories has resulted in a widespread under-utilization of capacity (45%). The Government for its part has not been able or willing to try to rectify the situation by an increase in the price paid the producers.

As a result, an increasing number of plantations have either been abandoned or simply destroyed. A recent SODEPALM report raises the alarm by stating that: 'It must be stressed that developments in the destruction of plantations have seriously accelerated during the past six months, particularly in the areas close to Abidjan.'[30]

Another important reason for the fall in production is the fact that the palm trees have now, after 10 to 15 years, reached a height where it is becoming increasingly difficult and burdensome to harvest the fruits by traditional techniques. In a situation where growing oil palms is considered by the peasants a troublesome and not very profitable affair, they have decided not to invest in the new techniques (the South East Asian bamboo technique) or hire the manpower necessary for the harvesting of the fruits. Many plantations are thus lying idle.

With the price paid to the producers kept constant, selling on the local market instead of supplying the SODEPALM system is becoming increasingly lucrative. It is estimated that for 1979-80 about 4% of total production was sold on the local market, where the price is roughly three times the official price. This percentage would probably be even higher were it not for the fact that the new SODEPALM varieties compared to the traditional varieties are not as suitable and do not have the taste required for home cooking.

Other factors contributing to the drastic decline in production since 1977 are the selling of the palm trees for manufacturing palm wine, parasitic diseases, an increasing number of plantations being difficult to reach by road, a lack of maintenance of the infrastructure, etc.

In all, it is estimated that in the 1978-79 season SODEPALM was deprived of around 110,000 tons of fruit caused by the factors mentioned above, only processing as a result 136,000 tons. During the period 1975-76 to 1978-79, productivity (measured in tons per hectare) declined from 7.64 to 4.87, resulting in such an extremely low yield that after allowing for the cost of fertilizers and labour there may have been a net loss for the peasants.

In a situation where most of the farmers are elderly and hence have to rely on employing labour for harvesting the fruit, it seems evident that family farming in oil palm production is on the decline — and that the peasants are not able to survive solely on the basis of oil palms, but will have to rely on other products. With the exception of rubber, however, the other products most commonly grown together with oil palms, cocoa and coffee, have also been hit by decreasing world market prices. In order to survive, many farmers have been forced to sell their trees for the production of palm wine as the price per hectare for this purpose is extremely high. Parallel to this, an increasing number of farmers are unable to pay the interest on their loans and as no government action against this is taking place, SODEPALM is witnessing an increasing number of defaults.

Bearing in mind the aspects of social differentiation in Ivorian agriculture described earlier, the case of oil palm production seems to illustrate that this differentiation may well have been furthered in recent years by the falling world prices for the major export products, and the resulting profound national economic difficulties. Since October 1978 several proposals for price increases in oil palm production have been made to the Ministry of Agriculture, which has not reacted so far. Up till the end of 1977 SODE-PALM's activities were highly profitable, and even for the years 1977-78 and 1978-79 preliminary analysis of the production costs of palm oil indicates that they were still marginally profitable. The oil palm case shows that the balance between, on the one hand international capital and the state, and on the other hand the peasants, is an extremely delicate affair. The balance can easily be disrupted if the peasants are squeezed to the extent described, with consequent increased tendencies towards marginalization and proletarianization, while the state — in a very irrational manner, it seems — is continuously trying to maximize its surplus whatever the costs.

The Class Nature of the State

As has been stressed, the state is the most dynamic factor in Ivorian economic development. It is not playing just a secondary role as a more or less passive tool for the local bourgeoisie or international capital, but is actively intervening in the economy, establishing a material basis for its own reproduction and hence relative autonomy which will enable the state to decide on socio-economic matters with a certain degree of freedom.

But what is the class nature of the state? Who are the classes or fractions of classes in the Ivory Coast determining state action? This very difficult question can only be tentatively answered by referring to the historically developing class structure of the country.

The struggle for independence was carried out by a layer of larger plantation owners, the persons who would mainly benefit from the abolition of colonial rule. The system of forced labour imposed by the French colonialists was hampering the development of an African planter class and with the cessation of the system in 1946 the African planter group grew in both size and importance.[31] It was this group of African planters, organized politically in the Syndicat Agricole Africain and numbering around 20,000 in the 1940s,[32] that carried through the opposition to French colonial rule and took over state power after independence.

While it is quite evident that it was this group of larger plantation owners who took over the colonial administrative apparatus and who gradually developed the state apparatus to what it is today, it is far less evident what is the class character of the Ivorian state at present.

One answer is given by Ikonicoff and Sigal,[33] who suggest that an administrative bureaucracy has taken over the colonial administration, and now controls state power in a situation where no other social groups have yet been solidly founded within Ivorian society. The administrative bureaucracy has according to this notion developed into a class in itself, with its own defined political and economic task to pursue.[34] The group of larger Ivorian plantation owners has not had the financial means to carry through an import substitution industrialization, which has therefore been left to international capital. It has been the major task of the state to attract international capital for this purpose and 'an objective alliance has developed between the bureaucracy founded within the State apparatus and the large multinational corporations'. It is, however, not possible for Ikonicoff and Sigal to confirm that the two social groups, the plantation owners and the bureaucratic layer, tend to develop into one class with compatible interests.[35] Rather, there is a 'transitional state' developing, able to transfer state power to a national bourgeoisie, the creation of which is in the hands of the very same state body.[36]

Referring to the works of Colin Leys on the 'post-colonial state', Bonnie Campbell is right in stating:

> While the class character of the state specifies the class which is dominant in a given social formation, since this dominance must be enforced by the state, the class origins, class ties or class ambitions of the individuals who compose the apparatus of the state are not necessarily the same as those of the dominant class, and the state power need not reflect their own class interests except in a secondary way.[37]

However, she continues with regard to the Ivory Coast that:

> The emergence in the post-colonial period of an important political and administrative group responsible for running an increasing number of state agencies and disposing, through the position which they occupy in the state apparatus, of considerable material wealth, does not necessarily imply, as some have suggested, that the basis of state power has shifted from rural to non-rural interests.[38]

This view is, at least implicitly, questioning the thesis put forward by Ikonicoff. To Campbell, the dominant class is still the *bourgeoisie de planteurs* which has been powerful enough to determine the class character of the Ivorian state:

> The nature of political power has certainly evolved with the development of the state apparatus. But the dominant class which assumed

power at independence maintains control over the export-oriented
pattern of growth and the particular pattern of surplus distribution
which it implies . . . . The dominant class may have been broadened in
its composition, but the interests of the planter bourgeoisie have
remained firmly dominant.[39]

Not only has the planter-politician group been successful in 'perpetuating
the past pattern of accumulation and distribution of surplus between their
foreign partners and themselves',[40] but it has also deliberately delayed or
hindered the emergence of a local group of entrepreneurs. According to
Campbell, this is because the development of 'a local entrepreneurial group
would threaten the economic authority of the Ivorian ruling group and more
fundamentally the foreign interests sanctioned by and backing this group'.[41]

One basic difficulty in discussing the class nature of the Ivorian state is
the lack of empirical evidence which might substantiate any of the above-
quoted positions. What is empirically obvious, however, is that the share of
private Ivorians in industrial investment is scanty, although the most recent
figures seem to indicate that their share has climbed to 13.19% of total
industrial investment for 1978-79 after having been nearly constant at around
11% for the past years.[42] But more basic studies on the possibilities for and
realities behind the development of a local bourgeoisie and its relations with
the state apparatus, possibly in conflict with the economic interests of the
African planter group and international capital, are still missing.

In the socio-economic studies quoted above in our oil palm case, one
major conclusion seemed apparent: namely that an increasing number of
functionaries and bureaucrats invested part of their gains in the (then) most
profitable parts of Ivorian agriculture, the agro-industrial plantations, which
promised the highest assured returns. That the prevention of similar investments in the profitable sectors of manufacturing should be a deliberate policy
of the dominant class — in flagrant contrast with the much talked-about Ivorianization and emphasis on developing a class of national entrepreneurs, as
expressed in the Development Plans — seems a bit odd. The group of large
Ivorian plantation owners is clearly losing ground, in that they do not
seem to be influencing the political decision-making process to the extent
they once did.[43] Bearing in mind the arguments from Chapter 1 in which the
new forms of internationalization of capital were presented, implying the substantial use of local funds (state or private) on the part of the multinational
corporations in the creation of new capitalist production and reproduction
centres, it seems not very likely that either the local planter bourgeoisie or
the international capital groups should object to the emergence of a local
entrepreneurial class capable of creating in conjunction with foreign capital a
dynamic base for continued capital accumulation. Of course, at the level of
negotiating with individual foreign capital groups a number of conflicts may
arise compared to the extreme licence hitherto granted these firms,[44] but at
a more generalized level different forms of joint ventures and other agreements involving local capital might constitute a more adequate response to

capital's present and future need.

We are therefore leaning more towards the suggestion offered by Ikonicoff that the Ivorian state is in a transitional phase, which will eventually result in the Ivorian commercial and industrial interests coming to the foreground to form a national bourgeoisie. This may well come about on the death of the ageing President, when the different classes and class fractions will have to do battle for their respective interests.

Conclusions

In the above treatment of the social differentiation process in the Ivory Coast and the class nature of the state, one fundamental precondition for the activities and intervention of the state has been missing: the political corollaries of the policy of economic growth.

For most Third World states political repression has proved a necessary prerequisite for the creation of an investment climate attractive to international capital. The repressive measures may vary from country to country, but it seems quite a general phenomenon that states are eager to curb political opposition by allowing only a single-party constitution, forbidding strikes for higher salaries (or any other purpose) (since the control of the wage level is an intrinsic part of the sound investment climate), suppressing trade union activities or incorporating them into the state-controlled political party, etc.

Although it seems to be a feature of Ivorian political repression that the press and other mass media do not report on strikes or any other acts which might be judged as subversive, many of the repressive functions listed above are nonetheless represented in the Ivory Coast.[45] Strikes are prohibited and illegal, political opposition is neutralized -- for example, the only existing trade union is part and parcel of the party, the P.D.C.I., which is the sole legal representative of workers' interests.

But strikes do occur — and so do attempted *coups* such as the ones reported in the early 1960s, which were followed by increased repression. Recently, student unrest has resulted in secondary schools being closed and the expulsion of students from the University of Abidjan. The repatriation of French university teachers of Marxist persuasion, the non-availability of certain books and periodicals, especially those critical towards government policies, are other examples.

The most recent example of a go-slow action was reported in early 1981;[46] this was a reaction to a government decision cutting salaries for some 30,000 state sector employees by between 50 and 60%. The action was accompanied by the distribution of leaflets, which — in the words of the article quoted — was 'a method of manifesting political discontent that has become a typical response to the severe restrictions that are imposed in Ivory Coast on the expression of political views'.[47] The leaflets called for, among other things, free trade unions and democracy in the Ivory Coast.

In spite of this, political 'stability' is a leading characteristic of Ivorian development in the 1960s and 70s and it reflects one of the major reasons for the continued interest of foreign capital in investing in the Ivory Coast.

The introduction of capitalist development in the Ivory Coast has thus in social terms been furthered by, on the one hand, the repressive policy of the Ivorian Government, and on the other hand, by the fact that the proletarianization process accompanying the introduction of capitalist relations of production has primarily taken place in the Ivory Coast's neighbours, thereby limiting hitherto the extent of Ivorian social transformation.

Notes

1. The World Bank, *Ivory Coast. The Challenge of Success. A World Bank Country Economic Report*, Bastiaan A. den Tuinder (Baltimore, The Johns Hopkins University Press, 1978), p. 122.
2. Ibid., p. 124; referring to the number as 50,000 in 1975.
3. The total population was 6.7 million in 1977. *La Côte d'Ivoire en chiffres, 1979-80*, p. 17.
4. The World Bank, op. cit., p. 130.
5. Ibid., p. 129. According to informal sources, the 1979 cost of for example E.E.C.-financed technical assistance personnel can well amount to U.S. $90,000 exclusive of fringe benefits.
6. Ibid., p. 134. The distribution of the total income is as follows:
   Lowest 40% receive 19.7% of the total
   Middle 40% receive 28.7% of the total
   Top 20% receive 51.6% of the total.
7. Hollis Chenery, *et. al.*, *Redistribution with Growth* (London, University of Sussex, 1974).
8. Abdoulaye Sawadogo, *L'Agriculture en Côte d'Ivoire* (Paris, Presses Universitaires de France, 1977).
9. *Recensement national de l'Agriculture, Vol. IV. Exploitation agricoles traditionelles* (Direction des Statistiques rurales, September 1976).
10. That is the coastal and forest belt south of Bouaké where most of the cash-cropping is concentrated.
11. *Recensement national de l'Agriculture, Vol. IV. Exploitation agricoles* ing the farmers' ability to buy according to their needs, to save money, to buy on credit, etc. and the number of holdings possessing different types of farm machinery
12. The estimates are computed on the basis of information in the Direction du Plan. Eddy Lee, 'Export-Led Rural Development: The Ivory Coast', *Development and Change*, Vol. II, 1980.
13. Lee, op. cit., pp. 626-7.
14. The figures are based on *Statistiques agricoles: Memento 1947-1977* (Abidjan, Ministry of Agriculture, 1978). The period covered is 1956/57-1976/77.
15. Lee, op. cit., p. 620.
16. *La Côte d'Ivoire en chiffres, 1979-80*, p. 263-5.

17. Lee, op. cit., pp. 620-1.
18. Lee, op. cit., p. 625.
19. E.E.C. internal working documents.
20. The World Bank, op. cit., pp. 139-40.
21. Lee, op. cit., p. 632.
22. Samir Amin, *Le Développement du capitalisme en Côte d'Ivoire*, 2nd edn (Paris, Editions de Minuit, 1969), p. 277.
23. Osendé Afana, *L'Economie de l'Ouest-africain* (Paris, Francois Maspero, 1977), p. 113.
24. Amin, op. cit., p. 277.
25. Lee, op. cit., p. 630.
26. Ibid., p. 632.
27. Table on the percentage distribution of planned public investment by major programme; The World Bank, op. cit., p. 150.
28. *Financial Times*, 9 December 1980. The total Government and Government-guaranteed external debt went up from 48.4 billion F C.F.A. in 1976 to 135.6 billion in 1979.
29. SODEPALM, *Les Plantations villageoises de palmier à huile. Evolution de la production* (Abidjan, January 1980).
30. Ibid., p. 27 (our translation).
31. For a description of this, see Bonnie Campbell, 'The Ivory Coast', in John Dunn (ed), *West African States: Failure and Promise* (Cambridge University Press, 1978).
32. With the later President of the Ivory Coast, Félix Houphouët-Boigny, as the leader and one of the wealthiest of the African farmers.
33. Moises Ikonicoff and Silvia Sigal, *L'Etat relais: un modèle de développement des sociétés péripheriques? Le cas de la Côte d'Ivoire* (Paris, IEDES, undated) and Moises Ikonicoff, 'Le système économique mondial: désordre ou rationalité?', *Revue Tiers Monde*, Vol. XXI, No. 81, January-March 1980.
34. Ikonicoff and Sigal, op. cit., p. 7. Ikonicoff in his later writings labels this administrative bureaucracy a *'technobureaucratique étatique'*, but without altering his opinion on the class character of the state; see Ikonicoff, op. cit., pp. 112 and 119.
35. Ikonicoff and Sigal, op. cit., p. 8.
36. 'L'Etat n'est conçu − par le pouvoir politique − que comme une "instance relais" devant transmettre les fonctions à une couche sociale que l'on pourrait appeler "bourgeoisie nationale" dont la création reviendrait à ce même Etat.' Ibid., p. 19.
37. Campbell, op. cit., p. 83.
38. Ibid.
39. Ibid., p. 89.
40. Ibid., p. 133.
41. Ibid., p. 110.
42. *La Côte d'Ivoire en chiffres, 1980-81*, p. 191.
43. One exception to this is of course the continuous dynamic and very influential role of the President in any decision of major importance. The recent Cabinet reshuffle in early 1981 and the preceding party elections in late 1980 seem, however, to confirm the view that an increasing number of younger 'turks' are entering the Ivorian political scene.

44. Already the economic difficulties of the Ivory Coast seem to have resulted in the drafting by the Ministry of Planning of a revised and more restrictive version of the Code of Investment.
45. In *West Africa*, 9 March 1981 the President, Félix Houphouët-Boigny, is quoted as saying that he is not aware of any strike ever in the Ivory Coast.
46. See *West Africa*, 2 March 1981, pp. 429-30.
47. As a result of strikes primarily in the economically very important cocoa and coffee export sector, the Government soon withdrew the plan.

6. A Changing Theoretical Paradigm? — From Dependency Theory to the Internationalization of Capital

In the previous chapter, our analysis mainly focused on empirical arguments concerning the possibility of transcending 'blocked development' in the countries of the Periphery, taking the Ivory Coast as our example. With Samir Amin and his work on West Africa, and the Ivory Coast in particular, as our main inspiration, we have — in the context of a theoretical understanding of the internationalization of capital and the activities of the peripheral state (supported by the international aid organizations) — tried to substantiate the argument that the Centre does not necessarily block capitalist development in the Periphery, but rather organizes it. We have tried to demonstrate that, with heavy influence from international capital, and with the Ivorian state as the most dynamic factor in the internal situation, the Ivory Coast has the potentiality in its agricultural and industrial sectors to transcend the 'blocked development' situation.

If our argument is correct, and if at least a few countries in the Periphery can develop into fully fledged capitalist social formations, resulting in a much more differentiated situation within the Periphery, this of course has severe repercussions for the Dependency School and its related theoretical concepts.

Therefore we will discuss the dependency theory and the theories of the internationalization of capital and the peripheral state, with a view to arguing for a basic change of theoretical paradigm in the understanding of relations between Centre and Periphery, and their impact on the internal development of the Periphery.

The Dependency Theory Re-examined

During the second half of the 1960s and the early 1970s the dependency theory completely dominated discussions of the relationship between the Centre and the Periphery within the Marxist-oriented tradition. As a result of the integration of the Periphery into the world market, this school of thought considered the development potential of the peripheral social formations to be 'blocked' due to the extraction by the Centre of the existing economic surplus.[1]

This theoretical approach developed in contrast to the then prevailing liberal development theories like the dual economy and stages of growth theories, and must be considered an important step forward.[2] It was particularly important that this new approach based its orientation on a historical analysis, specified and developed concepts for characterizing the internal socio-economic situation of the developing countries, and related the analysis of the industrialized countries to that of the Periphery.

In contrast to the classical imperialist theorists such as Rosa Luxemburg, Tugan-Baranowski, Grossmann, Lenin, and others, who sought explanations of the rise of imperialism in the general laws of capital accumulation, the post-war dependency theorists have concentrated on empirical analyses of the consequences of imperialism for the peripheral countries. In this way 'blocked capital accumulation' in the Periphery, 'the development of under-development', 'growth without development', etc. became the labels used to characterize the dependency of the Periphery, with only limited hope of overcoming this situation.

The material explanation for this in fact very static conception of imperialism can be looked for in the capitalist development of the Western countries, characterized by a long post-war period free of economic crises. This continuous and unrestricted accumulation process supported the view that the capitalist system had essentially reached the stage where state planning and intervention would ensure the continuation of a crisis-free situation.

Implicit in the concept of imperialism, which has been predominant during the 1960s, is a global system determined by factors in the Centre's accumulation process. But those factors have not been specified in any detail. Imperialism thereby becomes an unspecified 'system of exploitation', when the consequences for the Periphery are being analysed. The 'blocked accumulation' in the peripheral areas is, therefore, not incorporated into a theory of the movement of capital on the world market and is not explicitly placed within the field of the international reproduction of Centre capital. One of the authors most often quoted as representing the theory of blocked capital accumulation in the Periphery is Samir Amin. Through the 1960s he made many empirical studies of the development prospects of the mainly French-speaking West African countries, while at the same time he tried to establish a theoretical framework for understanding the worldwide expansion process.

In this respect, Samir Amin's model of the blocked peripheral accumulation of capital is a well-known and often cited example.[3] His model was developed at a time when the myth of crisis-free capitalist development still held sway. It confirmed Amin in his view that the basic relation between the developed and underdeveloped world was that of a system in equilibrium. In the Centre it was, according to Amin, in principle possible to continue the capitalist production and reproduction process indefinitely, while the Periphery was only linked to the Centre in terms of being minor profitable investment areas for the Centre because of the low wage level, thereby sustaining the condition for the continuance of blocked development.

The conception of the capitalist system as being a dynamic equilibrium seems on a theoretical level to be tied to Samir Amin's misinterpretation of the reproduction schemes. In his interpretation of the Marxist schemes of reproduction — which are explicitly his source of inspiration for his equilibrium conclusion[4] — Amin seems partially to have misunderstood Marx's level of abstraction. In the works of Marx,[5] the schemes of reproduction only represent the typological exemplification of an abstract, logical *possibility* for extended reproduction — period after period. The accumulation theory, however, and its related theory of periodic crises in capitalism is at a lower level of abstraction, clearly modifying this way of thinking. The reproduction schemes are therefore presenting the general conditions for a dynamic equilibrium system; they do not specify what is Samir Amin's central problematic — a historically based understanding of the demands of the Centre on the Periphery. Therefore, Samir Amin's analysis ends up in a mixture of logical conditions for general equilibrium and *historical* observations of the blocked economy.

Since Samir Amin ties his analysis to the reproduction schemes, he considers capital accumulation in the Centre as a steady ongoing process, and draws the conclusion that the peripheral state apparatus and bourgeoisie will conform to the fixed demands of the Centre's accumulation process. His choice of conceptual framework thereby leads to an overestimation of the stability of the system, and an underestimation of the role of the bourgeoisie and the state apparatus in the accumulation process of the peripheral social formations.

It is, however, quite difficult to trace and reproduce with great consistency Amin's theory and conceptual framework. In his earlier theoretical works[6] he uses the tendency of the rate of profit to fall as well as the organic composition of capital as primary concepts for the understanding of imperialism. In his most recent works,[7] however, these concepts are considered to be unimportant, representing an economistic viewpoint.

His latest theoretical analysis is a continuation of this fight against 'economism' or the 'Eurocentric' way of thinking, where imperialism is seen purely as a manifestation of 'economic laws'. In spite of his statement that he wants to view 'the historical materialism in its full totality and to its widest extent',[8] the battle against economistic thinking makes him consider the class struggle as the dynamo of development. In other words, the class struggle is without reservation seen as *the* 'independent variable', from which the concrete manifestation of imperialism can be deduced. In 1975, Amin expressed his central thesis as follows:

It is our thesis that the capitalist process of production does not have a 'need' for 'external' markets — and this goes for both commodities and capital. A dynamic equilibrium is in reality always possible . . . . Neither can expansionism be viewed as a problem of realization. The actual fight for foreign markets is a result of class struggle, because expansionism is the way in which 'internal' — that is national — conditions of capital accumulation show themselves in the global system of capitalism.[9]

In other words, Amin's thesis implies the primacy of the class struggle; it also implies that the capitalist system is essentially a dynamic equilibrium, which, referring to economic categories, does not have any built-in tendency towards expansion beyond the boundaries of national accumulation.

Summarizing Amin's viewpoint, it seems that he considers the class struggle to be global, which means that the class struggle will necessarily extend to the peripheral areas, where the revolutionary centre will be established. In contrast to this, capital is not at all necessarily international, as there exists a limitation on the continued expansion of Centre capital in the 'resistance by the producers of surplus value'. Because of the 'social democratic' solution to the conflict between capital and wage labour, such a resistance is considered an illusion. Likewise, according to Amin, the growing concentration and centralization of capital is a result of the class struggle, which means that the conditions of accumulation and movements in the rate of profit as a result of the competition between capitals are without any importance. In conclusion, he views the present crisis as a crisis of imperialism rather than of capitalism.[10] Although it is Amin's wish to view the development of capitalism in its totality, i.e. to analyse the economic categories as well as the political factors in their dialectical interrelationship, the result is obviously an overestimation of the political factors.

Amin's observation of the 'blocked accumulation' situation in the peripheral countries at the end of the 1960s might be correct for that period, but is not necessarily a proof or an expression of a *steady* state of affairs. The subsumption and dependency aspect is — as Olivier says[11] — viewed by Marx as a transitional period, in which the tendency of capitalism to subsume earlier modes of production and dissolve them is the dominant characteristic.

In one of his most recent articles,[12] Amin tries to tackle the latest developments in the international capitalist situation, not least the Third World demand for a New International Economic Order, in the light of his basic theoretical model. Amin asks the question whether the peripheral capitalist economies could 'become "self-reliant" without withdrawing from the world system of exchange of commodities, technologies, and capital? Could they do it by forcing the world system to readjust, by imposing an equal, and no longer unequal, division of labour? Could they attain this goal by means which define the programme of the new international economic order?' As Amin himself recalls, his basic theoretical model of peripheral capitalism excludes the possibility of a mature, autonomous capitalism in the Periphery. It asserts that a socialist break with this system is here 'objectively necessary'.

Therefore, the issue at stake is, of course, whether his model would still be valid, should the new international economic order come about.[13]

Having analysed and described the different phases of imperialist development, Amin argues that a new phase has now been reached, in which a certain industrialization is taking place:

> Experience shows that participation of *private* or *public local capital* — however subservient — in the process of import-substitution industrialization is quite common. It also shows . . . that . . . it [is] possible to create a sector producing capital goods. The latter is frequently brought into being by the state. But the development of basic industry and a public sector does not in any way mean that the system is evolving towards a mature self-reliant form, since the capital-goods sector is here used, not for the development of mass consumption but to serve the growth of export and luxury-goods production. So this . . . phase of imperialism is by no means a 'stage' towards the constitution of a self-reliant economy.[14] (Our italics.)

In other words, Amin now recognizes — contrary to his earlier writings — that a certain process of industrialization possibly based on local private or public capital is under way. But this development is not truly 'self-reliant', or truly capitalist either in the sense known from the classical period of capitalism in Western Europe or in the sense of 'mature capitalist formations similar to those of the developed centres'.[15] As Olivier has noted, we see that Amin is now giving examples of broader industrialization patterns in the Periphery although his original model only included the import-substitution industrialization strategy, which could not contribute to a break with the 'blocked development' situation. Now the question for Amin is whether these new trends are to be considered as a break away from blocked development, and whether they can lead to the 'mature self-reliant form' of capitalism familiar in the present 'developed capitalist economies [which] are indeed self-reliant, although not economically self-sufficient'.[16] Amin is not able to answer this in the affirmative, because of the lack of links between a *locally* controlled capital-goods sector and the development of mass consumption goods. When trying to answer the question as to whether mature capitalism is developing in some of the peripheral countries, it does not seem to us the most essential aspect to determine whether or not a linkage exists between Amin's two sectors, but rather to determine whether *capital accumulation* is taking place with an adequate material basis and locally controlled at least to the extent where further accumulation is made possible (i.e. extended reproduction). Amin consistently emphasizes the importance of *local* control of economic branches and sectors, and regards the extrovert nature of the peripheral countries (their export orientation and stress on attracting foreign investment) as the *primary* contradiction to be solved, should capitalist formations appear in the Periphery. Of course, the contradictions between national and foreign capitals are important in many specific situations, but it is questionable whether they are so important for the establishment of *mature capitalism* as such in the Periphery. Or in other words, is the nationality of an investor truly a determining factor? Is it not to be expected that an investor will act according to capitalist premises regardless of nationality? As expressed in the editorial of a journal on capitalism in Africa:

> Clearly it is the *consequences* of capital's investment that have to be studied by those who oppose capital, rather than the legalities of ownership. And clearly, too, these consequences are not governed by the presence or absence of patriotic sentiment, but rather by the laws of accumulation to which capital itself is bound, and which drive capitalists to compete.[17]

Among these consequences might be the establishment of a permanent process of capital accumulation, an extended reproduction of capital.

Amin occupies a central position in the Dependency School of thought, although this school contains a great variety of opinions, not least when one includes the Latin American scholars, who have been forced to modify their analyses in the light of recent examples of industrialization within their region. Like Amin, many of the dependency theorists have provided us with useful and important empirical information on the Periphery, but their analyses have generally only to a limited extent included an analysis of the developed capitalist countries. Development in the Periphery is, therefore, not seen as linked to the capital movements of the Centre, i.e. the conditions of capital accumulation in the Centre. The consequence of these theoretical shortcomings has been that the analysis has seldom been able to grasp sufficiently the essential *dynamic* elements of the system as a whole.

Increasingly, the shortcomings of the dependency theory are being debated in various theoretical and empirical contexts.[18] Recently, the development prospects of the Kenyan economy have given rise to an intense debate[19] presenting the various empirical arguments believed to support the conflicting views as to whether or not a national bourgeoisie is emerging and the role of the state in this process. Ironically, the empirical data presented seems capable of supporting both views, leaving the debate to be run at a conceptual level with much more generalized implications.

The theoretical attack in the Kenyan debate has to do with the tautological nature of the argument about the impossibility of 'real' capitalist development in the Periphery — that 'self-centred' and autonomous development is a kind of 'ideal type' of capitalist development applicable only to Western capitalist development.

This specific historical process in the West is generalized and idealized, when 'normal', or 'true' and 'self-centred' capitalist development is made uniquely specific to Western experience. This process of turning the variety of Western historical experiences into an ideal type model disregards the fact that capitalism grew up in the various countries in a variety of ways, under different historical settings, and with a varying degree of world market integration. To the extent that development in the peripheral economies does not correspond to this model, countries are judged to lack an 'autonomous capacity' and are hence 'dependent'.[20]

Another facet of dependency theory also brought out in the Kenyan debate is the lack of autonomy awarded local class forces and the peripheral state. The total subsumption of local forces in an external dynamic also excludes the possibility of the state acting fairly autonomously, intervening in the economy and trying to gear growth towards the creation of national productive and reproductive structures.

Theories of the Internationalization of Capital

The point of departure for theories of the internationalization of capital is to analyse at a very abstract level capital's tendency ever to broaden its sphere of operations, nationally as well as internationally, as a consequence of the basic laws of motion inherited in the process of capital accumulation.

Originally, this analytical point of departure dates back to the so-called classical theories of imperialism, formulated in the first quarter of the century. International economic developments since World War II — the increased quantities of foreign investment, changes in the export pattern of commodities and finance capital, cyclical developments in the process of capital accumulation (which for example has manifested itself in the recent economic crisis) — have resulted in this approach once more gaining momentum.

In particular, the changing economic and political relations between the West European countries and the U.S.A. in the post-war period has been discussed in terms of this analysis. So, too, with the analysis of the nation state and its changing role as a consequence of capital increasingly transcending national barriers. The relative decline in the economic importance of the U.S.A. compared to Western Europe and Japan since the end of the 1960s, the creation of the E.E.C. as a possible counterbalancing measure to U.S. domination, and the extraordinarily fast reconstruction of the West German economy, are all areas which have prompted efforts to restate the Marxist theory of accumulation.

Although these topics have a very concrete nature, a great number of authors have not succeeded in transcending convincingly a very abstract analysis, often devoting the major part of their work to the discussion of how to reread Marx and understand his scientific method when applied to capital's international movements.

The generally abstract nature of the analysis, its focus on the reasons for increases or decreases in productivity among the leading Western nations in the context of accumulation theory, and its exponents' partiality for analysing mainly economic factors, are among the aspects clearly limiting the scope and immediate relevance of these studies by themselves and when considering the peripheral countries.

Take, for example, the writings of Klaus Busch.[21] Having thoroughly analysed the economic relations between the European countries and the U.S.A. and the effect and importance of the E.E.C., he also tries to place the peripheral countries within his theoretical framework. According to him, the present phase in the development of capitalism is characterized by the replacement of commodity exports by direct investments as the determining relationship. This is especially the case in relationships between the industrialized countries, particularly since World War II.[22] His central thesis is that the laws that have created the international sphere of circulation, in which single or national capitals realize commodity capital, are also the laws governing the present tendency towards the internationalization of the production of surplus value in the form of productive foreign investments.[23]

Generally, the centralization of capital takes place in the same way internationally as within the nation state, where, according to Busch, it takes the form of stronger capitals ousting weaker ones. However, there are also differences between the way the centralization process takes place nationally and internationally, and these differences become crucial for Busch's theory.

His main argument in this respect is that the existence of nation states protects those countries which have the lowest labour productivity through the 'foreign exchange rate mechanism'.[24] For Busch the foreign exchange rate expresses the average level of productivity in a given country. From this perspective Busch presents three main points of view concerning the driving forces behind U.S. investments in Western Europe, and more generally, the mechanisms which make the industrialized countries invest in each other.

First of all, he stresses that for branches of industry with a productivity above the average within the nation state in question, there is a positive incentive to invest in other countries in order to stabilize and to extend supra-profits by letting local production replace commodity exports. In other words, there is an incentive to establish production geared towards the local market in the host country.

Secondly, Busch argues that, for branches with productivity below the average, the impulse to invest in other countries is the fear of being ousted in the home market. In this case, the foreign investments are geared towards production for the old home market or possibly new foreign markets, in which it is possible to compete as a result of the new conditions of production.

Thirdly, Busch argues that there is a general tendency towards centralization in order to strengthen one's own position in the export markets by buying up other firms and thereby taking over already existing market shares and established sales outlets.

In relation to the problem analysed in this book, it is of crucial importance to note that Busch makes a sharp division between the forces which generate direct investments by one Centre country in another, and the forces which lead firms in the Centre countries to invest in the Periphery. The latter is primarily caused by the magnitude of foreign investments in extractive industries in the Periphery, and by the protectionist policy vis-à-vis the world market pursued by the peripheral state, which forces the foreign enterprises to adhere to the import-substitution policy of the developing country in order to keep their share of the market.

In particular, the import-substitution policy of the peripheral countries seems to be the crucial factor in explaining the greater proportion of foreign direct investment which is now geared towards the Periphery. According to Busch, capital exports to the Periphery would be minimal were it not for this import-substitution policy.

The explanation offered by Busch seems, however, unsatisfactory, considering that we are now seeing the establishment of more profound patterns of industrialization in the Periphery, not only with labour-intensive and structurally weak industries being located in low-wage countries but also capital-intensive and export-directed industries. Busch omits the dimension of cheapening the cost of production by reducing the value of variable and constant capital, which has been the historical role of the Periphery within the Centre's reproduction process. This implies that Busch does not fully use the concepts that are inherited from his own theoretical frame of reference, and he thereby to some extent reduces explanations to factors grounded outside his own theory.

This aspect of cheapening the cost of production in the Centre by incorporating the Periphery in the Centre's reproduction process has, however, been an important element for other theorists.[25] In assessing the relative importance of the Periphery's raw materials, the so-called oil crisis has proved that a temporary blockage of the supply of raw materials at relatively predictable prices can strengthen symptoms of crisis inherent in the capitalist economy. This particularly affects Western Europe, which is heavily dependent on external raw materials for its industrial processes. This need for strategically important raw materials, even the need for tropical agricultural products and raw materials, is judged by Goralczyk[26] an important factor behind the internationalization of capital.

As we have seen, Busch is not fully consistent with his own theoretical point of departure (accumulation theory) since he takes as the most important explanatory element for capital exports external factors such as the peripheral state's import-substitution policy. The same criticism can be applied to the analysis of Schoeller.[27] Schoeller accepts the relatively blocked situation of productive forces in the Periphery and seeks explanations which can confirm this view, rather than factors which might contribute to the opposite situation. The explanatory power of the theory of internationalization of capital is therefore not at present developed to an extent which would allow us to understand the increasingly more complex situation in the Periphery.

Goralzcyk seems to be most useful within the tradition of the theory of the internationalization of capital. Besides the increased level of commodity exchange at an international level, Goralzcyk emphasizes the creation of adequate conditions of production in the Periphery as an important element. Among the factors contributing to capital exports to the Periphery he mentions: a well-developed physical infrastructure, a cheap but relatively well-educated labour force, an efficient and coherent functional linkage between state and capital, and a market structure allowing for local as well as international marketing of the products. Where these conditions are met, new patterns of industrialization of a more profound nature can take place in the Periphery.

Goralzcyk is, however, quite sceptical as to whether there exists in practice the possibility of a nationally based capital accumulation process in the Periphery. It is our argument, however, that the preconditions required by Goralzcyk as necessary for a local accumulation of capital are in *certain* countries established, mainly due to the intervention of the state. In other words, the time which has passed since Goralzcyk made his studies has shown more and more examples of peripheral state intervention creating the complex of factors which make up a favourable investment climate. Theoretically speaking, this implies that the internationalization of capital is a useful point of departure when supplemented with a theory of the peripheral state.

That Goralzcyk can be interpreted as being in accordance with this view is illustrated by the fact that he does not find the much-discussed (primarily by the Dependency School) rupture with the world market a realistic strategy. Instead, he stresses that it is essential to base a development strategy on a broad industrialization process, primarily geared towards the local market but also towards the already developed market economies. By following this approach he sees a possibility for peripheral social formations to be integrated in an adequate way into the international division of labour — although he emphasizes that this is probably only possible for a relatively small number of countries in the Periphery.

In a similar attempt to analyse the present material changes in the world economy, Fröbel, Heinrichs and Kreye[28] argue that capital has from its inception been global in character, and that centres of valorization and accumulation therefore exist in places around the world wherever opportunities for increased valorization at a particular point in time are the best possible. Their methodological point of departure is a study of the history of the world market, which leads them to the conclusion that only in the 1960s has a world market for labour and places of production been created which includes both the industrialized countries and the developing countries. This implies that it is only in the present period of the history of capitalism that it has become profitable to have production locations for particular industrial branches in the developing countries, and consequently possible for products originating there to compete on the world market.

As the important features constituting the new world market, Fröbel *et al.* list the following factors: the presence of a vast amount of manpower, a fragmentation of the industrial production process, which implies that elements of production can take place anywhere using unskilled labour, and the development of transport technology and communications, which reduces costs and allows for the use of the whole world as such as a sphere of production. They see the creation of the necessary conditions for new places of production as the key factor which leads capital to expand in the Periphery.

One consequence of this point is that they attribute only minor importance to changes in conditions of production in the Centre countries themselves. They are thus in opposition to Busch's main argument that the contemporary internationalization of capital is caused by differences in productivity between different national capitals in the Centre.

In contrast to this, they argue that a fall in the rate of profit in the Centre countries has to be rejected as the main cause for the internationalization of capital, and hence a new international division of labour. Rather it is quite simply a question of whether production can be pursued at a profitable level, that is at a level allowing for the accumulation of capital, regardless of the location of production. And the conditions described above make the Periphery, according to them, a suitable location of capitalist production.

They very clearly illustrate their main proposition with a historical parallel. They point to the fact that the European economic crisis in the 17th Century only marked the decline of Central and Southern Europe as the centre for accumulation and valorization and signified the rise of the Netherlands and primarily the United Kingdom as new centres. Similarly, it is possible today to observe indications of a new international division of labour, which takes its point of departure in the current phase of stagnation in valorization in the Centre and at the same time a relative and absolute increase in valorization and accumulation in the Periphery.

In other words, the shift in the centre of gravity from the traditional centres of accumulation to the traditional peripheries of accumulation through increasing investments, export-oriented industrialization, and growing utilization of the labour force there, is achieving increasing importance in a crisis which threatens the existence of even globally-operating capital, since it is precisely this capital which in these moves organizes itself in accordance with the changed conditions for valorization and accumulation. To use an expression from Fröbel *et al.*'s book: this process does not only imply but also presupposes that certain capitals — and in a figurative sense — even some countries will thereby be left behind 'on the battlefield'.[29]

In their empirical analysis Fröbel *et al.* give special emphasis to the creation of industrial free zones in the Periphery, which gained momentum in the 1960s, as well as the need for branches like the textile industry to move part of their production from the Centre countries to the industrial free zones in the Periphery as a result of the existence of such zones and the low wages of the readily available labour force. They therefore concentrate their analysis on industrial production in the Periphery geared towards exports and do not discuss thoroughly the relative importance of import-substitution or other kinds of industrial production geared towards the local market in the Periphery.

The strength of Fröbel *et al.*'s analysis is that they have studied a recent and concrete phenomenon in international economy: the industrial free zones. However, it seems that they exaggerate the importance of this phenomenon in two ways. First of all, they point to the existence in 1975 of 79 free zones and 39 under construction with a total labour force in the existing zones of 725,000, which is a relatively low figure compared to the total number of workers employed in the industrial sector in the Periphery. Secondly, they limit their analysis to export-oriented production and thereby exaggerate the importance of this, which has to be seen in relation to other kinds of industrial patterns in the developing countries.

In spite of the efforts of Busch, Schoeller, Goralzcyk, and Fröbel, Heinrichs and Kreye, it must be said that the theories of the internationalization of capital so far have not been able to place the peripheral countries satisfactorily within a global encompassing theory of the accumulation of capital. The great variety of development conditions and prospects in the Periphery obviously causes some problems with regard to avoiding a more or less mechanical global adaptation of capital's tendency ever to broaden its sphere of operations, ever to subsume new geographical areas and regions. At the same time, attempts to examine the changing conditions of capital accumulation in the Centre with the intention of relating them to development conditions of the Periphery have only been of a preliminary nature.

On this question, the present study implicitly suggests an approach that adds to and is more holistic than the theorizing mentioned. The analysis made so far has shown how the pattern of the internationalization of West European capital has been influenced by, on the one hand, the creation of the E.E.C. and the economic relations with the U.S.A., and, on the other hand, the impact of the present economic crisis. We have argued that there has been a marked tendency towards an increase in direct investments in various forms from the Centre to the Periphery during this crisis. And the importance of the intervention of the French state for the centralization of French capital has been shown, giving direction to the subsequent internationalization. The present study has led to the conclusion that the economic crisis in Western Europe, since the oil price rises following 1973, has implied new forms of internationalization of capital. From Europe, capital is now directed to a greater extent towards the peripheral countries in order to find *new* areas of investment and *new* markets. The consequence of this process is an increased differentiation among the countries in the Periphery. For the first time, a few countries are in the process of establishing the basis for national capital accumulation within a framework of capitalist development, while other countries seem to be remaining in the situation characterized by the theorists of the Dependency School as 'blocked development'. Therefore, what distinguishes our study from that of the Marxist theorists above is that we have reached the conclusion that, in the present changing historical conditions, dynamic possibilities exist for capital accumulation in the Western countries, particularly since the economic crisis following 1973, *as well as* in parts of the Periphery.

The conditions for capital accumulation in the Centre, as reflected in changes in the process of the internationalization of capital, together with relatively autonomous forces in the Periphery like the state, are creating new patterns of national accumulation of capital within a capitalist development process also in parts of the Periphery. At the theoretical level, this implies that the factors generating processes of the internationalization of capital are the primary moving force behind the international structuring of the capitalist system, not ignoring, however, the influencing and modifying of this by relatively autonomous factors such as the peripheral state.

Consequently, it is our opinion that the theory of the internationalization of capital represents a more useful theoretical approach than dependency theory, when studying the present changing international relations. Also it gives a better understanding of the need for increased state intervention in the Centre in relation to the actual development in patterns of accumulation. The tendencies which are explicitly embodied in the theory of the internationalization of capital, however, only manifest themselves *in the Periphery* to the extent that barriers to capital can be removed. It is the peripheral state, which in terms of its potential to actualize these tendencies and create attractive conditions for capital, that becomes the vital supplementary concept to be included in the theoretical framework.

Theories of the Peripheral State

As mentioned by Olle and Schoeller,[30] the development of capitalism in Western Europe was conditioned by the existence of an external market as well as by a protectionist and actively intervening state apparatus. The accumulation of money capital and the liberation of labour power from its feudal position were processes which both were necessary for capitalist development *and* presupposed a world market in its embryonic form.

The foreign adventures of merchant capital secured as much gold and other precious metals as possible, while later on the colonial areas also became markets for European industrial products. The discovery and exploitation of external markets was a process which had to be supported by a strong state, providing the military apparatus when necessary, extending credit facilities and guarantees for the private transactions of merchant capital, developing the means of circulation (money equivalents), etc.

With the consolidation of a national bourgeoisie taking on its natural role as the developer of capitalism — the destruction of feudal relations of production, the accumulation of capital, and the creation of the bourgeois state — a change took place in the role of the state. From being mainly protectionist, the state became more liberal in its policies towards both the national and international exchange of commodities.

The peripheral countries have right from the start been part and parcel of the Centre's development process. These countries have delivered raw materials for the industries of Western Europe and agricultural products to cheapen the reproduction costs of the labour force. This fact naturally poses the problem of the peripheral state differently. Historically as well as nowadays, the material basis for a national accumulation of capital in the peripheral countries has been external — the peripheral countries have been part of the reproduction process of the Centre. This has prevented the rise of a national bourgeoisie in the Periphery to take on its natural function as developer of capitalism. In this situation, the only instrument capable of creating a material basis for a national accumulation of capital seems to be the peripheral state.

When discussing the role of the peripheral state in furthering capitalist development, it is important to pose the question: which are the dominant classes in control of the state and why do their interests manifest themselves in an active interventionist state? In answering this question, it must be stressed that the dominant classes controlling the state will vary from country to country dependent on the particular historical circumstances. But different as they may be, they all have a class interest in widening their economic base in the economy by enlarging the activities of the state. At the same time it is often in their interest to limit the influence of foreign capital, whilst simultaneously working with foreign capital and international institutions. Hence it becomes a necessity for the dominant classes, even while opening up to foreign capital, to try to limit its influence and strengthen the national economic potential by means of the peripheral state.

In other words, the need for an active state interventionist policy in Third World countries manifests itself much more clearly and quite differently than was the case of the state in the transitional period towards capitalism in Western Europe. Similarly, the contradictions arising from the effects of the external economic dominance over the Periphery's socio-economic structure also poses the problem differently and much more markedly for the peripheral state.

The theoretical debate on the role of the peripheral state is mainly formulated within the context of the situation in post-colonial societies. The state apparatus in colonial times had as its main task the suppression of the indigenous classes. With formal decolonization, this state apparatus was inherited relatively unchanged initially, in spite of the fact that the new situation required new roles by the state. This continuation of some of the functions of the colonial state has led to the conclusion that the post-colonial state is 'overdeveloped'. Alavi has most clearly expressed this view:

> It might be said that the 'superstructure' in the colony is therefore 'overdeveloped' in relation to the structure of the colony, for its basis lies in the metropolitan structure itself, from which it is later separated at the time of independence . . . . The post-colonial society inherits that overdeveloped apparatus of the state and its institutionalized practices through which the operations of indigenous social classes are regulated and controlled.[31]

The fact that Alavi's thesis has been developed on the basis of material from the Indian Subcontinent may limit its general applicability. But apart from this, the theory has certain obvious shortcomings. The most serious one is that the so-called 'extra-societal' factors[32] and their influence on the role and function of the peripheral state are taken as an explicit theoretical point of departure, but are never specified in any detail. Rather, it is a general frame of reference which ensures that the 'global accumulation of capital' is not entirely lost to sight.

The debate on the 'overdeveloped state' has found some support with regard to East Africa.[33] The idea of the overdeveloped state has, however, been severely criticized. Colin Leys[34] considers it to be an empty category and argues against it from a theoretical as well as an empirical angle. With direct reference to Alavi, Leys questions the whole plausibility of his argument that the inherited state apparatus is larger and more coercive than would have been the case if there had not been a colonial state, for it would still be necessary to suppress and 'subordinate all the domestic classes in the pre-colonial formation'. This, together with the existence of a 'powerful bureau-cratic-military apparatus', makes Alavi believe — according to Leys — that the overdeveloped state is 'an accepted fact which his class analysis of its historical origins could then explain'.[35] Leys's theoretical argument against the concept of the overdeveloped state is directed towards this superficial and misleading approach where the descriptive dimensions and activity of the state are the point of departure for the construction of any theory:

> It is really that this whole way of approaching the question of the significance of the state, i.e. of starting out from its structure and scope, whether inherited from an earlier situation or not, is a mistake. In order to understand the significance for any state of the class strug-gle, we must start out from the class struggle, not the state. The idea of the 'overdeveloped state' functions, in both Alavi's and Saul's accounts, as an apparent reason for reversing the proper order of procedure . . . [36]

Leys also questions the idea of the overdeveloped state for empirical reasons. He says that 'the more of the total volume of surplus value which the State directly appropriates, the more it is likely to be immediately invol-ved in the class struggle'.[37] States in peripheral countries are, however, comparatively small with regard to population, the size of the economy, the surplus extracted, and the central government budget as a percentage of national income, etc. The central point to make, according to Leys, is never-theless that:

> The state is equally *important* in all class societies; it is no more 'cen-tral' in Tanzania than in Britain or the U.S.A. (or the U.S.S.R.). It may be more 'embracing' (i.e. may own more productive forces or intervene more directly in various areas in social life) in some societies than others, but in this respect it is typically less 'central' ('extensive' would be a better word here) in most post-colonial societies than in most advanced societies.[38]

The whole question of continuity which is implicit in Alavi's thesis is rightly criticized by Leys. If the bureaucracy of the peripheral state is extensive, then this is probably more a result of post-colonial expansion rather than a simple question of 'inheritance'. But this whole question of post-colonial expansion or, in other words, the particularly wide range of state functions which the peripheral state has to undertake because of the historical past as well as its contemporary position within the global capitalist reproduction process, is an aspect which Leys ignores in writing off the 'centrality' of the state. As Steven Langdon puts it — inspired by John Saul's article — the peripheral state has a 'further function in periphery economies, that of managing the meshing of capitalist and pre-capitalist modes of production. And that further function makes the colonial and post-colonial state more central in the direct process of surplus appropriation and capital accumulation than in advanced capitalist economies'.[39] But 'overdeveloped' is still rightly considered an empty category.

Although the form and function of the peripheral state in Alavi's analysis is considered to be primarily determined by the dominant structural relations in the capitalist world system, these 'extra-societal' factors are, as mentioned above, not specified in any satisfactory way. Nor does he systematically include the economic processes within the peripheral social formation, whether colonial or post-colonial. Although recognizing international as well as national economic processes as necessary preconditions for the complete understanding of the nature of the peripheral state, the result is a predominantly politicalistic analysis. Material explanations, and explanations which in the real sense of the word are total or holistic explanations, will necessarily have to include a description of the importance of world market integration for the peripheral nation (i.e. aspects of the internationalization of capital) as well as the delimitation of the peripheral state as an actively *economic* intervening factor, relatively autonomous, but in the last instance hemmed in by international capital. Within this materialist theoretical framework, the theory of the peripheral state becomes complete when the state's class relations and alliances are included in a dialectical way, i.e. as an extension of tendencies already present in the economic factors *and* as factors possibly transcending the economic base.

This is exactly the point of departure for W. Ziemann and M. Lanzendörfer.[40] These authors look at how the peripheral state is not merely relatively autonomous in the political sphere, but also how the internally available economic surplus is produced and appropriated by the state. Active state intervention in the national economy in peripheral societies is seen as 'structurally rooted in the historical disruption of the economic structure of peripheral society, i.e. the partially in deficit, and relatively stagnant expanded reproduction'.[41] The binding to the world market, historically as well as contemporarily, and the consequent particular socio-economic structures in the Periphery makes it a *sine qua non* for the state to try to maximize the surplus appropriation in whatever way it can. Whether this surplus is directed to productive purposes rather than being unproductively consumed by the state apparatus (the administrators, politicians and bureaucrats) is quite another question.

The peripheral societies' situation (in transition from precapitalist social formations to capitalism), therefore, poses particular problems for the state. The state is in many ways placed in a contradictory situation. One aspect of this is that, on the one hand in its effort to further a broader industrialization process, the state will necessarily have to break down the precapitalist relations of production. On the other hand, in order to avoid a process of proletarianization out of proportion with the more limited process of industrialization, the state has to preserve the precapitalist formations in which the farmers and also industrial workers often find their means of reproduction (and social security). This contradictory situation can be summarized in the dissolution/conservation tendency and is the basis for theories on the articulation of modes of production.[42]

Another aspect of the difficult position of the peripheral state is its primary dependence on world market conditions. There then arises the question of whether the state is pursuing a policy which is mainly to the benefit of the international bourgeoisie (i.e. acting as an instrument for the local comprador bourgeoisie), or whether, on the other hand, while being a part of the larger world economic system, it is nevertheless trying to act as a national state in pursuing a policy benefiting its own classes or fractions of classes. Most often this situation is seen as antagonistic, i.e. the state is acting on behalf of the international bourgeoisie to the exclusion of any possibility of acting as a national state at the same time. Ziemann and Lanzendörfer summarize the economic functions of the peripheral state as follows:

(1)   Linking the world market with the national economy by breaking down — as far as it is possible while maintaining the internal reproduction of the society — the political frontiers between the world market and the national economy (import-export policy, import of technology, foreign investment, etc.).

(2)   Securing the existence and expansion of the world market in the national economic area, directed to the reproduction of both internationally operating capital and national capital oriented to the world market.

(3)   Securing internal economic reproduction which is not automatically guaranteed through the economic process. This is directed, for instance, to the extended reproduction of national capital based on the home market (promotion of industry, infrastructure, etc.), the reproduction of the rural and industrial labour force, as well as of the independent and non-independent middle strata (wages policy, policy on food prices, etc.).

(4)   Securing structural heterogeneity, as a specific condition both for world-market and national reproduction, against the process of disintegration in the non-capitalist area (through partial agrarian reform, pricing policy, etc.) and in the backward capitalist areas of the national economy (subsidies, price and wage policies).[43]

From these mainly economic functions of the peripheral state, Ziemann and Lanzendörfer continue to discuss the political functions of the state — but still from the point of view of world market integration:

> The heterogeneous, world-market-dependent reproduction process produces and reproduces a fragmented and unstable class structure and a relative social weakness of classes, fractions of classes and groupings in the nation. The consequence is that interests are realized and accommodated less and less within the social process and are mediated more and more by the state. Thus the state becomes the actual forum of class struggle and class relations. This is manifested in a process of increasing concentration of political power in the state apparatus.[44]

Of particular importance in this respect is the state bureaucracy. To maintain its privileges, it has to extract surplus, most often from the agricultural sector or through other ways of raising revenue (taxes and import/export duties, etc.). This means that it is also in the bureaucracy's interest to find profitable investment opportunities for national and international capital while seeking other measures for the increase of production in other sectors. At the same time, however, the prevailing structure of society has to be maintained; social unrest and upheavals could threaten the powerful position of the bureaucracy. This implies both repression and active economic intervention by the state in co-operation with the powerful classes or fractions of classes. It is the opinion of Ziemann and Lanzendörfer that the state bureaucracy is in constant battle with other classes or fractions over the distribution of the (limited) state income. The bureaucracy's allies in this process are the economically most influential classes, which happen to be those oriented towards the world market.

It seems that the analysis of Ziemann and Lanzendörfer has taken a great step forward towards a more holistic conception of the peripheral state, in which economic and political factors are combined, and in which international as well as national economic conditions are integrated. From this, more detailed and historically concrete analyses of peripheral social formations can be made.

In just one aspect, however, their analysis does not seem to depart very far from the position of Dependency theory. In their concluding chapter — when discussing the contradictions of capitalist reproduction in the Periphery — they only see an either/or solution to these contradictions: 'The resultant impulses to development tend towards an expansion of capitalist production relations, without the non-capitalist production relations being suppressed (growth without development, or dynamic stagnation), or towards a separate development of the capitalist and non-capitalist sectors with a deepening of the economic crisis (improvement growth).'[45] A tendency towards transcending blocked development — partly the result of the new trends in the international division of labour — is therefore excluded from their analysis, which is obviously a shortcoming vis-à-vis the theoretical approach we have been advancing of the internationalization of capital.

The work of Olle and Schoeller[46] sticks much more to this theoretical framework. They see the fundamental problem as being one of achieving industrial development in the Periphery in the face of competition from products on the world market produced under conditions of superior reproduction costs. The fact that the peripheral countries right from the start, i.e. right from their first linking together with the colonial powers, were 'a direct and integral component of the total social process of reproduction in the industrial nations . . . allows us to identify the most important functions of the state: the creation of conditions which will permit *accumulation* and *extended reproduction.*'[47]

Since the peripheral nations are inevitably included in the reproduction process of the industrialized capitalist countries (the Third World countries deliver raw materials necessary for the continued accumulation of the industrial nations as well as agricultural products for the reproduction of their labour force), their socio-economic structures are externally directed and not internally integrated. In fact, the Third World countries are missing a reproductive sector themselves. Lacking this reproductive sector of their own, these countries have to import this from the outside in the form of means of production. In order to increase their opportunities to import means of production on an increased scale — and thereby the possibility of an increase also in the productivity of labour — the peripheral countries have to raise their export earnings, by an increased productivity in the agricultural and mining sectors. The import purchasing power of the peripheral countries is, therefore, closely bound to the success of the state in raising (exportable) national output.

This productivity increase in agriculture most often takes place through importing technology and machinery, high-yielding varieties of seed, pesticides, etc. The international aid organizations often finance package programmes intended for this purpose; and the local processing of raw materials is financed through foreign direct investment, or combinations of investment such as state/foreign or state/private-national capitals.

The lack of an internal reproductive sector is also the reason behind the need for foreign investment if a capitalist industrialization strategy is to succeed. Only by creating an investment climate favourable for international capital can the peripheral state get industries which, although geared towards the world market, could contribute to the beginnings of an interlinking of the different economic branches domestically. The precondition for the establishment of attractive investment conditions is, however, repressive measures by the state, whereby the trade unions are suppressed and the wages kept down to a level acceptable to the foreign investor. Therefore — apart from the creation of the necessary infrastructure, participation in key industries, organization of the capital market, financial support for locally developed technological innovations — the *primary* function of the peripheral state is to increase the productivity of labour, while at the same time controlling wage rises.

157

In conclusion, our main conception of the peripheral state is as an instrument which, in the absence of a national bourgeoisie, can actively intervene in the economy and establish capitalist relations of production. The state has, of course, to be seen also in relation to the underlying class structures in the peripheral country in question. But different as the dominant classes may be in various countries, they all have – to repeat – a class interest in widening their economic base in the economy by enlarging the activities of the state, and limiting the influence of foreign capital, even while working with it in certain contexts. In our case study of the Ivory Coast, it has clearly been demonstrated that the heavy involvement in the national economy of foreign capital has not prevented the dominant classes from limiting its influence and strengthening the national economic potential by means of the peripheral state.

Towards a Changing Theoretical Paradigm

In our empirical analysis of the socio-economic development of the Ivory Coast, we have argued that, by virtue of (and not in spite of) its world market integration, the Ivory Coast seems to have the potential for breaking with the 'blocked accumulation of capital' situation. In the previous sections of this chapter we have tried, mainly on theoretical grounds, to substantiate this view by discussing the main exponents of the Dependency School and of the very different theories on the internationalization of capital and the peripheral state.[48]

It is, of course, not possible to generalize from the experience of the Ivory Coast without reservations. Compared to most other countries in the Third World, the Ivory Coast is in a unique position with respect to the general shortage of manpower. The very favourable climatic conditions for the development of tropical agriculture are another obvious advantage. These conditions have supplemented by a development policy which favours the use of technologically developed inputs in agriculture (the lack of manpower has led naturally to a policy of mechanization), and increase in productivity and the widespread diversification of products have contributed to the linking of agriculture with industrial development.

The special conditions under which this development has taken place in the Ivory Coast are, however, not so very unique. Other countries have also had some success in pursuing a capitalist-oriented development policy, which has also resulted in a much broader industrialization pattern than has up till now been recognized in the development literature inspired by the Dependency School. It is our contention that the changing historical conditions for capital accumulation in the Centre have led to a situation in some of the peripheral social formations, where more mature capitalist relations of production are rooting themselves. The consequence for the Periphery is a growing internal heterogeneity in which a few countries with conditions particularly attractive to capital – for example mineral resources or a state-initiated favourable investment climate — constitute the *nouveau riches* of this unequal development of capitalism, while other countries have in every way a stagnant economy with only limited hope for overcoming their completely constricted situation.

In West Africa, we can distinguish three broad categories of countries. At the top we have countries (like the Ivory Coast and Nigeria), with impressive growth rates and development potentials resulting from large inflows of foreign capital, establishing the material preconditions for a capital accumulation process which could transcend their blocked development. Secondly, we find countries (for example, Senegal) which are trying to attract foreign capital by means of free production zones, but where development prospects — so far at least — do not seem to show obvious tendencies towards a break away from the blocked situation. And lastly, there are the countries — most often in the Sahel area — which act as huge labour reserves for the richer and wealthier coastal nations, and where blocked development as characterized by Amin seems obviously still to prevail.

If our analysis is correct, it has severe repercussions on the concepts used within development theory. The changes in the international division of labour, with the consequent establishment of a profound capitalist development in some countries of the Periphery, suggest that this new situation has to be understood within the framework of capitalism's global reproduction. The role of the Periphery, in the context of this theory of the internationalization of capital, cannot primarily be analysed with concepts like dependency, underdevelopment, or blocked development. Rather, capitalism's basic tendency to unequal development must be stressed, the consequences of which are both an equalization process (where conditions of production such as technological development, wage levels, profit, etc. equalize) and a differentiation process, in the Centre as well as in the Periphery. Capitalism's global expansion thereby causes the establishment of an international reproductive hierarchy, in which tendencies towards equalization are constantly succeeded by new differentiation patterns, and in which these basic conceptions express themselves at the regional, national and international level.

The basic dynamic in this international reproductive hierarchy, in which the Centre and the Periphery are a single entity, is the historically concrete accumulation and crisis process, which supports or impedes capitalism's expansionist tendencies. The consequence of this is that not only is the equalization tendency taking root in the Periphery, but the differentiation process is also creating new inequalities within the Centre countries (and, of course, also among the peripheral countries), creating 'peripheral' structures within specific regions of particular Centre countries.

The bourgeoisie and/or the peripheral state are looked on in the dependency literature primarily as serving international capital (comprador bourgeoisie), and playing an unimportant part in furthering a peripheral accumulation process. The restructuring of the international division of labour, however, implies a strengthening of the state's economic, social and political functions, not only in the Centre but even more in the Periphery.

159

The peripheral state is the instrument capable of providing the necessary infrastructure, extracting an economic surplus, offering investment opportunities, etc. — factors which all contribute to the actualization of the tendencies in the internationalization of capital. While the internationalization of capital is closely linked to the development of the global accumulation process (and the crises inherent in it), it may only realize itself in the creation of peripheral capitalist structures when the specific circumstances within the peripheral socio-economic setting are sufficiently attractive.

It is in the theory of the internationalization of capital, therefore, that we find the conditions in the Centre's accumulation process which contribute to capital's efforts to seek new investment opportunities (the necessity for capital ever to broaden its sphere of production and realization). The creation of favourable investment and accumulation opportunities (in the Periphery and elsewhere) is the key attractive factor which can take advantage of this tendency of the internationalization of capital — and it is the peripheral state which under the present historical conditions is the instrument of this development.

Notes

1. See for example Andre Gunder Frank, *Capitalism and Underdevelopment in Latin America* (New York, Monthly Review Press, 1969).
2. In this debate Frank was very active; see his *Sociology of Development. Underdevelopment of Sociology* (Stockholm, Zenit Press, Farsta Reprint, 1969) and 'The Wealth and Poverty of Nations. Even Heretics Remain Bound by Traditional Thought', *Economic and Political Weekly*, Special Number, July 1970.
3. Samir Amin, *Le Développement Inegal* (Paris, 1973).
4. Samir Amin, 'Le modele theorique d'accumulation', *Revue Tiers Monde*, 52, October-December 1972.
5. Karl Marx, *Das Kapital II* (Marx-Engels Werke, Band 24) (Dietz Verlag, 1963), pp. 485-517.
6. Samir Amin, *L'Accumulation à l'échelle mondiale* (Dakar, IFAN, 1970) and *Le Développement Inegal* (Paris, Editions de Minuit, 1973).
7. See for example Samir Amin, *L'Echange inegal et la loi de la valeur* (Paris, Editions Anthropos, 1973).
8. Samir Amin, 'La Crise de l'impérialisme' (Minuit 9, May 1974).
9. Ibid. (Our translation)
10. In other recent works of Samir Amin, like 'C'est une crise de l'impérialisme', *Minuit*, No. 14, May 1975, he is explicitly stressing the point that in capitalism there is no built-in tendency towards the internationalization of capital, neither in the form of productive capital nor in commodities. The present crisis is, according to Amin, not a crisis of capitalism, but of imperialism, created and caused by the centre class relations. In contrast to this, however, in his 'Towards a New Structural Crisis of the Capitalist System?', in Samir Amin and Widstrand (eds), *Multinational*

Firms in Africa (Uppsala, Scandinavian Institute of African Studies, 1975) he stresses the fundamental contradictions between the development of the productive forces and that of the relations of production as the basis for a structural crisis in *capitalism*.

11. Jean-Pierre Olivier, 'Afrique: Qui exploite qui?', *Les Temps modernes*, No. 346, May 1975.

12. Samir Amin, 'Self-Reliance and the New International Economic Order', *Monthly Review*, July/August 1977.

13. Ibid., pp. 2-3.

14. Ibid., p. 10.

15. Ibid., p. 13.

16. Ibid., p. 2.

17. *Review of African Political Economy*, No. 8, 1977, pp. 1-2.

18. Among the recent critics of the dependency theoretical position and the position of Samir Amin in particular, are Jonathan Schiffer, 'The Changing Post-war Pattern of Development: The Accumulated Wisdom of Samir Amin', *World Development*, Vol. 9, No. 6, 1981 (confronting the factual development in the course of the 1960s with the arguments and conclusions of Amin), and Sheila Smith, 'The Ideas of Samir Amin: Theory or Tautology?', *Journal of Development Studies*, Vol. 17, No. 1, 1980 (attacking Amin from a purely theoretical perspective).

19. The Kenya debate started with Colin Leys: 'Underdevelopment and Dependency: Critical Notes', *Journal of Contemporary Asia*, Vol. 7, No. 1, 1977; and Colin Leys, 'Capital Accumulation, Class Formation and Dependency: The Significance of the Kenyan Case', *Socialist Register*, 1978; followed by Nicola Swainson, 'The Rise of a National Bourgeoisie in Kenya', *Review of African Political Economy*, No. 8, 1977, and *The Development of Corporate Capitalism in Kenya, 1918-1977* (London, Heinemann, 1980). Among the critics of the Leys/Swainson position, adhering more to a traditional dependency notion are Ralph Kaplinsky, 'Capitalist Accumulation in the Periphery: the Kenyan Case Re-examined', IDS, mimeo, 1979; and Steven Langdon, 'Multinational Corporations in the Kenyan Political Economy', in Ralph Kaplinsky (ed), *Readings on the Multinational Corporation in Kenya* (Nairobi, O.U.P., 1978) and Langdon, 'Multinational Corporations and the State in Africa', in J. Willamil (ed), *Transnational Capitalism and National Development* (Sussex, Harvester Press, 1979). The debate has been continued at a seminar in Dakar in December 1980, discussing capitalist development prospects in the Ivory Coast, Nigeria and Kenya.

20. Björn Beckman, 'Imperialism and Capitalist Transformation: Critique of a Kenyan Debate', *Review of African Political Economy*, No. 19, 1980.

21. Klaus Busch, *Die multinationalen Konzerne. Zur Analyse der Weltmarktbewegung des Kapitals* (Frankfurt, Suhrkamp Verlag, 1974) and *Die Krise der Europäischen Gemeinschaft* (Frankfurt, EVA-Verlag, 1978).

22. Busch, 1974, op. cit., pp. 95-106.

23. Ibid., p. 98.

24. Ibid., p. 89-94.

25. The element of cheapening the cost of production in relation to securing the necessary raw materials in the Centre is of crucial importance for Harry Magdoff, *The Age of Imperialism* (Danish version, Copenhagen, Demos, 1970) and Pierre Jalée, *Imperialism in the 1970s* (Danish version, Copenhagen, Demos, 1970).

26. Dietmar Goralzcyk, *Weltmarkt, Weltwährungssystem und Westeuropäischen Integration* (Giessen, Focus Verlag, 1975), p. 73.

27. Wolfgang Schoeller, *Weltmarkt und Reproduktion des Kapitals* (Frankfurt, EVA-Verlag, 1973). His later writings with Werner Olle are much closer to the viewpoints argued in this study; see Werner Olle and Wolfgang Schoeller, *World Market, State and National Average Conditions of Labour*, Economic Research Bureau, University of Dar es Salaam, Occasional Paper No. 77.1, October 1977, and Werner Olle and Wolfgang Schoeller, 'World Market, Reproduction of Capital and the Role of the Nation State', unpublished manuscript, undated.

28. Folker Fröbel, Jürgen Heinrichs and Otto Kreye, *Die neue internationale Arbeitsteilung. Strukturelle Arbeitslosigkeit in den Industrieländern und die Industrialisierung der Entwicklungsländer* (Reinbeck, Rowohlt, 1977).

29. Ibid., p. 65.

30. Olle and Schoeller, 1977, op. cit.

31. H. Alavi, 'The State in Post-Colonial Societies: Pakistan and Bangladesh', *New Left Review*, No. 74, 1972.

32. By which is meant the influence of and determination by the world capitalist system as such.

33. John Saul, 'The State in Post-Colonial Societies: Tanzania', *Socialist Register*, 1974.

34. Colin Leys, 'The "Overdeveloped" Post Colonial State: A Re-evaluation', *Review of African Political Economy*, No. 5, 1976.

35. Ibid., pp. 41 and 43.

36. Ibid., p. 43.

37. Colin Leys, 'The State and Capitalism in Kenya', *Review of African Political Economy*, No. 8, 1977.

38. Ibid., p. 92.

39. Quoted in W. Ziemann and M. Lanzendörfer, 'The State in Peripheral Societies', *Socialist Register*, 1977, p. 147.

40. Ibid., p. 161.

41. Ibid., pp. 161-2.

42. For a summary of these theories, see for example Aidan Foster-Carter, 'The Modes of Production Controversy', *New Left Review*, No. 107, 1978.

43. Ziemann and Lanzendörfer, op. cit., p. 165.

44. Ibid., p. 167.

45. Ibid.

46. Olle and Schoeller, 1977, op. cit.

47. Ibid., p. 14.

48. For another approach attacking issues similar to those discussed here see B. Warren, *Imperialism: Pioneer of Capitalism* (London, New Left Books, 1980).

7.   The Political Implications

At the time of independence for the countries in Asia and Africa there were great expectations concerning the possibilities of their rapid economic development. However, in spite of either self-proclaimed capitalist or socialist development strategies, the results of the first years of independence were in most countries meagre. The new states experienced economic stagnation or in some cases direct setbacks in production, as well as difficulties with state finances and the balance of payments, and all in all, a high degree of dependence on the Western world.

The importance of independence lay, therefore, rather in the creation of a new privileged group, consisting of the bureaucracy, whose wealth and power was dependent on support from abroad. Colonialism, therefore, did not give way to political and economic independence, but rather to accelerated dependence and underdevelopment, as has been argued by the dependency theorists.

We have concentrated on Samir Amin as one of these theorists, but André Gunder Frank and Arghiri Emmanuel should also be mentioned. The three of them have been especially preoccupied with the issue of how under-development of the peripheral countries has been brought about and the consequences of this process for the countries concerned. Politically and strategically, as a consequence of their analysis they concentrated on the possibilities for a peripheral country to break with the world capitalist system.

This emphasis on the Third World implies that these theorists do not deal in much detail with the issue which — ever since Lenin wrote *Imperialism: The Highest Stage of Capitalism* — has been the most important for an understanding of contemporary imperialism, that is, an understanding of capitalist development in the Centre countries, their unequal development and contradictions, and the changing conditions for class struggle in that part of the world.

The shift in revolutionary perspective by the dependency theorists to the developing countries must be seen as a result of the long period of prosperity in the Centre since the Second World War, the non-existence (until the mid-1970s) of symptoms of crisis, and the weakened class struggle there.

In other words, the contradictions in the world capitalist system manifested

themselves predominantly in the Third World, and the revolutionary theore-
ticians of the 1960s therefore based their analyses on these countries and their
populations. Amin, Gunder Frank and Emmanuel all developed their theories
on the basis of personal experience of living in various parts of the Third
World, and they aimed at elaborating a revolutionary perspective for the
broad masses.

From the middle of the 1970s, however, it has been possible to observe a
change in orientation in many studies, where less importance is given to the
way surplus is appropriated from the developing countries — as originally
analysed by Frank, Amin and Emmanuel. Increasingly, greater emphasis is
now being given to changes in the economic and political developments of
the Centre countries, and the resulting changes in commodity and capital
exports to the Periphery. This change in the focus of many studies has, first
of all, as its background a political reassessment of the role of the European
working class, which started at the time of the May 1968 events in Paris.
Secondly, the deepening of the world economic crisis also contributed to
this change in focus. Both these factors showed that the dependency
theorists had overestimated the stability of the Centre, and underestimated
the possibility for a change in the relations between Centre and Periphery,
and through this the internal economic dynamic in the countries of the
Periphery.

Where the dependency theorists saw the relations between Centre and
Periphery as a situation of deadlock, in which the countries of the Third
World were continuously being deprived of their economic surplus — a
situation they could only avoid by breaking with the world market — our
study indicates that there seems to exist now a possibility for a capital
accumulation process within the context of capitalist development, at least
in some countries of the Periphery, by virtue of the world market. As we
have argued throughout the book, the present economic crisis and the
limited markets in the Centre have made it essential to an increasing extent
to integrate the Periphery into the accumulation process of the Centre, by
means of for example new investments and the sale of turn-key factories. In
some Third World countries, the dominant classes have been able to use the
state to take advantage of this tendency and are in the process of breaking
with the situation of blocked development.

These tendencies imply that the common interest of Third World workers,
peasants and the bourgeoisie — so often postulated by the dependency
theorists — in breaking with the world market remains a myth in a situation
where the bourgeoisie in the Periphery is strengthening its material base to
an ever increasing extent.

This leads to the conclusion that, while the dependency theorists saw the
dominant contradiction as being between developed and developing
countries, the material changes in the world economy on the threshold of the
1980s are bringing about a situation where the internal class contradictions
are becoming manifest in the Centre as well as in the Periphery — and, in the

process, pushing aside the predominance of nationalist and populist ideology and bringing to the forefront the necessity of socialism.

As we have seen in the case of the Ivory Coast, the classes having an interest in furthering capitalist development are still very strong. They are, however, challenged by an increasing opposition directed against them. Whether the relations of forces can change over time in favour of the workers and peasants still has to be seen. What is clear, however, is that it is in the aspiration for socialism that the toiling masses of the Ivory Coast — and elsewhere in the Third World — have a genuine interest.

Statistical Annex

A. Foreign Direct Investment Flows by country, 1961-79 (%)

DAC Country	1961-67	1968-73	1974-79
Canada	2.3%	4.5%	6.2%
United States	61.1	45.8	29.3
Japan	2.4	6.7	13.0
Australia	0.7	1.4	1.6*
Belgium	0.3†	1.4	2.5
France	6.9	5.2	7.8
Germany	7.2	12.5	17.0
Italy	3.6	3.3	2.0
Netherlands	4.4	6.8	9.6**
Sweden	2.0	2.4	3.7††
United Kingdom	8.7	9.1	9.2
Spain	0	0.3	0.6
Norway	0	0.3	0.9

* From 1974 to 1976.
† From 1965.
** From 1974 to 1978.
†† From 1974 to 1977.

Source: *International Investment and Multinational Enterprises: Recent International Direct Investment Trends* (Paris, OECD, 1981), p. 40.

B. Average Annual Growth Rates of Foreign Direct Investment from DAC
Countries to LDCs, 1960-78 (current $)*

Period	Growth Rate
1960-68	7.0%
1968-73	9.2
1973-78	19.4

* The DAC countries include Australia, Austria, Belgium, Canada, Denmark,
Finland, France, Germany, Italy, Japan, Netherlands, New Zealand,
Norway, Switzerland, United Kingdom, United States.

Source: *International Investment and Multinational Enterprises: International Direct Investment Trends* (Paris, OECD, 1981) p. 43.

C. Total DAC Foreign Direct Investment by country of origin, 1967-76 ($ billion and %)

Country of origin	Billions of dollars					Percentage distribution				
	1967	1971	1973	1975	1976	1967	1971	1973	1975	1976
United States	56.6	82.8	101.3	124.2	137.2	53.8%	52.3%	51.0%	47.8%	47.6%
United Kingdom	17.5	23.7	26.9	30.8	32.1	16.6	15.0	13.5	11.9	11.2
Germany, Federal Republic of	3.0	7.3	11.9	16.0	19.9	2.8	4.6	6.0	6.2	6.9
Japan*	1.5	4.4	10.3	15.9	19.4	1.4	2.8	5.2	6.1	6.7
Switzerland	5.0	9.5	11.1	16.9	18.6	4.8	6.0	5.6	6.5	6.5
France	6.0	7.3	8.8	11.1	11.9	5.7	4.6	4.4	4.3	4.1
Canada	3.7	6.5	7.8	10.5	11.1	3.5	4.1	3.9	4.1	3.9
Netherlands	2.2	4.0	5.5	8.5	9.8	2.1	2.5	2.8	3.2	3.4
Sweden	1.7	2.4	3.0	4.4	5.0	1.6	1.5	1.5	1.7	1.7
Belgium–Luxembourg	2.0	2.4	2.7	3.2	3.6	1.9	1.5	1.4	1.2	1.2
Italy	2.1	3.0	3.2	3.3	2.9	2.0	1.9	1.6	1.3	1.0
Total above	101.3	153.3	192.5	243.8	270.4	96.2	96.8	96.9	94.3	94.2
All other (estimate)	4.0	5.1	6.3	15.1	16.8	3.8	3.2	3.1	5.7	5.8
Grand total	105.3	158.4	198.8	258.9	287.2	100.0	100.0	100.0	100.0	100.0

* Fiscal year beginning 1st April of the year indicated.

Source: *International Investment and Multinational Enterprises: Recent International Direct Investment Trends* (Paris, OECD, 1981) p. 39.

D. Net External Financial Receipts of LDCs by type of flow, 1970-79 ($ billion and %)

	$ billion				Share of total in %			
	1970	1974	1978	1979	1970	1974	1978	1979
ODA	8.13	14.94	23.44	27.97	42.6	44.1	29.5	34.6
1. DAC bilateral	5.67	8.24	13.12	15.91	29.7	24.3	16.5	19.7
2. OPEC bilateral	0.35	3.02	2.97	4.02	1.8	8.9	3.8	5.0
3. Multilateral	1.07	2.85	5.99	6.10	5.6	8.4	7.5	7.5
of which: OPEC financed	–	0.12	0.96	0.25	–	0.4	1.2	0.3
4. Other	1.04	0.83	1.36	1.94	5.5	2.5	1.7	2.4
of which: CMEA financed	1.04	0.83	1.26	1.84	5.5	2.5	1.5	2.3
Non-concessional	10.95	18.98	56.16	53.01	57.4	55.9	70.5	65.4
1. Bank lending	3.00	10.00	22.51	16.67	15.7	29.5	28.3	20.6
2. Bonds	0.30	0.28	3.03	(3.00)	1.6	0.8	3.8	3.7
3. Export credits	2.71	3.25	12.93	10.76	14.2	9.4	16.3	13.3
of which: Private	2.16	2.49	9.97	9.42	11.3	7.3	12.6	11.5
Official	0.55	0.70	2.96	1.50	2.9	2.1	3.7	1.8
4. Direct Investment	3.69	1.10*	11.15	13.49	19.3	3.3*	13.9	16.7
5. OPEC bilateral	0.20	0.92	1.02	0.80	1.0	2.7	1.3	1.0
6. Multilateral	0.69	1.81	3.41	4.20	3.6	5.3	4.3	5.2
of which: OPEC financed	–	0.02	0.49	(0.30)	–	0.1	0.6	0.4
7. Other	0.36	1.42	2.11	3.93	1.9	4.8	2.7	4.9
of which: CMEA financed	0.11	0.09	0.10	0.10	0.6	0.3	0.1	0.1
Total receipts	19.08	33.92	79.60	80.98	100.00	100.00	100.00	100.0
Per cent of GNP	4.0	3.5	5.1	4.6				

* Figure significantly below trend because of nationalisation (disinvestment) of major companies' assets by certain oil-exporting countries.

Source: *Development Co-operation* (Paris, OECD, 1980) p. 85.

E. Total DAC Private Direct Investment* in LDCs by country, 1978 ($ million)

Europe			Seychelles		12
Cyprus		90	Sierra Leone		82
Gibraltar		30	Somalia		(100)
Greece		1,050	Sudan		60
Malta		120	Swaziland		50
Portugal		560	Tanzania		170
Spain		5,700	Djibouti		10
Turkey		450	Togo		100
Yugoslavia		170	Uganda		(10)
Total Europe	9%	*8,170*	Upper Volta		20
			Zaire		(1,250)
Africa, North of Sahara			Zambia		330
Algeria**		385	*Total South of Sahara*	5%	*4,668*
Libya**		660			
Morocco		350			
Tunisia		280	Central America		
Egypt		245	Bahamas†		2,060
Total North of Sahara	2%	*1,920*	Barbados †		180
			Belize		75
Africa, South of Sahara			Bermuda†		4,300
Angola		(100)	Costa Rica		290
Benin		34	Dominican Republic		390
Botswana		57	El Salvador		150
Burundi		26	Guadeloupe		55
Cameroon		370	Guatemala		290
Central African Empire		(70)	Haiti		80
Chad		(26)	Honduras		270
Congo (P.R.)		170	Jamaica		900
Ethiopia		(100)	Mexico		6,000
Gabon**		780	Neth. Antilles		2,500
Gambia		15	Nicaragua		(90)
Ghana		280	Panama†		3,140
Guinea		200	Trinidad and Tobago		1,300
Guinea (Eq.)		20	West Indies (Br.)		970
Ivory Coast		530	*Total Central America*	26%	*22,860*
Kenya		520			
Lesotho		4	South America		
Liberia†		1,230	Argentina		3,340
Malawi		100	Bolivia		140
Mali		10	Brazil		13,520
Mauritania		25	Chile		1,440
Mauritius		24	Colombia		1,510
Mozambique		(100)	Ecuador**		660
Niger		100	Guyana		230
Nigeria*		1,130	Paraguay		110
Rhodesia		(400)	Peru		2,150
Rwanda		25	Surinam		420
Senegal		340	Uruguay		330

Total DAC Private Direct Investment* in LDCs by country, 1978 (*continued*)

Venezuela**		3,620	Brunei	300
Total South America	*31%*	*27,470*	Burma	65
			Fiji Isl.	220
Middle East			Fr. Polynesia	45
Bahrain†		210	Hong Kong†	2,100
Iran**		(1,000)	India	2,500
Iraq**		150	Indonesia**	5,760
Israel		1,000	Korea (Rep. of)	1,500
Jordan		70	Malaysia	2,680
Kuwait**		180	Nepal	10
Lebanon		(100)	New Caledonia	145
Oman**		50	New Hebrides	40
Qatar**		150	Pakistan	790
Saudi Arabia**		250	Papua–New Guinea	860
Syria		70	Philippines	1,820
United Arab Emirates**		190	Singapore†	1,900
Total Middle East	*1%*	*1,220*	Sri Lanka	70
			Taiwan	1,850
Asia (including Oceania)			Thailand	445
Afghanistan		(20)	*Total Asia*	*26%* *23,000*
Bangladesh		(80)		
			GRAND TOTAL:	*100%* *89,308*

* Includes DAC Secretariat estimates for reinvested earnings.
** OPEC Member.
† Off-shore banking centre.
Note: Stock figures represent estimated book values.

Source: *International Investment and Multinational Enterprises: International Direct Investment Trends* (Paris, OECD, 1981) p. 46.

F. LDC Share in Total Foreign Investment of Leading DAC capital-exporting
    Countries, 1966-77.

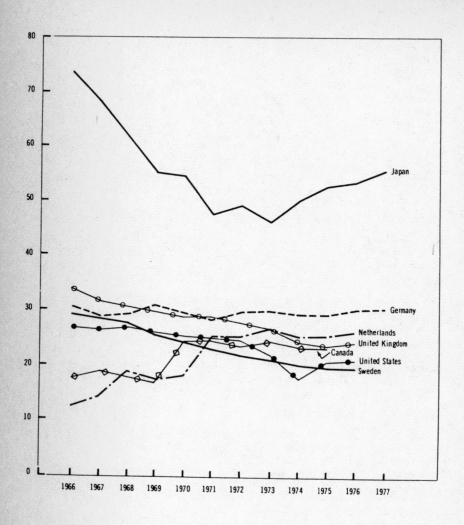

Source: *Internationale Direktinvestitionen, Ergänzungsband 1978/79,* by
    Henry Krägenau, Institut für Wirtschaftsforschung, Hamburg, in:
    *International Investment and Multinational Enterprises: International
    Direct Investment Trends* (Paris, OECD, 1981) p. 54.

Bibliography

Books and Articles

O. Afana, *L'Economie de l'ouest africain* (Paris, Francois Maspero, 1977).

H. Alavi, 'The State in Post-Colonial Societies: Pakistan and Bangladesh, *New Left Review*, No. 74, 1972.

V. Amagou and G.-L. Gleizes, 'Le Groupe SODEPALM et l'agroindustrie du palmier à huile', *Economies et Sociétés*, Series AG, No. 13, 1976.

S. Amin, *L'Accumulation à l'échelle mondiale* (Dakar, IFAN, 1970).

S. Amin, *Le Développement du Capitalisme en Côte d'Ivoire*, 2nd edition (Paris, Editions de Minuit, 1971).

S. Amin, 'Le modèle théorique d'accumulation', *Revue Tiers Monde*, No. 52, 1972.

S. Amin, *Le développement inégal* (Paris, Editions de Minuit, 1973).

S. Amin, *L'échange inégal et la loi de la valeur* (Paris, Editions Anthropos, 1973).

S. Amin, *La Crise de L'Imperialisme* (Paris, Editions de Minuit, 1975).

S. Amin, 'Towards a New Structural Crisis of the Capitalist System?', in S. Amin and C.G. Widstrand (eds), *Multinational Firms in Africa* (Uppsala, Scandinavian Institute of African Studies, 1975).

S. Amin, 'C'est une crise de l'impérialisme', *Minuit*, No. 14, May 1975.

S. Amin (ed), *L'agriculture africaine et le capitalisme* (Paris, Editions Anthropos, 1975).

S. Amin, 'Self-Reliance and the New International Economic Order', *Monthly Review*, July/August 1977.

O.M. Andersen, 'EFs generelle toldpræferencer og deres betydning for lavindkomstlandene' (The GSP and its Importance for the Low Income Countries), *Den ny Verden*, No. 1, 1975-76.

B. Beckmann, 'Imperialism and Capitalist Transformation: Critique of a Kenyan Debate', *Review of African Political Economy*, No. 19, 1980.

K. Busch, *Die multinationalen Konzerne: Zur Analyse der Weltmarktbewegung des Kapitals* (Frankfurt, Suhrkamp Verlag, 1974).

K. Busch, *Die Krise der Europäischen Gemeinschaft* (Frankfurt, EVA-Verlag, 1978).

B. Campbell, 'The Social, Political and Economic Consequences of French Private Investments in the Ivory Coast 1960-70: A Case Study of Cotton and Textile Production', PhD thesis, University of Sussex, 1973.

B. Campbell, 'Neo-Colonialism, Economic Dependence and Political Change:

A Case Study of Cotton and Textile Production in the Ivory Coast 1960-70', *Review of African Political Economy*, No. 2, 1975.

B. Campbell, 'The Ivory Coast', in John Dunn (ed), *West African States: Failure and Promise* (Cambridge, Cambridge University Press, 1978).

F. Capronnier, *La Crise de l'industrie cotonnière francaise* (Paris, Editions Génin, 1959).

H. Chenery *et al.*, *Redistribution with Growth* (London, 1974).

J. Chevassu and A. Valette, *Les industriels de la Côte d'Ivoire: Qui et pourquoi?* (Abidjan, ORSTOM, Sciences humaines, 1975).

J. Chevassu and A. Valette, *Les relations intermédiaires dans le secteur industriel ivoirien* (Abidjan, ORSTOM, Sciences humaines, 1975).

J. Chevassu and A. Valette, *Les revenues distribués par les activités industrielles en Côte d'Ivoire* (Abidjan, ORSTOM, Sciences humaines, 1975).

J. Chevassu and A. Valette, 'Les Modalités et le contenu de la croissance industrielle de la Côte d'Ivoire', *Cahiers ORSTOM, Sciences Humaines*, Vol. XIV, No. 1, 1977.

Commonwealth Secretariat, *The Export Earnings Stabilization Scheme and the Lomé Convention* (London, Secretariat, General Section, Commodities Division, undated).

H. Coppens, G. Faber and E. Lof, 'Security and Raw Material Provision, Development and the Lomé Convention', Paper delivered at the 8th International Colloquium of John F. Kennedy Institute, Center for International Studies, New York, 1975.

J.Y. Darrake, 'Le lien entre rentabilité et modification de la structure des emplois', *Critiques de l'économie politique*, No. 23, 1976.

G. Delanoë, *Etude sur l'évolution de la concentration dans l'industrie du textile en France* (Luxembourg, C.C.E., 1975).

F. Deppe (ed), *Europäische Wirtschaftsgemeinschaft (EWG)* (Reinbeck, Rowohlt, 1975).

F. Deppe, *Arbeiterbewegung und westeuropäischen Integration* (Köln, Pahl. Rugenstein Verlag, 1976).

J.F. Drevet, *Enquete socio-économique dans les plantations villageoises de Basse Côte d'Ivoire* (Paris, SEDES and SODEPALM, 1975).

M. Dumas, 'Le Nouvel Ordre économique internationale', *Revue Tiers Monde*, No. 66, April-June 1976.

M. Dupire and J.-L. Boutillier, *Le Pays Adioukrou et sa palmeraie: Etude socio-économique* (Paris, L'Homme d'Outre-Mer, ORSTOM, 1958).

A. Foster-Carter, 'The Modes of Production Controversy', *New Left Review*, No. 107, 1978.

A.G. Frank, *Capitalism and Underdevelopment in Latin America* (New York, Monthly Review Press, 1969).

A.G. Frank, *Sociology of Development: Underdevelopment of Sociology* (Zenit Press, 1969).

A.G. Frank, 'The Wealth and Poverty of Nations: Even Heretics Remain Bound by Traditional Thought', *Economic and Political Weekly*, Special Number, July 1970.

F. Fröbel, J. Heinrichs and O. Kreye, *Die neue internationale Arbeitsteilung: Strukturelle Arbeitslosigkeit in den Industrieländern und die Industrialisierung der Entwicklungsländer* (Reinbeck, Rowohlt, 1977).

D. Goralzcyk, *Weltmarkt, Weltwährungssystem und Westeuropäischen*

Integration (Giessen, Focus Verlag, 1975).

M. Ikonicoff and S. Sigal, *L'Etat relais: un modèle de développpement des sociétés péripheriques? Le cas de la Côte d'Ivoire* (Paris, IEDES, undated).

M. Ikonicoff, 'Le système économique mondial: désordre ou rationalité?', *Revue Tiers Monde*, Vol. XXI, No. 81, January-March 1980.

P. Jalée, *Imperialism in the 1970s* (Danish version, Demos, Copenhagen, 1970).

R. Kaplinsky, 'Capital Accumulation in the Periphery: The Kenyan Case Re-Examined', mimeographed, University of Sussex, 1979.

R. Kühn, 'Voraussetzungen, Resultate und Perspektiven der Assozierung Afrikanischer Staaten an die EG', in Linhard and Voll (eds), *Weltmarkt und Entwicklungsländer* (Rheinstetten, Berliner Studien zur Internationale Politik, 1976).

R. Kühn, 'Afrika: Franc Zone, Währungsunion und Abhängigkeiten', Arbeiten aus der Abteilung Entwicklungsländerforschung, No. 45, Forschungsinstitut der Friedrich Ebert Stiftung, Bonn, 1977.

S. Langdon, 'Multinational Corporations in the Kenya Political Economy', in R. Kaplinsky (ed), *Readings on the Multinational Corporation in Kenya* (Nairobi, Oxford University Press, 1978).

S. Langdon, 'Multinational Corporations and the State in Africa', in J. Villamil (ed), *Transnational Capitalism and National Development* (Sussex, Harvester Press, 1979).

G.H. Lawson, 'La Côte d'Ivoire: 1960-1970: Croissance et diversification dans africanisation', in J. Esseks (ed), *L'Afrique de l'indépendance politique à l'indépendance économique* (Grenoble, 1975).

E. Lee, 'Export-Led Rural Development: The Ivory Coast', *Development and Change*, Vol. II, 1980.

C. Leys, 'The "Overdeveloped" Post-Colonial State: A Re-evaluation', *Review of African Political Economy*, No. 5, 1976.

C. Leys, 'The State and Capitalism in Kenya', *Review of African Political Economy*, No. 8, 1977.

C. Leys, 'Underdevelopment and Dependency: Critical Notes', *Journal of Contemporary Asia*, Vol. 7, No. 1, 1977.

C. Leys, 'Capital Accumulation, Class Formation and Dependency: The Significance of the Kenyan Case', *Socialist Register*, 1978.

H. McArthur and B.R. Scott, *Industrial Planning in France* (Paris, Dalloz, 1974).

H. Magdoff, *The Age of Imperialism* (Danish Version, Copenhagen, Demos, 1970).

E. Mandel, 'International Capitalism and "Supranationality" ', in H. Radice (ed.), *International Firms and Modern Imperialism* (London, Penguin, 1975).

M. Mazoyer, 'Développement de la production et transformation agricole marchande d'une formation agraire en Côte d'Ivoire', in S. Amin (ed), *L'agriculture africaine et le capitalisme* (Paris, Editions Anthropos, 1975).

H.S. Marcussen and J.E. Torp, 'Den internationale arbejdsdeling og Lomé samarbejdet' (The International Division of Labour and the Lomé Co-operation), *Forum for Utviklingsstudier*, No. 3-4, 1977.

K. Marx, *Das Kapital II* (Marx-Engels Werke, Band 24) (Berlin, Dietz Verlag, 1963).

C.A. Michalet and M. Delapierre, *The Multinationalization of French Firms* (Chicago, 1975).

L.K. Mytelka, 'Crisis and Adjustment in the French Textile Industry', Working Paper, Carleton University, 1980.

O.E.C.D., *Development of Local Engineering Capabilities for Industry: Case Study of the Ivory Coast*, O.E.C.D. Development Centre, Industry and Technology, Occasional Paper No. 20, February 1978.

O.E.C.D. , *International Investment and Multinational Enterprises* (Paris, O.E.C.D., 1981).

J.-P. Olivier, 'Afrique: Qui Exploite Qui?', *Les Temps Modernes*, No. 346, May 1975.

W. Olle and W. Schöller, *World Market, State and National Average Conditions of Labour*, Economic Research Bureau, University of Dar es Salaam, Occasional Paper No. 77.1, October 1977.

W. Olle and W. Schöller, 'World Market, Reproduction of Capital and the Role of the Nation State', unpublished manuscript, undated.

C. Oman, 'Changing International Investment Strategies: The "New Forms" of Investment in Developing Countries', O.E.C.D. Development Centre, Conference Document No. 2, 2nd Meeting of Experts on Foreign Investments and its Impact on Development, Paris, 1980.

Y. Pehaut, 'Les Oléagineaux dans les pays d'Afrique occidentale associés en Marché Commun', Thesis, University of Lille III, 1974.

M. Pescay, *Etude socio-économique des plantations villageoises de palmier à huile* (Paris, SEDES and SODEPALM, 1968).

A.-M. Pillet-Schwartz, 'Capitalisme d'état et développement rural en Côte d'Ivoire', Ph.D. thesis, University of Paris, 1973.

N. Poulantzas, *Classes in Contemporary Capitalism* (London, New Left Books, 1975).

G.L. Reuber, *et al.*, *Private Foreign Investments in Development* (Oxford, 1973).

J.D. de la Rochère, *L'Etat et le développement économique de la Côte d'Ivoire* (Paris, Pédone, 1976).

U. Rödel, 'Die Verschärfung der internationalen Konkurrenz', in Volkhard Brandes (ed), *Handbuch 1: Perspektiven des Kapitalismus* (Frankfurt, EVA-Verlag, 1974).

J. Saul, 'The State in Post-Colonial Societies: Tanzania', *Socialist Register*, 1974.

A. Sawadogo, *L'Agriculture en Côte d'Ivoire* (Paris, Presses Universitaires de France, 1977).

J. Schiffer, 'The Changing Post-war Pattern of Development: The Accumulated Wisdom of Samir Amin', *World Development*, Vol. 9, No. 6, 1981.

W. Schoeller, *Weltmarkt und Reproduktion des Kapitals* (Frankfurt, EVA-Verlag, 1973).

SEDES, *Etude socio-économique des plantations villageoises de palmier à huile* (SEDES, undated).

SIGES, *Etudes sur la sous-traitance en vue de la création d'une bourse de sous-traitance à Abidjan* (Abidjan, SIGES, 1970).

S. Smith, 'The Ideas of Samir Amin: Theory or Tautology?', *Journal of Development Studies*, Vol. 17, No. 1, 1980.

A. Statz, 'Zur Geschichte der Westeuropäischen Integration bis zur Gründung der EWG', in F. Deppe (ed), *Europäische Wirtschaftgemeinschaft (EWG)* (Reinbeck, Rowohlt, 1975).

H. Stordel, 'Preference in the Lomé Convention and the Generalized System of Preferences and the World Trade System', Paper delivered at the 8th International Colloquium of John F. Kennedy Institute, Centre for International Studies, New York, 1975.

J. Suret-Canale, *Afrique noire: De la colonisation aux indépendances 1945-1960* (Paris, Editions Sociales, 1972).

N. Swainson, 'The Rise of a National Bourgeoisie in Kenya', *Review of African Political Economy*, No. 8, 1977.

N. Swainson, *The Development of Corporate Capitalism in Kenya: 1918-1977* (London, Heinemann, 1980).

C. Uhlig, *Monetäre Integration bei wirtschaftlicher Abhängigkeit: Probleme einer währungspolitischen Strategie dargestellt am Beispiel der Franc Zone* (München, Weltforum Verlag, 1976).

Y. Ullmo, *La Planification en France* (Paris, Dalloz, 1974).

U.N., *Transnational Corporations in World Development: A Re-Examination* (New York, U.N., 1978).

UNIDO, *Technical and Economic Aspects of the Oil Palm Fruit Processing Industry* (New York, U.N., 1974).

H.H. Walker, 'Entwicklung, Wirtschaftliche Bedeutung und Zukunft von Palmöl und Palmkernelöl in Rahmen des Weltmarktes an Olen und Fetten', *Zeitschrift für ausländische Landwirtschaft*, Vol. 16, No. 2, April-June 1977.

D. Wall, 'The E.E.C. – A.C.P. Lomé Convention: A Model for the New International Economic Order?', The Halifax Conference, Canada, 1975.

B. Warren, *Imperialism: Pioneers of Capitalism,* (London, New Left Books, 1980).

G. Wiedensohler, 'Westafrikanische Staaten als Vertragspartner ausländischer Privatunternehmen', *Afrika Spectrum*, No. 2, 1977.

World Bank, *Ivory Coast: A Basic Economic Report* (New York, February 1978).

World Bank, *The Challenge of Success: A World Bank Country Economic Report*, Bastiaan A. den Tuinder (Baltimore, The Johns Hopkins University Press, 1978).

World Bank, *World Development Report, 1980* (New York, June 1980).

W. Ziemann and M. Lanzendörfer, 'The State in Peripheral Societies', *Socialist Register*, 1977.

Periodicals and Official Documents

Afrique Agriculture (Paris).
Afrique Industrie.
Analyse de Marchés.
Banque Centrale des Etats l'Afrique de l'Ouest, *Statistiques, économiques et monétaires*, various issues, Dakar.
Bulletin de l'Afrique Noire.
Bulletin for de europæiske Fællesskaber.
La Côte d'Ivoire en Chiffres, various years.

The Courier.

Eurostat A.C.P., *Statistical Yearbook 1970-76* (Luxembourg, 1977).

L'Express (Paris).

Financial Times (London).

Fraternité Matin (Abidjan).

How to do business in the Ivory Coast (Abidjan, Société africaine d'édition).

L'Industrie Ivorienne (Abidjan, Chambre d'Industrie, various years.

IPW Berichte.

Marchés Tropicaux (Paris).

Ministère de l'économie et des Finances, *Statistiques et Etudes Financières* (Paris, Ministère de l'Economie et des Finances; Banque de France).

Ministry of Finance, Economic Affairs and the Plan, *Private Investments in the Ivory Coast: Investments Law* (Abidjan, undated).

Le Monde (Paris).

Le Monde Hebdomadaire (Paris).

Recensement National de l'Agriculture, Vol. IV. Exploitations agricoles traditionelles (Abidjan, Direction des Statistiques rurales, September 1976).

Société Générale de Banques en Côte d'Ivoire, *Industrie Textile en Côte d'Ivoire* (Abidjan, April 1976).

Statistiques Agricoles: Memento 1947-1977 (Abidjan, Ministry of Agriculture, 1978).

Telex Africa.

UN Yearbook of International Trade Statistics.

West Africa (London).

Index

Abidjan, 99-100
Absentee farmers, 94
Accumulation of capital, 17-24, 114-17, 140-50, 158-60
A.C.P. countries, 43
Afana, Osende, 128
African Development Bank, 79
Agache, Willot, 37, 42, 106
Agrarian bourgeoisie, 115
Agriculture, 69, 74-89
Alavi, Hamza, 152-4
Algeria, 35
Amin, Samir, 48, 68, 74-5, 97, 103, 114-16, 128, 139-44, 159
A.O.F. area, 40
Arusha Declaration, 53

Bank lending, 26
Benin, 42, 77, 89, 105
Berlin Group, 87
Blocked development, 114, 116, 140-3, 159
Blohorn, André, 84-5
Blue Bell Côte d'Ivoire, 45, 107-8, 111-13
Bourgeoisie, 69, 73, 115, 155, 158-9
Boussac Company, 37, 104
Brazil, 29, 33-4, 75
Busch, Klaus, 22, 145-7, 150

Caisse, la, 40, 69, 83, 88, 101 102
Cameroun, 42, 56, 68
Campbell, Bonnie, 133-4
Capital accumulation, see accumulation of capital

Capital in general, 22
Capitalist development, 18
Capitalist relations of production, 76, 136, 158
Cash crops, 93
C.C.C.E., 84
C.F.A.O., 38, 45, 102, 106
C.F.C.I., 106
C.F.D.T., 104
Chevassu, Jean, 100
Cheysson, Claude, 52
C.I.T.E.C., 104
Class, 115, 132-4, 142, 152-3, 158
Cocoa, 69-72, 75, 93, 95, 128-9, 131
Coffee, 69-72, 75, 93, 95, 128, 130-1
Colombia, 75
Common Agricultural Policy, 54
Comprador bourgeoisie, 102, 155, 159
Concentration of capital, 18-24
C.O.T.I.V.O., 45, 105, 106, 112
Cotton, 103, 129
Crisis, 23, 25-6

Darrake, J.Y., 38
Delapierre, Michel, 33, 35
Dependency theory, 9-10, 139-45, 156, 158
Deppe, Frank, 22
Diawara, 68
Direct investments, 25, 115
Dollfus-Mieg et Cie, 37-8, 42

Eastern Europe, 18
E.E.C., 12-13, 17-21, 48-64

E.E.C. aid, 48-64, 80, 88
Established Agreements, 112
Export credits, 26-7
Extended reproduction, 116, 157
European Coal and Steel Union, 18
European Development Fund, 54-5,
    79, 82, 84, 88
European Investment Bank, 60-1,
    79-80, 82, 88

F.C.C.R.I., 70
F.I.T.E.X.H.A., 109
France, 25, 32-46, 49-51, 54-5,
    101-3
Franc Zone, 22, 34, 49-51
Frank, André Gunder, 9, 10
French Economic and Social Fund,
    41
French Economic and Social
    Development Fund, 41
French State, 39-42
French textile industry, 35-46
French trading companies, 103
Fröbel, Folker, 148-150

Gabon, 66-8, 82
General Scheme of Preferences, 57
Ghana, 13, 68, 75, 79, 129
Gonfreville, Ets., 38, 104, 105, 106,
    108
Goralzcyk, 147, 148, 150
Grossmann, 140
Growth and equity, 123
Growth without development, 68

Heinrichs, Jürgen, 148, 150
Hong Kong, 29
Houphouët-Boigny, Félix, 84

I.C.O.D.I., 105, 107
I.D.A., 79
Ikonicoff, Moises, 73, 133
I.L.O. Convention on Working
    Conditions, 63
I.M.F., 11
Imperialism, 140, 145
Implementing Convention, 54
Indochina, 35
Indonesia, 26, 77
Industrial bourgeoisie, 102

Industrial Free Zones, 149, 159
Internationalization of capital,
    9-12, 24-8, 33-6, 145-51
International division of labour, 12,
    28-30, 48-53, 62-4
I.R.C.T., 104
I.R.H.O., 78, 80, 87
Italy, 23
Ivorian Agricultural Census, 124
Ivorian Code of Investment, 72, 110
Ivorian State, 69-74, 110-13, 132-5
Ivorian Trade Unions, 72
Ivory Coast, 44-6, 60-2, 66-136

Japan, 13, 17, 23, 105, 145

Kenya, 29, 53, 68, 144-5
Korean War, 21
Kreye, Otto, 148, 150

Langdon, Steven, 154
Lanzendörfer, M., 154, 155
Lee, Eddy, 124-8
Lenin, 140
Leys, Colin, 133, 153
Liberal development theories, 140
Liberia, 87
Linkage effects, 98, 115
Lomé Convention, 48-64
Lomé Convention II, 63
Luxemburg, Rosa, 140

Madagascar, 56, 105
Malaysia, 77
Mali, 105
Mandel, Ernest, 21
Marshall Plan, 18
Marx, Karl, 141
Matrilineal system, 90
Mexico, 29
M.I.C.E., 108
Michalet, Charles Albert, 33, 35
Migrant workers, 127
Multifibre Agreement, 42, 63

National bourgeoisie, 135, 155
Netherlands, the, 78, 149
New International Economic
    Order, 48, 62-3
Niger, 105

Nigeria, 29, 61, 66, 77, 89, 103, 129, 159

O.E.C.D., 24
Olivier, Jean-Pierre, 142
Olle, Werner, 151, 157
O.P.T.O.R.G., 45, 106
O.R.S.T.O.M., 94

PALMINDUSTRIE, 79, 82
Palmivoire, 82
Palm oil, 73, 76-97, 130
Pascal, Paul, 107
Patrilineal system, 90
Pehant, Yves, 80
Perennial crops, 93
Peripheral state, 14-15, 151-60
Permanent labourers, 126
P.H.C.I., 84
Plan Palmier, 78, 80, 82, 84, 88
Planter bourgeoisie, 128, 134
Portfolio investments, 26
Portugal, 33-4
Poulantzas, Nicos, 21, 22
Pre-capitalist relations of production, 155
Proletarianization, 89, 95, 97, 136, 155

Reproduction schemes, 141
Rural bourgeoisie, 97, 128

S.A.B., 108
Sanu, E.D., 58
Saul, John, 154
Sawadogo, Abdoulaye, 124
Schaeffer, 37, 42
S.C.O.A., 45, 106
Schoeller, Wolfgang, 147, 157
Schumann, Robert, 18
S.E.D.E.S., 91, 94, 95, 96
Self-centred development, 97, 115
Senegal, 13, 56, 68, 103, 113, 159
Sigal, S., 73
Singapore, 29
Skilled work force, 80
Social differentiation, 123-9
S.O.C.I.T.A.S., 38, 106
S.O.D.E.P.A.L.M., 76, 80-2, 84-5, 87, 96, 130, 132
S.O.D.E.R.I.Z., 84

S.O.D.H.E.V.E.A., 84
South Korea, 29
Spain, 33-4
S.P.H.C.I., 78
S.T.A.B.E.X., 49, 58-9
Sterling Area, 22
Sunflower oil, 77
Syndicat Agricole Africain, 132

Taiwan, 29
Tanzania, 53
Technology, 76, 87-9, 115
Texunion, 37
Timber, 129
Togo, 129
Transcending 'blocked development', 139, 156
Treaty of Rome, 19, 53
T.R.E.F.O.R., 108
Tugan-Baranowski, 140

Uganda, 53
U.N.D.P., 79
Unequal development of capitalism, 29-30, 159
Unilever, 83
United Kingdom, 25, 33, 77, 78, 149
U.N.I.W.A.X., 45, 105, 106, 107
Upper Volta, 73, 75, 82
U.S.A., 17, 23, 25, 83
U.S.S.R., 17
U.T.E.X.I., 45, 105, 106, 107

Valette, Alain, 100

Wall, David, 59
West Germany, 23, 25, 78, 145
Working class, 20
World Bank, 79, 84, 123, 124, 125, 128, 129
World War II, 17

Yaounde Convention, 49
Yaounde Convention II, 80
Yugoslavia, 33-4

Zaire, 56, 61, 77, 113
Zambia, 68
Zieman, W., 154, 155

INTERNATIONAL RELATIONS/IMPERIALISM TITLES
FROM ZED BOOKS

Albert Szymanski
IS THE RED FLAG FLYING?
The Political Economy of the Soviet
Union Today
Hb and Pb

V.G. Kiernan
AMERICAN — THE NEW
IMPERIALISM:
From White Settlement to World
Hegemony
Hb

Satish Kumar
CIA AND THE THIRD WORLD:
A Study in Crypto-Diplomacy
Hb

Dan Nabudere
THE POLITICAL ECONOMY OF
IMPERIALISM
Hb and Pb

Yan Fitt et al
THE WORLD ECONOMIC CRISIS:
US Imperialism at Bay
Hb and Pb

Clyde Sanger
SAFE AND SOUND
Disarmament and Development in the
Eighties
Pb

Frederick Clairemonte and John
Cavanagh
THE WORLD IN THEIR WEB:
The Dynamics of Textile
Multinationals
(Preface by Samir Amin)
Hb and Pb

Henrick Secher Marcussen and Jens
Erik Torp
THE INTERNATIONALIZATION
OF CAPITAL:
Prospects for the Third World
Hb and Pb

Malcolm Caldwell
THE WEALTH OF SOME
NATIONS
Hb and Pb

Georgi Arbatov
COLD WAR OR DETENTE: THE
SOVIET VIEWPOINT
Hb and Pb

Rachel Heatley
POVERTY AND POWER:
The Case for a Political Approach to
Development
Pb

Ronald Graham
THE ALUMINIUM INDUSTRY
AND THE THIRD WORLD:
Multinational Corporations and
Underdevelopment .
Pb

Petter Nore and Terisa Turner
OIL AND CLASS STRUGGLE
Hb and Pb

Rehman Sobhan
THE CRISIS OF EXTERNAL
DEPENDENCE:
The Political Economy of Foreign Aid
to Bangladesh
Hb and Pb

AFRICA TITLES FROM ZED

Dan Nabudere
IMPERIALISM IN EAST AFRICA
Vol. I: Imperialism and Exploitation
Vol. II: Imperialism and Integration
Hb

Elenga M'Buyinga
PAN AFRICANISM OR NEO
COLONIALISM?
The Bankruptcy of the OAU
Hb and Pb

Bade Onimode
IMPERIALISM AND
UNDERDEVELOPMENT IN
NIGERIA
The Dialectics of Mass Poverty
Hb and Pb

Michael Wolfers and Jane Bergerol
ANGOLA IN THE FRONTLINE
Hb and Pb

Mohamed Babu
AFRICAN SOCIALISM OR
SOCIALIST AFRICA?
Hb and Pb

Anonymous
INDEPENDENT KENYA
Hb and Pb

Yolamu Barongo (Editor)
POLITICAL SCIENCE IN AFRICA:
A RADICAL CRITIQUE
Hb and Pb

Okwudiba Nnoli (Editor)
PATH TO NIGERIAN
DEVELOPMENT
Pb

Emile Vercruijsse
THE PENETRATION OF
CAPITALISM
A West African Case Study
Hb

Fatima Babikir Mahmoud
THE SUDANESE BOURGEOISIE
— Vanguard of Development?
Hb and Pb

No Sizwe
ONE AZANIA, ONE NATION
The National Question in South
Africa
Hb and Pb

Ben Turok (Editor)
DEVELOPMENT IN ZAMBIA
A Reader
Pb

J. F Rweyemamu (Editor)
INDUSTRIALIZATION AND
INCOME DISTRIBUTION IN
AFRICA
Hb and Pb

Claude Ake
REVOLUTIONARY PRESSURES
IN AFRICA
Hb and Pb

Anne Seidman and Neva Makgetla
OUTPOSTS OF MONOPOLY
CAPITALISM
Southern Africa in the Changing
Global Economy
Hb and Pb

Peter Rigby
PERSISTENT PASTORALISTS
Nomadic Societies in Transition
Hb and Pb

Edwin Madunagu
PROBLEMS OF SOCIALISM: THE
NIGERIAN CHALLENGE
Pb

Mai Palmberg
THE STRUGGLE FOR AFRICA
Hb and Pb

Chris Searle
WE'RE BUILDING THE NEW SCHOOL!
Diary of a Teacher in Mozambique
Hb (at Pb price)

Cedric Robinson
BLACK MARXISM
The Making of the Black Radical Tradition
Hb and Pb

Eduardo Mondlane
THE STRUGGLE FOR MOZAMBIQUE
Pb

Basil Davidson
NO FIST IS BIG ENOUGH TO HIDE THE SKY
The Liberation of Guinea Bissau and Cape Verde:
Aspects of the African Revolution
Hb and Pb

Baruch Hirson
YEAR OF FIRE, YEAR OF ASH
The Soweto Revolt: Roots of a Revolution?
Hb and Pb

SWAPO Department of Information and Publicity
TO BE BORN A NATION
The Liberation Struggle for Namibia
Pb

Peder Gouwenius
POWER OF THE PEOPLE
South Africa in Struggle: A Pictorial History
Pb

Gillian Walt and Angela Melamed (Editors)
MOZAMBIQUE: TOWARDS A PEOPLE'S HEALTH SERVICE
Pb

Horst Drechsler
LET US DIE FIGHTING
The Struggle of the Herero and Nama Against German Imperialism (1884-1915)
Hb and Pb

Andre Astrow
ZIMBABWE: A REVOLUTION THAT LOST ITS WAY?
Hb and Pb

Rene Lefort
ETHIOPIA: AN HERETICAL REVOLUTION?
Hb and Pb

Robert H. Davies, Dan O'Meara and Sipho Dlamini
THE STRUGGLE FOR SOUTH AFRICA
A Reference Guide to Movements, Organizations and Institutions
Hb and Pb

Joseph Hanlon
MOZAMBIQUE: THE REVOLUTION UNDER FIRE
Hb and Pb

Henry Isaacs
LIBERATION MOVEMENTS IN CRISIS
The PAC of South Africa
Hb and Pb

Toyin Falola and Julius Ihonvbere
THE RISE AND FALL OF NIGERIA'S SECOND REPUBLIC, 1979-83
Hb and Pb

Dianne Bolton
NATIONALIZATION: A ROAD TO SOCIALISM?
The Case of Tanzania
Pb

A.T. Nzula, I.I. Potekhin and A.Z. Zusmanovich
FORCED LABOUR IN COLONIAL AFRICA
Hb and Pb

Jeff Crisp
THE STORY OF AN AFRICAN WORKING CLASS
— Ghanaian Miners' Struggles, 1870-1980
Hb and Pb

Aquino de Braganca and Immanuel Wallerstein (Editors)
THE AFRICAN LIBERATION READER
Documents of the National Liberation Movements
Vol I: The Anatomy of Colonialism
Vol II: The National Liberation Movements
Vol III: The Strategy of Liberation
Hb and Pb

Faarax M.J. Cawl
IGNORANCE IS THE ENEMY OF LOVE
Pb

Kinfe Abraham
FROM RACE TO CLASS
Links and Parallels in African and Black American Protest Expression
Pb

Robert Mshengu Kavanagh
THEATRE AND CULTURAL STRUGGLE IN SOUTH AFRICA
A Study in Cultural Hegemony and Social Conflict
Hb and Pb

A. Temu and B. Swai
HISTORIANS AND AFRICANIST HISTORY: A CRITIQUE
Hb and Pb

Robert Archer and Antoine Bouillon
THE SOUTH AFRICAN GAME
Sport and Racism
Hb and Pb

Ray et al.
DIRTY WORK 2
The CIA in Africa
Pb

Raqiya Haji Dualeh Abdalla
SISTERS IN AFFLICTION
Circumcision and Infibulation of Women in Africa
Hb and Pb

Christine Obbo
AFRICAN WOMEN
Their Struggle for Economic Independence
Pb

Maria Rose Cutrufelli
WOMEN OF AFRICA
Roots of Oppression
Hb and Pb

Asma El Dareer
WOMAN, WHY DO YOU WEEP?
Circumcision and Its Consequences
Hb and Pb

Miranda Davies (Editor)
THIRD WORLD — SECOND SEX
Women's Struggles and National Liberation
Hb and Pb

Organization of Angolan Women
ANGOLAN WOMEN BUILDING THE FUTURE
From National Liberation to Women's Emancipation
Hb and Pb